Bugsplat

Bugsplat

The Politics of Collateral Damage in Western Armed Conflicts

BRUCE CRONIN

OXFORD
UNIVERSITY PRESS

OXFORD
UNIVERSITY PRESS

Oxford University Press is a department of the University of Oxford. It furthers
the University's objective of excellence in research, scholarship, and education
by publishing worldwide. Oxford is a registered trade mark of Oxford University
Press in the UK and certain other countries.

Published in the United States of America by Oxford University Press
198 Madison Avenue, New York, NY 10016, United States of America.

© Oxford University Press 2018

CIP data is on file at the Library of Congress
ISBN 978–0–19–084911–5 (pbk.); 978–0–19–084910–8 (hbk.)

1 3 5 7 9 8 6 4 2

Paperback printed by Webcom, Inc., Canada
Hardback printed by Bridgeport National Bindery, Inc., United States of America

CONTENTS

Bugsplat

Introduction

No phrase in international politics simultaneously sounds so banal yet evokes such powerful images as the term "collateral damage." It is both coldly technical—a flippant "oops" figuratively uttered by political and military leaders—and hotly emotional. It is a political concept that explains inadvertent civilian casualties during war, while also providing a legal loophole for the combatants who produced these casualties. The very use of the term is an acknowledgment that civilians should be immune from military action (which is why the damage is "collateral"), while at the same time it also represents a bold assertion that some level of civilian losses are acceptable. In short, it justifies the deaths and injuries of civilians caused by armies who are otherwise committed to following the principle of civilian immunity and the laws and customs of war.

The US Department of Defense defines collateral damage as "unintentional or incidental injury or damage to persons or objects that are not lawful military targets."[1] It includes loss of civilian life, injury to civilians, destruction of civilian property, and other types of noncombatant casualties that result from (1) the spillover or collateral effects of attacks against legal military targets; (2) accidents; (3) misidentification of targets; and (4) weapons malfunctions that occur during military operations. In a broader sense, it also encompasses damage to infrastructure and public facilities that primarily serve the civilian population, as well as long-term reverberation effects (such as disease and starvation) on the civilian population that can be directly traced to specific military actions. Finally, collateral damage also includes casualties that result from attacks on individuals and groups who are misclassified as combatants, but who are actually civilians. Collateral damage therefore includes both those actions that are the foreseeable result of planned attacks—justified under the principle of proportionality—and the unplanned unintended consequences which are accidental or unforeseen.[2]

Collateral damage differs from casualties produced by deliberate attacks on civilian populations or indiscriminate assaults against neighborhoods, towns, and cities in that they are unintended and the result of otherwise legal behavior according to the laws of armed conflict. Although the term does not appear in any treaty or official diplomatic documents, in practice collateral damage is part of the legal calculus factored into the warfighting strategies of many military organizations.[3] This calculus enables states to adopt the principle of civilian immunity within their military services while at the same time implement policies that allow for a certain level of civilian losses. For this reason collateral damage may be incidental, but it is also usually foreseeable and therefore preventable.

Various military organizations have devised methods to calculate probable civilian casualties prior to launching attacks, none more infamous than the computer program designed by the United States called Bugsplat.[4] This software examines a potential target by analyzing the surrounding terrain, the direction and angle of the proposed attack, and the particular characteristics of the munition selected for the strike, and then generates a bloblike image of an irregular-shaped "probable damage field" that "looks like insects hitting a car windshield at high speed."[5] Thus its unfortunate name. The decision to brand the software with this moniker was likely made without malice, but it does symbolize the indifference toward civilian casualties that is the theme of this book. The software (which has since been renamed Fast Assessment Strike Tool—Collateral Damage) was created by computer engineers to enable Pentagon officials to better predict the level of collateral damage during its operations, allowing commanders to assess how the attack will impact noncombatants and help them determine whether the attack should proceed as planned or be altered. Yet as the following pages will demonstrate, the experience of armed conflicts fought by technologically advanced states committed to following the laws of war suggest that the problem of civilian casualties is not one that can be addressed through sophisticated computer software. The problem is political, not technical.

This book examines why states that are committed to the principle of civilian immunity and the protection of noncombatants end up killing and injuring large numbers of civilians during their military operations. I argue that despite the efforts of Western military organizations to comply with the laws of armed conflict, the level of collateral damage produced by Western military operations are the inevitable outcome of the

Western method of warfare—that is, the strategies and means through which their military organizations fight wars. Drawing on their superior technology and the strategic advantage of not having to fight on their own territory, such states employ highly concentrated and overwhelming military force against a wide variety of political, economic, and military targets under conditions that are likely to produce high civilian casualties. In doing so, they eschew the traditional military objectives of annihilating or eroding the enemy's military forces, instead targeting all of the applicable elements of the adversary's national power: diplomatic, economic, military, and information. This involves attacking buildings, infrastructure, and dual-use targets located deep within heavily populated towns and urban areas, inevitably producing high levels of civilian casualties and damage to civilian objects.

Since this book examines collateral damage rather than deliberate civilian targeting, it will necessarily focus on those states that demonstrate a clear commitment to the principle of civilian immunity and the adherence to the laws and customs of war. States demonstrate such a commitment by (1) incorporating the main provisions of the international law of armed conflict into their military manuals and cadet training programs; (2) including military lawyers at planning meetings where war-fighting strategies are discussed and targets chosen; and (3) having an independent judicial process that has the authority to interpret the rules and sanction violators.

In this vein, the focus will be on the Western powers—primarily the United States, members of the North Atlantic Treaty Organization (NATO), and Israel—because they best represent the paradox between a commitment to the laws and customs of war and high rates of civilian casualties produce during military operations. Moreover, as the states that lead the world in military capabilities many times over (NATO countries alone account for more than 70% of all military spending and possess by far the most technologically advanced militaries in the world),[6] the behavior of Western military organizations establishes a baseline from which others determine the means and methods though which they will fight. Quite simply, Western actions provide a standard for future armed conflicts fought by a wide range of states.

The temporal focus will be on armed conflicts initiated after 1989, the year the Cold War officially ended at the Malta Summit, and the beginning of the Geneva Protocol regime.[7] Although the idea of civilian immunity dates back many centuries, it was not until the ratification of the First and

Second Protocols to the Geneva Conventions of 1977 that this principle was detailed, codified, and defined in international law and incorporated into the military manuals of the major powers.[8] Many of the principles— such as distinction, military necessity, and proportionality—had existed informally as part of customary international law prior to this period; however, it was the overwhelming ratification of the Protocols over the following two decades that created near-universal acceptance.

Prior to 1989, fewer than a dozen states had ratified the First Protocol, most of whom were from Scandinavia, and primarily included countries that had not fought an armed conflict since the Second World War. Within five years following the end of the Cold War, however, the number of sig- natories jumped to more than 40 (eventually reaching 173), and even among the nonratifiers, many states explicitly expressed support for the legal authority of the Protocol's main principles by incorporating them into their military manuals and making public statements to that effect.[9]

Collateral Damage in Recent Conflicts

The proliferation of collateral damage and other forms of civilian casual- ties during conflicts involving the major military powers over the past sev- eral decades is troubling, if not alarming. According to a study conducted by the *Public Library of Science (PLoS) Medicine* journal, for example, an estimated 11,516 civilians were killed by direct attacks from US-led coalition forces between 2003 and 2008 during the invasion and occu- pation in Iraq, and of these, 7,252 deaths occurred during the first year the conflict, when the types of military operations discussed in this book were conducted.[10] During the 34-day war between Israel and Hezbollah in Lebanon in 2006, Israeli attacks resulted in approximately 1,183 civil- ian fatalities.[11] Approximately 1,523 more civilians were killed by Israeli air and artillery attacks on Gaza during the Israeli–Hamas war of 2014 (known by Israelis as Operation Protective Edge).[12]

In the course of the two-month war that led to the overthrow of the Afghani Taliban in 2001 (October–December 2001), attacks by NATO forces produced between 1,000 and 1,300 civilian deaths.[13] Others esti- mate that 3,000 to 3,400 civilians were killed during the entire five-month bombing campaign (October 2001 through March 2002).[14] NATO's two-and-a-half-month air war against Serbia in 1999 left between 500 and 1,500 civilians dead.[15] According to the most recent estimates, about 3,600 Iraqi civilians were killed by coalition forces over the month-and-a-half-long Persian Gulf War of 1991.[16] Although the exact figures will probably never be known, nongovernmental organizations estimate that approximately 300 civilians were killed during the 12-day US invasion of Panama in 1989.[17]

This pattern also extends to less formal conflicts, such as the "drone wars" fought by the United States against al Qaeda and Ansar al-Sharia in Pakistan and Yemen. According to a study conducted by Bureau of Investigative Journalism, US drone attacks in Pakistan from 2004–2017 killed between 424 and 966 civilians, including 172–207 children.[18] More recently, the United Nations Office of Coordination of Humanitarian Affairs estimated that Saudi Arabia's air war against the Houthis in Yemen during the first three months of 2015 killed approximately 364 civilians and injured thousands of others. By September, the number of civilian deaths inflicted by these air strikes rose to an estimated one thousand.[19] These attacks were conducted in close consultation with US and other Western advisors, and followed the standard Western approach to war.[20]

While some of these casualties were the result of isolated acts by individual soldiers unconnected to general strategy, most were caused by combatants following the rules of engagement proscribed by their commanders. These figures challenge the belief by authors such as Christopher Coker that the contemporary Western approach to war is more humane and less destructive than conflicts of the past.[21]

None of these figures include injuries, or damage to civilian homes, schools, hospitals, infrastructure, or other nonmilitary institutions. Nor do they include the secondary effects and long-term consequences to civilians that were the direct result from the destruction of these facilities. Although such damage is far more difficult to quantify than immediate deaths and injuries, investigations by international and nongovernmental organizations do provide a snapshot of the depth of collateral destruction to civilian institutions in recent conflicts. These snapshots paint a picture of widespread damage and destruction to the facilities and institutions necessary for the survival and well-being of the civilian population. For example, in the aftermath of NATO's air war against the Taliban in 2001 an estimated 3,200 Afghan civilians died of "starvation, exposure, associated illnesses, or injury sustained while in flight from war zones" as a direct result of coalition airstrikes.[22]

In all cases, the casualties and damage were inflicted by military organizations that were committed to the principle of civilian immunity and to the protection of noncombatants imposed by the laws and customs of war. The official military doctrines of all 28 members of NATO, as well as the state of Israel, not only specifically prohibit targeting civilians and attacking civilian facilities, but also mandate that its combat forces attempt to minimize incidental civilian losses. Indeed, much of the text in their respective military manuals is drawn verbatim from the applicable treaties that comprise the international law of armed conflict.[23] In implementing these policies, the armed services of these 29 nations have generated procedures and guidelines for minimizing civilian casualties during military operations, conducted extensive training programs to instruct their soldiers on the laws and customs of warfare, and developed complex rules of engagement for each conflict to ensure that their actions are consistent with these laws.

For example, following the uproar over the 1968 My Lai massacre in Vietnam, the US Department of Defense issued an order requiring that all members of the military be trained in the laws and customs of war and instructing its soldiers to report war crimes and investigate allegations as they arise. This directive was updated in 2006.[24] In July 2012, the US Army released a Civilian Casualty Mitigation manual (CIVCAS), outlining what they call an "integrated approach" to reducing noncombatant deaths that would operate at various levels of preparation, planning, and implementation of military action.[25] At the same time, the US Department of Defense has also developed a "collateral damage estimate methodology" that outlines standards, methods, techniques, and processes for its commanders to conduct a collateral damage estimate prior to authorizing attacks for the purpose of mitigating incidental damage to noncombatants.[26] According to the US State Department, "the goal to mitigate the effects of civilian, or 'collateral' damage, as it is euphemistically referred to, is ingrained in the U.S. military from the first officer whose task it is to identify appropriate targets to the individual in theater who finally presses the button to launch a strike."[27]

As a result, several academic studies conclude that this has led to an internalization of noncombatant immunity within the US military's organizational culture, particularly among its officers.[28]

Moreover, during each of the above cited conflicts, military lawyers were closely involved in the planning stages for developing attack strategies. The United States and Israel, for example, regularly includes judge advocates (military lawyers) in meetings to determine target selection, charging them with making judgments regarding the legality of specific targets.[29] During the 2003 US invasion of Iraq, the Pentagon developed a list that detailed each potential target, and submitted this list to military lawyers for review. Accompanying this list was another one that specified objects, buildings, and infrastructure that would be off limits to attack.[30]

In addition to these legal restrictions, there is nearly universal agreement among Western military experts that inflicting harm to civilians and their facilities is almost always counterproductive from both a practical and political standpoint.[31] Civilian casualties make it difficult for the attacking state to maintain support from both allied governments and their own populations, and produce strong condemnation from intergovernmental and international nongovernmental organizations.[32] According to the United States Army, for example, Army units must mitigate civilian casualties because they "undermine national policy objectives," "incite increased opposition to Army units," and "create lasting repercussions that impair post-conflict reconstruction and reconciliation . . . leading to ill will among the host-nation population and political pressure that can limit freedom of action of military forces."[33] For this reason, as Jessica Stanton demonstrates, in many civil wars both governments and rebels avoid targeting civilians in the hope of winning support from domestic and international audiences.[34]

Given all of this, why are civilian casualties and damage to civilian facilities so consistently high in conflicts fought by the Western powers?

How High Is High?

The first cut to answering this question is to determine how high is high. Brookings Institution Senior Fellow Michael O'Hanlon referred to the approximately 1,000 civilians killed by coalition air attacks in Afghanistan in October and November of 2001 as a *"mercifully low number*," demonstrating that "the war caused relatively *modest harm to innocents*."[35] Vice chair of the Joint Chiefs of Staff, General Joseph Ralston, said of NATO's war against Serbia that "despite the weight of bombs dropped, Serbian civilian casualties were *amazingly light*, estimated at 1,500 dead."[36] Commenting on the approximately 3,500 Iraqi civilians killed by coalition forces during the two-month 1991 Persian Gulf War, the Pentagon stated in its final report to Congress that "although the death or injury of any civilian is regrettable, *the apparently low number* clearly reflects Coalition efforts to minimize civilian casualties."[37]

Indeed, many members of the military argue that focusing on civilian deaths is itself a "fundamentally flawed approach and therefore the number of casualties in and of themselves is not relevant."[38] RAND Corporation analyst Benjamin Lamberth further laments that "thanks to unrealistic efforts to treat the normal friction of war as avoidable human error, every occurrence of unintended collateral damage became overinflated as front-page news."[39] Former Defense Department attorney Marine Colonel W. Hays Parks argues that compliance with the laws and customs of war is "not determined by the amount of the devastation or the number of deaths, but by the direction of the action itself, i.e., by what is deliberately intended and directly done."[40] Another military official put it this way: "I've approved targets that could have caused some 3,000 civilian casualties, and I've raised questions about targets predicted to risk fewer than 20 civilian lives. The issue is the importance of the target."[41] Former US Defense Department intelligence analyst Anthony Cordesman agrees, holding that "counting every bit of collateral damage as if it was important is pointless."[42]

This view is reflected in policy. Western military organizations do not measure or catalog civilian casualties, nor do they consider them a factor in evaluating the success of an operation, except in cases where they cause a public uproar. While militaries conduct many different types of evaluations both during and after a conflict, such as battle damage assessments (BDA), there is no standard method for conducting a civilian casualty assessment. Rather, military effectiveness is calculated by measuring the inputs—such as the total number of sorties, total munitions, and percentage of precision strikes—against specific effects, specifically the degree to which they can destabilize the political and economic systems on which the enemy relies.

This brings us back to the question, how high is high? Although raw numbers alone cannot necessarily answer this, there are at least two statistical indicators that can help us assess the degree to which the civilian casualties produced by Western military operations are the outcome of excessive military force:

(1) *The civilian casualty ratio*, which compares the number of civilian deaths to those of enemy soldiers, thereby calculating the percentage of total enemy casualties that were civilian. A high civilian to soldier ratio suggests that the attacking force did not take feasible precaution in attempting to limit collateral damage.

(2) *The risk transfer ratio*, which measures the relationship between civilian deaths caused by military attacks to those suffered by one's own soldiers. Risk transfer occurs when a belligerent minimizes the risk to their soldiers by increasing the dangers to the civilian population. Although it is difficult to statistically determine the amount of risk a military force assumes in an armed conflict—much less making a direct connection between this and civilian casualties it inflicts—this ratio can offer a crude illustration of whether civilians or combatants are placed in the greater danger during the conflict. A high ratio that is heavily slanted toward civilian deaths suggests that the attacking force faced a minimal risk in relation to the one it posed to the civilian population.[43]

Assessing the Statistics

The preliminary evidence suggests that there is a clear prima facie case that the level of collateral damage and other noncombatant deaths in Western-initiated armed conflicts has been exceptionally high given the civilian casualty and risk transfer ratios. This is particularly evident inasmuch as in all cases, the conflicts were fought solely on the territory of the enemy, thereby giving the attacking forces the luxury of choosing the time and circumstances of each attack without having to worry about defending their own territory or populations.

During the two-month air war over Afghanistan in 2001, 3,000 to 4,000 Taliban and al Qaeda fighters were killed by coalition attacks,[44] meaning that 27% of the enemy casualties were civilian on the low end, and 43% on the high end. NATO's 1999 air war against Serbia killed approximately 576 Serbian soldiers,[45] resulting in a 46 to 61% civilian death rate, depending on which civilian casualty figure one uses. Approximately 22,000 Iraqi soldiers were killed by coalition attacks during the 1991 Gulf war,[46] meaning that 14% of the casualties were civilians, by far the lowest ratio of the group. This lower percentage, however, can be attributed largely to the devastating around-the-clock air attacks against Iraqi soldiers in the desert that caused extremely high military casualties; virtually all of the civilian casualties were in Iraq's major cities, far from the battlefield, where they were separated from their country's military forces. These attacks produced a far higher rate of civilian deaths in relation to military casualties.

Approximately 450 Panamanian Defense Force soldiers died in action during the 1999 invasion,[47] leading to a 40% rate of civilian deaths. The first five years of the 2003 Iraq war saw 23,000 pro-Saddam Iraqi soldiers and anti-coalition insurgents killed,[48] producing a 33% civilian fatality rate.[49] During the 2006 Israeli–Hezbollah conflict approximately 500 Hezbollah fighters were killed,[50] making 67% of the casualties civilian. An estimated 669 Hamas fighters were killed during the 2014 Gaza war, producing a civilian death toll of 69%.[51] According to the Bureau of Investigative Journalism, the drone wars fought by the United States in Pakistan from 2004 to 2017 produced between 1,535 and 3,579 noncivilian (thus military) deaths, bringing the civilian casualty ratio between 11% on the low end and 39% on the high end; the New American Foundation puts the ratio at 32% up through 2012.[52]

The risk transfer ratios are equally revealing. During the 2001 Afghan war, 30 NATO soldiers were killed by hostile action (not including accidents or friendly fire).[53] When compared to the number of civilian deaths (above), this computes to a 43–1 risk transfer ratio. That is, 43 civilians died for every coalition soldier. No NATO troops died in combat during the 1999 air war against Serbia,[54] which computes to a 500–1,500–0 civilian to military casualty ratio, depending on which estimate of civilian casualties one uses.

During the 1991 Persian Gulf War, 240 coalition soldiers died from hostile fire,[55] a ratio of 22 civilian deaths for every coalition solder killed. Over the first seven and half years of the second Iraq war, 3,842 coalition troops lost their lives in hostile incidents,[56] meaning that three times as many Iraqi civilians died by coalition attacks as coalition fatalities at the hands of their adversaries. During the 2006 Lebanon war, 119 Israeli soldiers (and 43 Israeli civilians) were killed in combat,[57] a 10–1 Lebanese civilian-Israeli soldier combatant ratio. Sixty-four Israeli soldiers (and one civilian) did in battle during the 2014 war with Hamas in Gaza, suggesting that 23 times more civilians than Israeli soldiers died in the conflict. The 1989 Panama invasion cost 23 American lives, meaning that 13 civilians died for every US soldier.[58] Obviously by definition, the drone wars did not produce any American casualties, which put the civilian to military death ratio at approximately between 423 and 965–0 for the period in question. On this measure at least, in all of these cases, civilian casualties appear to have been consistently high relative to the threats posed to the attacking armies. These statistics are summarized in Table 1.1.[59]

On their face, these figures also suggest that the rate of civilian casualties in wars fought by Western powers—measured in relation to military deaths on both sides—has not decreased over the past few decades. Indeed in some cases we have seen an increase. Thus the use of precision-guided bombs, computer-generated collateral damage models, and other types of advanced technology does not appear to have had any effect on reducing collateral damage in armed conflicts.

Military leaders, public officials, and legal their advisors usually attribute collateral damage and other causes of civilian harm to factors beyond their control, by arguing that although they take unprecedented steps to avoid harming civilians, noncombatant casualties are an inevitable side effect of all armed conflicts. Michael Schmitt argues that collateral damage is the result of three factors: uncertainty as to what is being hit, the inability of the attacker to precisely meter the amount of force applied, and lack of absolute certainty that the target can be hit.[60] These factors are present in all conflicts, he and other military leaders assert, and as long as they follow the basic laws of armed conflict, there is little that combatants can do to prevent them. Similarly, former Director of British Army Legal Services, Major General A. P. V. Rogers, argues that "although they are not military objectives, civilians and civilian objects are subject to the general dangers of War in the sense that attacks on military personnel and military objectives may cause incidental damage. It may not be possible to limit the radius of effect entirely to the objective to be attacked."[61]

Table 1.1 Civilian Casualty Ratios in Western Conflicts

Conflict	Year(s) of Conflict	Civilian Deaths	Coalition Military Deaths	Enemy Military Deaths	Ratio Civilian–Coalition Deaths	% Enemy Deaths Civilian
US–Panama	1989	300	23	450	13–1	40
Gulf War	1991	3,600	240	22,000	22–1	14
NATO–Serbia	1999	500–1,500	0	576	500–0	46
US–Taliban	2001–2002	1,000–1,300	30	3,000–4,000	43–1	27–43
Second Iraq War	2003–2010	11,516	3,842	23,000	3–1	33%
Israel–Hezbollah	2006	1,183	119	500	10–1	67%
Drone wars	2004–2017	424–966	0	1,535–3,579	424–966–0	11–39%
NATO–Libya	2011	72	0	?	72–0	?
Israeli–Hamas	2014	1,523	64	669	23–1	69%

The Israeli Foreign Ministry argued in a report defending their conduct in the 2008 war against Hamas in Gaza that "in the heat of battle, commanders must make agonising, complex and hazardous decisions affecting the lives of their soldiers, the achievement of their military mission and the safety of civilians ... even the most sophisticated systems and the most rigorous training cannot prevent all civilian casualties and damage to public and private property."[62] Law professor Kenneth Anderson took a more affirmative position, defending collateral damage by comparing Western military practices to those of their adversaries. In reference to the Gulf War, he argued that "there is no moral equivalence between stray missiles aimed in good faith, using the best technology, and using human shields, shelling civilians to prevent them from fleeing Basra, and rape or summary executions of prisoners."[63]

Political and military officials also attribute civilian casualties to the behavior of their adversaries, arguing that unlike their own organizations, their enemies intentionally comingle their military forces with civilians, thereby putting their own populations at risk. Weaker parties employ this tactic to protect their fighters and military resources from attack by using churches, mosques, hospitals, and schools as hiding places, weapons-storage facilities, and combat positions.[64] In doing so, they exploit the Western commitment to minimize collateral damage, thereby discouraging their vastly stronger adversaries from launching assaults that could result in significant civilian casualties.

Jefferson Reynolds argues that this use of what he terms "concealment warfare" by weaker parties in conflicts with Western states is the primary cause of civilian casualties over the past few decades.[65] Thus, responsibility for most collateral damage lies with the West's adversaries. As the US Air Force asserts, a party to a conflict that puts its own population at risk by failing to segregate military and civilian activities automatically accepts collateral damage caused as a result of attacks on military objects.[66] Similarly, Yoram Dinstein and Margaret Artz argue that in cases of comingling, the definition of "excessive injury" (to civilians) should be relaxed due to the fact that the presence of civilians is beyond the control of the attacker and the result of illegal activity.[67] Israel Foreign Minister Tzipi Livni adds, "It's difficult to target like a surgery. Unfortunately, civilians sometimes pay the price of giving shelter to terrorists."[68]

In the following pages, I will demonstrate that while accidents and concealment warfare can increase the likelihood of civilian casualties, they only account for a very small percentage of collateral damage and other forms of noncombatant deaths and injuries. Rather, I will show that the primary explanation for the high rate of collateral damage in conflicts fought by Western states is the reckless war-fighting strategies adopted by their military organizations. This determination of cause and effect cannot be made by employing statistical calculations. Instead, we must examine the details of how and why civilians were killed in each particular conflict. This is the goal of chapters 3 through 6.

Setting the Standard for Civilian Protection

The key factor in determining whether the level of civilian casualties and damage to civilian objects is excessive, is the degree to which these casualties were foreseeable, preventable, and unnecessary. The standard for making this determination is international humanitarian law (IHL), the body of multilateral treaties, customary practices, and normative principles that regulate the means and methods that combatants may employ during an armed conflict.[69] The primary goal of IHL is to protect those who are not directly participating in hostilities either because they are not combatants (that is, civilians or medical personnel) or because they have been rendered *hors de combat* (incapable of performing any military activities as a result of being wounded, sick, or detained as prisoners of war).

International humanitarian law provides the best guide to minimizing civilian casualties because it carefully balances the requirements for effective military action with humanitarian concerns. This has always been a delicate task. Military operations are about violence and destruction while humanitarian concerns are about minimizing the effect of this destruction on noncombatants. From the military perspective, combat missions are designed to defeat the enemy in the most efficient manner with the lowest cost to its own soldiers and resources. The laws of armed conflict were never designed to ensure a fair fight between belligerents, and for that reason its creators were careful to avoid creating rules that would provide an opportunity for one party to gain a tactical advantage over the others.[70] Since there are obviously no referees to determine winners and losers, the combatants themselves must establish their own goals, choose the means through which they will attempt to secure them, and determine when their goals have been met. This provides a significant amount of leeway for combatants to pursue various strategies for achieving their aims.

At the same time, the international community has long agreed that the right of combatants to choose their means and methods of warfare is limited.[71] Specifically, it is subject to the regulations imposed by legally binding treaties and customary practices, all of which reflect prevailing international norms regarding human rights and technological advancements in warfare. The decision by political leaders to steadily increase special protection for noncombatants, even at the expense of military necessity, is the result of such advancements. Although history is filled with cases of marauding armies massacring civilians and laying siege to entire cities, until the twentieth century combatants lacked the means to target and kill large numbers of noncombatants in a short period of time, particularly those located far from the front line of the battlefield. As a result, prior to the introduction of aerial warfare, military objectives were usually confined to such targets as troop concentrations, fortified buildings, arms depots, military installations and infrastructure, and command centers.[72]

This changed with advancements in both the technology and organization of armed conflict. Technologically, the development of mechanized armies, rocket and jet propulsion, satellite and computer guidance systems, and high-yield explosives made it possible to target and destroy any object at any time, even those deep within the towns and cities of the adversary. This was coupled with the adoption of "total war" strategies as the primary means for pursuing victory. Total war is a type of combat that is directed against an adversary's entire society. Its goal is not only to gain an advantage on the battlefield, but also to destroy the enemy's morale, disrupt its productive capability, destabilize its governmental and civil functions, and undermine the ability of the society to sustain the war effort.[73] In practice, this involved targeting virtually anything supporting the war effort, including infrastructure, social institutions, industry, labor, and the will of the adversary's population. In this context, during the first half of the twentieth century, most states considered attacking civilians to be an acceptable strategy insofar as it affected the morale and support of the enemy population.

World War II took this concept to a new level, not only by introducing massive aerial bombing of major towns and cities by both sides of the conflict, but also by employing large-scale reprisals against civilian population centers in retaliation for attacks by the other side.[74] As a result, World War II was the most destructive conflict in human history. In addition to the tens of millions of soldiers and civilians killed or injured, thousands more civilians were raped, imprisoned, or held as sex slaves by Japanese soldiers during its occupations of Korea and China.[75] Such mistreatment greatly surpassed previous modern conflicts in their scale and level of cruelty.

As a result, since the mid-twentieth century, international law has moved steadily toward increasing the protection of noncombatants as the dominant principle underlying the laws of armed conflict. Indeed, civilian protection has come to dominate both the discourse and progressive development of international law in this area. Moreover, the rapid proliferation of global and regional intergovernmental organizations such as the United Nations and the Organization of American States—coupled with the growth of nongovernmental organizations such as the International Committee of the Red Cross and Human Rights Watch—have increased the management and monitoring of armed conflict in favor of greater civilian protection.[76]

This has caused concern among some military officials, who complain that the laws of war have become too restrictive by giving too much protection to civilians at the expense of military necessity. For example, military lawyers Michael Schmitt and Lieutenant Colonel Joseph Holland both object that the very term "international humanitarian law" (as opposed to the more neutral "laws of armed conflict") symbolizes the priority that contemporary international law gives to humanitarian factors over military advantage.[77] W. Hays Parks further charges that since IHL tends to be developed by international lawyers, political leaders, and diplomats rather than military officials, it fails to reflect the realities of combat that those with battlefield expertise and experience would better understand. "War is something that cannot be trifled with by individuals who do not understand it," Parks charges. "It is complex and lacking in order not given to simple rules that govern all circumstances at all levels of conflict."[78] Air

Force Major (and military lawyer) Jefferson Reynolds goes even further, arguing that compliance with the letter of IHL can provide a significant military advantage to weaker parties in an asymmetric conflict.[79]

It should not be surprising that military officials and their legal advisers would prefer to have maximum flexibility to pursue their combat strategies with a minimum of restrictions; that is their job. However, this perspective on IHL and its goal of minimizing civilian casualties misses several important factors.

First, armed conflicts do not exist independently from the political systems that nurture them; they reflect the prevailing norms, political environments, and practices of states, as well as the increasing influence of intergovernmental and nongovernmental organizations. The movement toward greater humanitarian protection over the past half century has clearly had overwhelming support within the international community from both governments and officials from international organizations. Since the late nineteenth century, states have developed more than 100 treaties and other legal agreements designed to regulate armed conflict. All states in the world (194) have ratified the 1949 Geneva Conventions, and an overwhelming majority are also parties to the first and second Protocols (173 and 167, respectively). Even most of the nonsignatories to the two Protocols (such as the United States and Israel) have implicitly accepted most of its provisions by incorporating them verbatim into their military manuals and by publicly stating their legality.[80]

In addition to these formal agreements, over the past few decades the major principles protecting the lives and welfare of civilians during armed conflict have become firmly established in international customary law through both state practice and resolutions of multilateral organizations.[81] Customary law is binding on all countries and their political leaders regardless of whether they are parties to particular treaties, reflecting the consensus of the international community of states. As the United Nations Special Court for Sierra Leone declared, "it is well settled that all parties to an armed conflict, whether states or non-state actors, are bound by international humanitarian law, even though only states may become parties to international treaties."[82]

Second, armed conflicts almost always occur alongside corresponding diplomatic and political processes involving the belligerents, intergovernmental organizations, and neighboring states. Military power is not the only method available for a state to achieve its goals, and therefore constraints on the use of armed force do not prevent states from using other means for promoting their interests. Although military force may be preferred in some cases, particularly by those states with the ability to dominate in that area, contemporary norms preclude its use if it cannot be employed without producing extensive civilian casualties.

Studying Civilian Casualties

Most academics, journalists, and political analysts who study the impact of armed conflict on civilians focus on the victimization of noncombatants by those who brazenly ignore or flout the principle of civilian immunity. From the front pages of the daily newspaper to the activities of the International Criminal Court to the volumes of research produced by security studies scholars, the horrors of armed conflict are usually represented by the shocking war crimes committed in conflicts such as those in the former Yugoslavia, Rwanda, Sierra Leon, Chechnya, Uganda, Somalia, Syria, and elsewhere.[83] However, shocking as these actions may be, these types of violations are in many ways the least interesting from both a policy and scholarly perspective, because such violations are usually unambiguous, easily detected, and difficult to defend. Governments and international organizations have developed a wide range of institutions to address these flagrant war crimes: courts martial and military tribunals, economic and diplomatic sanctions, prosecution by international criminal courts, and even military intervention. More insidious are practices that produce extensive civilian casualties under the shroud of legality and concern for the innocent. There is little available—other than bad publicity or the resentment of local populations—to deal with them.

In other cases, some research focuses on the issue of civilian casualties without distinguishing between those that are deliberate and those that are inadvertent. For example, John Tirman's broad study of civilian casualties inflicted during armed conflicts fought by the United States doesn't distinguish between those caused by deliberate attacks against noncombatants and those that were produced inadvertently.[84] This is at least in part because his timeline begins during World War II and includes the wars in Korea and Vietnam, all conflicts in which the United States did engage in indiscriminant attacks against population centers in enemy towns and cities. As a result, although the study is well-researched and illuminating, by not distinguishing between deliberate and inadvertent casualties it misses an important nuance in US warfare, particularly the efforts by policymakers and military officials to minimize civilian casualties after Vietnam. Moreover, he fails to link civilian casualties to any specific political policies or military strategies, leaving us wondering why, beyond indifference, US wars produce so many noncombatant deaths and injuries.

The most comprehensive study of collateral damage to date has been undertaken by Neta Crawford, who focuses on the moral responsibility and culpability of military organizations for the collateral damage inflicted on civilians during US wars since 2001.[85] She does so by developing a theory of collective moral responsibility. Crawford argues, in part, that collateral damage is less the product of immoral acts by individual soldiers than the result of bureaucratic decisions, rules of engagement, and expanded definitions of "military necessity" made by military organizations at the organizational and command levels. Crawford holds that most of the civilian casualties she studied were foreseeable, but accepted by US officials under the principle of proportionality.[86]

Crawford makes a compelling case for how we should apportion moral responsibility for collateral damage, and her work provides a strong starting point for taking a broader view of the phenomenon. *Bugsplat* builds upon and expands the study of unintended civilian casualties by broadening its scope and linking them specific practices that have defined the Western approach toward warfare since the end of the Cold War. Although Crawford's work is extremely well-researched and detailed, its focus on the United States after September 11, 2001 is narrow in that it does not fully capture the full scope of the phenomenon. The practices that lead to high levels of collateral damage by military organizations that accept the principle of civilian immunity began well before 2001, and are have been adopted by a wider group of states beyond the United States. For this reason, this book expands the focus to include the Western powers, broadly conceived (the United States, Canada, the European members of NATO, Australia, and Israel) since the end of the Cold War in 1989.

This is not simply an extension of the timeline and scope of the study. I argue that there is a well-defined approach toward armed conflict that characterize the practice of the advanced Western democracies that in turn accounts for the levels of collateral damage. By focusing on these practices (articulated in chapter 2), *Bugsplat* is less concerned with moral responsibility or culpability than with the consequences of strategy.

Although I employ international law as the standard for defining legitimate behavior, this book is not intended to be a legal analysis, nor does it attempt to evaluate the degree to which Western military organizations conform to the specific provisions of treaty and customary international law. Rather, I try to demonstrate how such organizations exploit the collateral damage exemption in IHL that enables them to generally follow the rules while still causing extensive civilian casualties and damage to civilian property and infrastructure.

Organization of the Book

This book argues that the level of collateral damage produced by Western armies in a given conflict is the direct outcome of the reckless war-fighting strategies pursued by its military organizations. Chapter 2 discusses the specific practices pursued by Western states that result in high levels of civilian casualties and argues that given the Western method of fighting wars, such levels are inevitable. The next four chapters examine specific cases, exploring the degree to which the theories advanced in chapter 2 explain the level of civilian casualties and damage to civilian facilities in Western armed conflicts. It is not the purpose of these chapters to provide new information about the cases. All of them have been extensively researched by military analysts, human rights investigators, and security scholars. Rather, the case studies are narrowly designed to focus on the degree to which the civilian casualties can be explained by the practices theorized in chapter 2, rather than the more commonly accepted factors cited by military and government leaders above. In pursuing this task, I use existing data (both primary and secondary source) and studies to trace the causes of collateral damage in armed conflicts fought by the Western powers.

Western states have been involved in 10 armed conflicts since the end of the Cold War, not including peacekeeping missions, retaliatory air strikes, limited operations conducted by Special Forces, and other uses of force that fall short of sustained, ongoing hostilities (for example, the 1993 Operation Restore Hope in Somalia or the 1994 Operation Deliberate Force in Bosnia).[87] This study will examine five of them, grouped into four chapters. These case studies are designed to determine how and why the level of civilian casualties reached the levels that they did, and the degree to which they were preventable. As such, they will examine whether there is a link between the casualty rates and the strategies pursued by the belligerents as manifestations of the Western method of warfare that has existed since at least 1989. The specific cases were chosen because they each represent a different type of conflict fought by the 30 states that comprise what has popularly been referred to as the Western democracies.

The first conflict in the study was prosecuted by a broad, Western-led coalition against a moderately strong state in what military analysts label a "medium-intensity conflict" (the 1991 Gulf War). The next two cases are one-sided clashes initiated by NATO that consisted exclusively of sustained air attacks against Serbia and Libya. The fourth case involves a war between a nation-state and a nonstate actor (Israel and Hezbollah). The final case is an example of what Michael Ignatieff has called a "virtual war," fought exclusively with remotely piloted drones over a range of territories in the absence of any battlefield. In all cases, the conflicts were fought using the specific Western approach to warfare.

Of the 10 armed conflicts fought by the Western democracies since 1989, only four involved protracted fighting using ground troops. This book will examine one of them in detail, the 1991 Gulf War; however, since the ground war only lasted four days and virtually all of the collateral damage was produced by air attacks over Iraq's cities, most of the chapter will focus on the air campaign that preceded the fighting by ground troops. The empirical section of the book will not include the other two conflicts involving sustained ground combat—the Second Iraq War (2003–2011) and the US–NATO war against the Taliban in Afghanistan (2001–2014).

I am excluding Afghanistan largely because there is little data on the causes of civilian casualties after the initial air campaign of 2001, specifically on how, why, and under what circumstances civilians were killed during the 14 years US and NATO forces were engaged in combat.[88] There is a similar problem with the US war against Iraq. As mentioned above, the most reliable figures attribute at least 11,516 of civilian deaths to attacks by coalition forces, however, the same sources estimate that 68,396 (74%) of the total civilian deaths were caused by "unknown perpetrators."[89]

Chapter 3 examines the Gulf War of 1991, viewed by many military analysts at the time as the prototype for the new Western way of war in the post-Cold War era. It was the most concentrated use of military force employed by the West since the US war in Vietnam two decades earlier, and provided the first opportunity to employ the new warfighting strategies discussed in the next chapter.

Chapter 4 analyzes NATO's air campaigns against Serbia in 1999 and Libya in 2011. Both conflicts are distinctive in several ways. First, both relied exclusively on air attacks against a wide variety of targets, with little risk to the attackers. No ground troops were involved. This gave NATO complete control in choosing targets and initiating attacks. Second, both campaigns were waged in the name of humanitarian goals—that is, to save civilian lives—making civilian casualties all the more problematic. Third, as purely NATO actions, all aspects of the campaigns were theoretically subject to consensus decision-making involving all members of the alliance.

Chapter 5 examines the 2006 war between Israel and Hezbollah in Lebanon, a conflict between a state and a nonstate militia involving both air attacks and ground combat. This is a prototypical example of what analysts refer to as an "asymmetrical conflict," that is, one in which there is a wide disparity in both the legal status of the belligerents (state vs. nonstate) and the resources employed (primarily military power, but also economic, political and diplomatic assets).[90]

Chapter 6 focuses on the war between the United States and al Qaeda between 2001 and 2017, focusing on the US strategy of "targeted killings." Unlike our conventional understanding of warfare, this war was not waged against a single, centralized entity, but rather an amorphous group that included al Qaeda, Taliban, and associated forces located in many parts of the world without any specific territory or institutional center. At the same time, the administrations of both George W. Bush and Barak Obama classified this confrontation as an armed conflict and as such, it was regulated by international humanitarian law. This chapter will examine civilian casualties during this effort, which began in 2001 and is still ongoing. Since the conflict involves many levels of activity, this chapter will only focus on those that can be classified as military action (not law enforcement) against discreet entities that fulfill the criteria for a "transnational" armed conflict.[91] As such, it will center mostly on the drone wars inasmuch as this has been the primary means employed by the United States and its allies to prosecute the military aspects of the conflict.

Chapter 7 provides a conclusion and summary of assessing collateral damage.

The case studies draw from a variety of documentary sources, primarily official reports, interviews, and on-site investigations by international agencies and international nongovernmental organizations, as well as those issued by government agencies. I also make considerable use of research conducted by various policy analysts and scholars. Like most researchers, I view government reports with a fair amount of skepticism, inasmuch as they are likely to be self-serving and biased. At the same time, they do articulate the perspectives of the public officials and military officers who write them, and we can learn a lot about strategy and motives by carefully scrutinizing their content.

I found the most useful reports and investigations to be those that are conducted by nongovernmental organizations such as the International Committee of the Red Cross (ICRC), Human Rights Watch, and Amnesty International. Certainly the objects of such reports, particularly the military organizations involved, often argue that these organizations are biased against the use of military force in general, and that this taints their investigations. W. Hays Parks, for example, charges that the ICRC has a "fixation against the employment of airpower" and wants to restrict "if not prohibit the use of airpower beyond the immediate battlefield."[92] Yet these organizations offer the most neutral perspectives, inasmuch as they are neither parties to any of the conflicts nor do they have any specific relationship to any of the sides involved. As such, they have no particular interest in the outcome of their studies. Their critiques are nonpartisan and are almost always levied at all parties involved. Similarly, reports and investigations by intergovernmental organizations such as the United Nations offer the perspective of an agency that is not a party to the any of the conflicts, except the Gulf war.

In addition, I draw from a considerable number of studies of each conflict conducted by international law scholars, security analysts, and nonprofit research organizations such as the Council on Foreign Relations, the Brookings Institution, the RAND Corporation, the Project on Defense Alternatives, the Bureau of Investigative Journalism, and the New American Foundation. This literature tends to draw from empirical work, some of which was conducted by the above sources, but offers critical analysis that is useful in developing a fuller understanding.

Collateral Damage and Western War-Fighting Strategy

The level of civilian casualties and damage to civilian objects produced during an armed conflict is determined by the specific war-fighting strategies that are employed by political and military organizations. Although a wide range of actors—from individual soldiers to commanding generals—can be responsible for the deaths and injuries to noncombatants and damage to civilian facilities, it is the conduct of government officials and top military commanders that have the greatest impact on how combatants fight. It is their policies and approaches to combat that either pose the greatest threat to—or provide for the strongest protection of—the bedrock principle of civilian immunity. This chapter will examine how these policies and strategies determine the level of civilian casualties in armed conflicts fought by Western states who are committed to the laws and customs of war.

Civilian casualties can result from at least five different types of actions and policies: civilian targeting, depraved indifference, reckless attacks, inadvertent spillover effects, and accidents.

Civilian targeting is a calculated strategy to inflict suffering on the general populace by deliberately focusing attacks on population centers and public facilities such schools, commercial areas, hospitals, residential neighborhoods, and refugee camps.[1] Such attacks are executed with the belief that mass killing, destitution, and terror are appropriate—or at least necessary—responses to military and political problems.[2] This type of warfare flouts the principle of distinction by making the civilian population, individual civilians, nondefended localities, and demilitarized zones the object of attack. This brazen violation of IHL has been employed in a variety of conflicts over the past two decades. In conflicts such as the

1992–1995 war between Bosnia and Serbia, for example, civilian casualties were not collateral damage, but rather the primary goal of the Serbian forces attacking defenseless towns and cities in Bosnia-Herzegovina.[3] Similarly, during the 10-year civil war in Sierra Leone in the 1990s, rebel forces systematically murdered, mutilated, and raped civilians during their military offensives.[4] These types of violations have been the primary focus of research by academics and journalists, as well as disciplinary action taken by international organizations against violators.

Depraved indifference warfare occurs when attackers exhibit a wonton disregard for civilian lives by executing massive indiscriminant attacks on towns and cities for the purpose of progressively degrading the adversary's infrastructure and political and economic institutions. In criminal law, depraved indifference is defined as an act that presents a very high risk of death to others, and is "so wanton, so deficient in a moral sense of concern, so lacking in regard for the life or lives of others, and so blameworthy as to warrant the same criminal liability as that which the law imposes upon a person who intentionally causes a crime."[5] Launching such attacks on heavily populated towns and cities—including those aimed at facilities that are essential for the survival of the population—suggests a wanton indifference to the lives of noncombatants.[6] Unlike civilian targeting, depraved indifference warfare is defined by the risk that is intentionally created by the perpetrator's conduct, rather than a specific malevolent intent or the injuries actually resulting from the action. In both cases, however, the damage is intentional rather than collateral. For example, the widespread attacks against major towns and cities employed by Russian forces during the Second Chechen War in 1999 were aimed at terrorizing the population and punishing them for supporting secessionist groups.[7] Although the purpose of their attacks was not specifically aimed at killing civilians, the lack of concern for the effect of their attacks on civilians that Russian military officials knew they were inflicting was evidence of a depraved indifference to human life.

Reckless attacks are those that are executed with the knowledge that they will likely create a substantial risk of injury or death to those other than the target. Whereas there is no specific intent to cause harm, the action demonstrates a reckless disregard for the foreseeable consequences of one's actions.[8] They differ from depraved indifference attacks in that they are the result of negligence and recklessness rather than a wonton disregard of human life. While they may be irresponsible, they are not necessarily illegal. In some cases, the resulting casualties can be considered a form of collateral damage if they are unintentional or inadvertent. For example, as I discuss in chapter 4, NATO's bombing of Serbia's Radio and Television (Radio Televisija Srbije or RTS) headquarters in a densely populated neighborhood in downtown Belgrade during the 1999 war exposed hundreds of civilians to grave risk, even though the attack was executed with precision-guided munitions, and the military attempted to minimize the damage to civilians. This form of combat is one of the primary focuses of this book inasmuch as most civilian casualties produced in Western conflicts tend to be the result of recklessness in executing the strategies discussed later in this chapter.

Accidents are unforeseen mishaps caused by weapons or equipment malfunctions, misidentification of targets, or other types of human or mechanical error. To the extent that they are the result of events beyond the control of the combatants, they are considered by some to be unpreventable tragedies. However, if they occur in the course of reckless attacks, they may not be unforeseeable. For example, a number of the civilian deaths caused by US drone attacks in Pakistan in the first decade of the twenty-first century were the result of misidentification of targets by the operators, all of whom were located thousands of miles from the scene. The deaths were likely accidental; however, as I will discuss in chapter 7, these types of accidents were frequent enough as to be predictable, even though no one knew in advance which specific attacks would produce this result.

Spillover effects are the unintended (although not necessarily unanticipated) secondary consequences of attacks launched against legitimate military targets. They occur whenever an attack produces casualties or damage beyond the range of the intended target, whether the targets are buildings, weapon systems, military vehicles, or soldiers. This is the classic form of collateral damage. As discussed in chapter 6, a number of Israeli air attacks on Hezbollah targets in Lebanon in 2006 produced explosions that radiated to nearby civilian homes, killing or injuring many of those living inside. Unlike accidents, spillover effects can be roughly calculated in advance even if they cannot be precisely predicted. For example, military planners can estimate the spillover effects that might arise from a particular attack through two measures: (1) lethal blast range, the radius around the detonation point of a bomb or other munitions at which a 100% mortality rate can be expected; and (2) the effective casualty radius, the radial distance from the point of detonation in which it may be expected that at least 50% of the exposed personnel will be casualties.[9] Moreover, one can calculate the probable effects of an explosion that would occur if a weapon missed its target by a statistically probable range. Based on this, planners often make calculations on what they would consider to be an acceptable rate of noncombatant losses given the importance of the target under the principle of proportionality (see next section).

The Standard for Culpability: International Humanitarian Law

A combatant's culpability for the casualties or damage to civilian facilities they cause during these types of actions is largely determined by the degree to which the casualties were preventable, legal, or necessary. As mentioned in chapter 1, this judgment is determined by the degree to which the combatants adhere to the standards established by IHL, which provides a common standard that is universally applicable to all armed conflicts regardless of the identity of the combatants, the nature or origin of the conflict, or the righteousness of the cause.[10] Distinctions between just and unjust war, aggression and self-defense, or good and evil are irrelevant in determining the means through which combatants may prosecute a conflict. The rules are binding on all sides. Thus, while there is some room for interpretation of a particular rule or its application in a specific circumstance, the provisions that provide for the protection of noncombatants is not subject to differing conceptions of morality, philosophy, political orientation, or culture. International law is the one common language for all states and their military organizations.

In addition to establishing a firm standard for behavior, IHL provides the best guide to minimizing civilian casualties because it carefully tempers the requirements for effective military action with humanitarian concerns. It does so through the legal principles of distinction, military necessity, proportionality, and feasible precaution. The degree to which combatants adhere to these principles—not just their own interpretations of specific text—largely determines the level of collateral damage in a particular conflict.

Distinction requires combatants to distinguish at all times between civilians and combatants and between military objectives and civilian objects in planning and executing attacks. In doing so, they must explicitly identify the status of any target prior to launching any strikes. All attacks must be limited to military targets, which are defined as those that by their nature, location, purpose, or use make an effective contribution to military action *and* whose destruction or neutralization offers a definite military advantage in circumstances ruling at the time.[11] This "two-pronged test" mandates that even if an object is of military value, it cannot be attacked if it's the military advantage is general or theoretical rather definite.[12] Any object that does not fall into this category is considered to be civilian and therefore not a legitimate target. In implementing this principle, belligerents are prohibited from (1) launching indiscriminate attacks against territories or objects; (2) deliberately attacking civilians or civilian objects unless they are specifically used for military purposes; (3) launching attacks which treat as a single military objective a number of clearly separated and distinct military objects located in populated areas; and (4) initiating attacks or threats whose primary purpose is to spread terror among the civilian population.[13]

Secondly, the use of force by combatants must be strictly limited to goals that are consistent with *military necessity*, that is, the amount and kind of force necessary to compel the submission of the enemy with the least possible expenditure of time, life, and money, subject to the laws of war.[14] Although central to IHL, this principle has been subject to re- or misinterpretation and manipulation by combatants. This is because the concept of military necessity is both empowering and restrictive. On the one hand, it empowers militaries to employ a wide range of actions and strategies designed to (a) kill enemy combatants or render them *hors de combat*; (b) weaken, neutralize, or destroy objects that play a direct role in sustaining the war effort; and (c) force the adversary into submission or surrender by destroying their capacity to fight or defend themselves.

On the other hand, the principle of military necessity also limits military action to those measures which are *indispensable* for securing the ends of the war, and which are lawful according to the modern law and usages of war. This excludes any act of hostility which makes the return to peace unnecessarily difficult.[15] Thus, the concept of military necessity cannot be a legal justification for taking *any* kind of action that combatants might view as beneficial to securing victory or the aims of the war effort. There must be some reasonable connection between the destruction of a particular object and the defeat of the enemy's military forces.

These restrictions must be followed even if it results in the loss of a battle or even a war.[16]

If combatants adhere to these principles, they are not held legally liable for "inadvertent" or "incidental" civilian casualties or the unintentional destruction of civilian objects that might result from a particular action. This is the collateral damage exemption in the law of armed conflict. Under IHL, such casualties are considered to be *inadvertent* if they are unanticipated or accidental.[17] Civilian losses are *incidental* if they are the unintended (although not necessarily unforeseen) side effect of an attack that is executed according to plan that abides by the principles of international humanitarian law. The primary criterion for determining whether such effects are collateral (as opposed to intentional or depraved) is the degree to which the attacker conformed to the principles of distinction, military necessity, and proportionality. Thus, a missile strike on an arms factory that kills civilian workers inside is legal because the facility was a legitimate military target and the civilians were not the object of the attack, but an attack on factory workers in their houses or on their way home from work is a violation of IHL because they were.

In addition, the responsibility of the attacker for civilian losses can be mitigated by two factors: the failure of the defenders to clearly separate military from civilian objects, and the use of civilian facilities for military purposes. According to IHL, the defending state or belligerent has an obligation to protect its own populations from an attack by removing civilians from the vicinity of military objects and avoiding the placement of military facilities and personnel near civilian areas.[18] This is known as the principle of passive precaution. In addition, under the principle of military necessity, civilian objects can become military ones when by their nature, location, purpose, or use such objects make an effective contribution to military action. This could theoretically include purely civilian facilities such as apartment buildings if they are used by combatants as staging areas or attack positions. Under certain conditions, combatants can legally target a site, facility, or object even if they anticipate that civilian casualties will result from such an attack.

Military action against legal targets that could result in civilian casualties or damage to civilian objects creates a very uneasy tension between military necessity and civilian immunity, a tension that is mediated by the third principle of IHL, the principle of proportionality. Proportionality holds that in *all* circumstances, the anticipated military advantage of an attack or action must be balanced against the probable or expected civilian losses. The expected civilian casualties or damage to civilian property from an attack cannot be "excessive" in relation to said advantage gained from the attack.[19] Combatants may not attack even a legitimate military target if the collateral damage to civilians is likely to be disproportionate to the specific military gain from the attack.[20] In other words, a target may be legal but the effects of an attack on noncombatants disproportionate and therefore illegitimate.

The failure of a defender to clearly separate civilian and military objects does not relieve the attacker of its obligation to adhere to the principle of proportionality. Attackers are still required to exercise extreme discretion before deciding to target a military object if they foresee that it would put civilians at risk.[21] The proportionality principle therefore raises the standard for declaring an object to be a legitimate target. Moreover, the increasing intolerance of collateral damage within the international community, by both states and international organizations, becomes a factor in determining proportionality. The greater the expected collateral damage, the narrower the definition of military advantage.[22] Attackers do not have an unlimited right to attack a facility or object even if it is being used for military purposes; combatants are still always required to consider the possibility of civilian casualties.[23]

In implementing this principle, combatants must make precise calculations concerning the likely effects of their attacks on civilian lives and objects, and then balance anticipated military gains with expected civilian losses *prior* to launching a strike. The attacker must make all reasonable efforts to ensure that such expected losses are not excessive—a term that is obviously difficult to quantify and which provides a loophole for legal liability. Therefore, while high civilian losses in and of themselves do not indicate a violation of the distinction principle, they may very well suggest a disproportionate attack.

Proportionality is the most difficult of the main principles to evaluate in practice because it requires balancing two incompatible values: civilian casualties and military necessity. Since there is no objective way of evaluating the value of a military target vis-à-vis the collateral damage it would likely cause, it provides military commanders with a loophole for engaging in attacks that they know will result in high civilian casualties by claiming that military necessity outweighed the expected losses. For example, Alexander Downes holds that the greater the military advantage associated with an object, the more collateral damage is legally permissible in an attack.[24] This is one way the collateral damage exemption is applied in practice. Of course, such an approach challenges spirit of proportionality inasmuch as it can be stretched to justify almost any type of attack, so long as a commander declares that the military value of the target is high enough.

In addition, the proportionality rule contains at least two other subjective elements that are difficult to weigh and easy to exploit. First, combatants are required to evaluate the *anticipated* military advantage against *expected* civilian losses. Determining what is anticipated and expected can be manipulated by those with an interest in a particular outcome. At the same time, there are limits to how far military commanders can go in doing so. Like all areas of law, there is an assumption of reasonableness in interpretation and application that provides boundaries for even the most subjective judgments. For example, the International Criminal Tribunal for the former Yugoslavia ruled that when determining whether an attack was proportionate, "it is necessary to examine whether a reasonably well-informed person in the circumstances of the actual perpetrator, making reasonable use of the information available to him or her, could have expected excessive civilian casualties to result from the attack."[25]

Second, although civilian losses may not be excessive, there is no firm measure for what this constitutes. As International Criminal Court Chief Prosecutor Luis Moreno-Ocampo held, "Under international humanitarian law and the Rome Statute, the death of civilians during an armed conflict, no matter how grave and regrettable, does not in itself constitute a war crime. International humanitarian law and the Rome Statute permit belligerents to carry out proportionate attacks against military objectives even when it is known that some civilian deaths or injuries will occur."[26]

War-Fighting Strategies and Collateral Damage

Despite the efforts of Western military organizations to comply with the laws of armed conflict, its war-fighting strategies inevitably lead to significant civilian casualties and long-term effects that threaten the lives and well-being of the civilian population. Such strategies are the result of the way it employs its dominant military technology pursuing what Martin Shaw calls the new "Western way of war." Shaw argues that since the end

of the Cold War, Western governments' difficulties in mobilizing public support for armed conflicts in the absence of clearly defined security
threats requires them to strictly limit the effects of war on their econo-
mies and societies.[27] In particular, Michael Ignatieff and Colin McInnes
hold that Western military technology and the lack of substantive threats
to their homelands encourage them to engage in "virtual wars" that
attempt to shield them from the devastating effects of armed conflict.[28]
This argument is supported by a variety of studies revealing that both
the military and civilian elite believe that the public support for military
action is conditioned, at least in part, on maintaining low casualty rates
among their own soldiers.[29] For these reasons, it has become a staple of
Western military strategy to ensure that conflicts be of short duration, are
fought in territories that are far removed from the Western heartlands,
and result in few casualties among their own soldiers. I would add to this
that its conflicts result in a decisive outcome, as opposed to a negotiated
solution.

Janina Dill expands this analysis, arguing that since the end of the
Vietnam War, Western states have exploited the ambiguities within IHL
to adopt a new "logic of efficiency" over the more traditional "logic of
sufficiency." The latter holds that the laws and customs of armed conflict
are designed to regulate war as a military competition that permits only
that degree of harm which is necessary and sufficient to achieve military
victory. The logic of efficiency, on the other hand, advocates that belligerents prioritize political over military goals, and that targets and tactics
should be focused on achieving these goals in the fastest, easiest, and
most direct way.[30]

To implement this strategy, advanced Western states draw on their
superior technology and the strategic advantage of not having to fight on
their own territory, and employ highly concentrated and overwhelming
military force against a wide variety of political, economic, and military
targets in what military theories refer to as "effects-based operations."
Such operations employ military force for the purpose of undermining
the political and economic foundations of the adversary's base of power,
and define success by the degree to which they can destabilize the systems
and "centers of gravity" on which the enemy relies. This includes objects
that are highly valued by both the adversary's military forces and their
populations.[31] In doing so, they eschew the traditional military objectives
of annihilating or eroding the enemy's military forces, instead targeting

all of the applicable elements of national power: diplomatic, economic, military, and information.[32]

This approach relies heavily on the use of air power against key political and economic systems to produce paralysis on the target state or organization's ability to function.[33] In many ways, this approach is a contemporary adaptation of the old idea of strategic bombing, a method of warfare designed to break the will of a people and its government by destroying its vital centers.[34]

In the words of former Air Force lawyer Major General Charles Dunlap, the "erosion of the will of an adversary through the indirect effects of aerial bombardment on civilians is a key element of victory in modern war."[35] Such attacks are not only designed to impeded the means of the adversary to maintain their ability to fight—the traditional function of military force—but also the ability of the "entire spectrum of a society at each level to have control of its vital functions."[36] Ward Thomas argues that this is a contemporary version of an older tactic designed to depress civilian morale that dates back to World War II, known as "duress bombing." In the contemporary era, however, duress bombing is designed to inflict hardship on the civilian population without actually killing or injuring individual civilians, thus noncombatants are not actually the target of the attacks.[37]

The US Defense Department maintains that the propriety of such tactics depends upon the circumstances, and thus attacks that may appear to be improper and result in civilian casualties may in fact be consistent with its definition of military advantage. For example:

> The military advantage from an attack may result from harm to the morale of enemy forces. Diminishing the morale of the civilian population and their support for the war effort does not provide a definite military advantage. However, attacks that are otherwise lawful are not rendered unlawful if they happen to result in diminished civilian morale. The military advantage expected to be gained from an attack might not be readily apparent to the enemy or to outside observers because, for example, the expected military advantage might depend on the commander's strategy or assessments of classified information.[38]

Therefore, whether massive bombing of infrastructure and public facilities is aimed at destabilizing the society or using the population to press their leadership to capitulate, any resulting casualties would be counted as unintentional.

US Air Force Colonel John Warden's widely adopted five strategy rings theory takes this approach a step further, promoting the massive use of air power to paralyze each of the adversary's five centers of gravity, which he portrays as a series of concentric circles: military forces, population, supporting infrastructure, "system essentials" such the national economy, and political leadership.[39] According to this approach, the military forces of the adversary (the outer ring) are less important than the social and political centers of gravity (the inner rings), and therefore the military should skip the outer ring and focus their attacks on the political leadership, infrastructure, and foundations of "popular support."

Similarly, the US strategy of rapid dominance (from which the phrase "shock and awe" emerged) that was developed by military planners in 1996 involves "the capability to deny an opponent things of critical value . . . Shutting the country down would entail both the physical destruction of appropriate infrastructure and the shutdown and control of the flow of all vital information and associated commerce so rapidly as to achieve a level of national shock akin to the effect that dropping nuclear weapons on Hiroshima and Nagasaki had on the Japanese."[40] This would entail disrupting "means of communication, transportation, food production, water supply, and other aspects of infrastructure."[41] The appropriate balance of shock and awe "must cause the perception and anticipation of certain defeat and the threat and fear of action that may shut down all or part of the adversary's society or render his ability to fight useless short of complete physical destruction."[42]

General Dunlap justifies this by arguing that such uses of force would be reserved for those societies possessing "malevolent propensities." "We must hold at risk the very way of life that sustains their depredations and we must threaten to destroy their world as they know it. This means the air weapon should be unleashed against entire new categories of property that current conceptions of LOAC (law of armed conflict) put off limits."[43]

While neither of these strategies advocate either violating IHL or deliberately targeting civilians, they are an example of what Robert Pape calls "risk coercion," whose purpose is to degrade infrastructure and economic targets in order to convince the leadership that more severe damage will follow if they fail to make the demanded concessions.[44] Though the United States can to be sensitive to the political and humanitarian costs of the destruction of power plants and other infrastructure, US military doctrine places great importance on the use of such attacks to disrupt an enemy's command and control capabilities, air defenses, and weapons production. In addition, many US military planners also see an advantage to placing pressure on an enemy's civilian population. Attacks against economic infrastructure enable the attacker to bypass the enemy's fielded military forces by influencing the enemy populace and its leadership's decision-making.[45]

This strategy all but guarantees a significant amount of collateral damage inasmuch as targeting "population, supporting infrastructure, system essentials such the national economy, and political leadership" both directly threatens their lives and indirectly endangers their livelihood and survival. This is because infrastructure, government ministries, economic institutions, and communications and transportation systems are usually located in heavily populated areas, and because these system essentials are often necessary to the survival of the civilian population.

These types of strategies stretch the principle of military objectives to include undermining the enemy leadership, demoralizing the population, and degrading civilian and economic targets in an effort to coerce the adversary's government to capitulate.[46] The US military justifies this interpretation of military objective by expanding the definition from "war-fighting" to include "war-supporting" and "war-sustaining" capabilities.[47] This includes "economic targets of the enemy that indirectly but effectively support and sustain the enemy's war-fighting capability."[48] According to US Air Force doctrine, "Location as well as prior uses are important factors in determining whether objects are military objectives. Thus, dwellings located within a heavily contested contact zone need not be presumed to be civilian objects."[49] This broadens the accepted definition of military target, which requires that the operation or function of the object have a direct impact on hostilities and presents a definite *military* advantage. According to the International Committee of the Red Cross, it implies a causal relationship between the activity engaged in and the harm done to the personnel and equipment of the armed forces at the time and place where the activity takes place.[50]

Equally significant is that this type of strategy relies heavily on targeting dual-use facilities, without placing the operation of these facilities within any kind of specific context. A dual-use object is one that can have either a military or civilian function, such as electrical power stations, bridges, and telecommunications installations. Such objects often fulfill both of these functions, although not necessarily at the same time. Attacks on dual-use facilities are a major cause of collateral damage inasmuch as these types of facilities are not only usually located in populated areas, but are also used regularly by civilians in the course of their daily lives.

"Dual-use" is not a separate legal category; strictly speaking there are only two types of targets, military and civilian. Military planners will often designate a primarily civilian dual-use facility (such as an electrical power plant) to be a military target if it could be used by the armed forces at some future point. For example, W. Hays Parks argues that the follow-ing dual-use facilities are *"always* military objectives" regardless of the cir-cumstances: power sources, communications networks and equipment, industry (not only military, but also those that are geared toward export), railroads, waterways, and highways that are known or suspected enemy avenues of approach or withdrawal.[51] To this list, A. P. V. Rogers adds ports, airfields, main roads, tunnels and canals, television stations, and telephone networks that *could* be used for military communications.[52]

Both Parks and Rogers are correct that some dual-use facilities could be legitimate targets if such facilities directly contribute to the war effort. A bridge that is used for moving soldiers and weapons to a conflict zone, for example, is clearly a legal military target. However, the question of whether a target or series of targets is legitimate requires a contextual evaluation rather than a blanket policy that *all* dual-use facilities are *always* legal military objects, particularly if the real purpose of the attacks is to disrupt the political and social life of the population. For example, a bridge in a major town or city that could be used to transport enemy trucks might serve a military goal; however, under the principle of pro-portionality the legality of attacking such a structure is more ambiguous if the bridge is also the primary means for the population to receive food and medical supplies. Under this condition, in the absence of overwhelm-ing necessity, an attack on such a facility is irresponsible and reckless, par-ticularly for belligerents who completely control the airspace and can therefore easily select other targets.

This is especially true when the military use of the bridge or other dual-use facility is primarily theoretical, that is, when there is a lack of evidence that the adversary is actually using the object for a hostile purpose or that the destruction of such an object provides a definite and concrete military advantage that cannot be obtained through other means. Just because the

military may make use of an object at some future point does not automatically mean that the object becomes a military objective.

It is not the purpose of this book to engage in the debate over the
degree to which targeting war-supporting and war-sustaining facilities
is legal. Rather, I am simply arguing that the Western strategy to target
such facilities—particularly those that are located deeply within civilian
areas—is one of the main explanations for the level of collateral damage
its combatants produce during attacks. I hold that this probability, based
on past experience and empirical evidence, makes such attacks reckless.

Reckless Endangerment Warfare

It is not only the choice of targets that leads to high rates of collateral damage. The massive use of airpower against targets located in towns and cities inevitably produces significant civilian casualties. For example, during
the first two weeks of the attack on Afghanistan in 2001, NATO aircraft
dropped 22,000 bombs.[53] Similarly, NATO delivered 23,000 bombs during its 1999 air campaign against Serbia, mostly in the cities of Belgrade
and Novi Sad. During the 1991 Persian Gulf War aircraft engaged in 2,695
strikes against fixed targets in populated areas, many of them in the city
of Baghdad.[54] Over a two-day period Israel launched more than 7,000
air attacks and 2,500 naval bombardments on heavily populated towns
throughout Lebanon during its 2006 war against Hezbollah, including
the capital city of Beirut.[55] In each case, this was done over a period of
only two to six weeks and many of these attacks occurred in or near civilian areas. While the number of bombs employed does not in and of itself
indicate recklessness, when done in densely populated towns and cities,
high levels of collateral damage are both foreseeable and inevitable.

Thus use of such approaches represents the implementation of war-
fighting strategies that focus on attacking infrastructure, government ministries and economic institutions, all of which are in close proximity to
civilian objects and population centers. Under these conditions, the rate
of collateral damage can increase quickly regardless of how high-tech and
precise the delivery systems are. As Boston University historian Howard
Zinn observed during NATO's 1999 air campaign against Serbia:

> [It is time] we stopped using the word "accidental" to
> describe NATO bombing of Yugoslavian hospitals, residential

neighborhoods, buses, trains, trucks, and refugees . . . An accident implies something unforeseen. True . . . the hospital bombed in Belgrade may have been unforeseen as a specific consequence of bombing the city. But it was foreseeable, given the magnitude and nature of the bombing, that some hospital, school, village, or bus would at some point be hit, and civilians would die. If I drive my car 80 miles an hour down a street crowded with children and 10 of them are killed, I cannot dismiss this as an accident, even if I had not intended to kill these particular children. When an action has inevitable and terrible consequences, it cannot be excused as "accidental."[56]

The use of overwhelming military force against an adversary is obviously not in and of itself an issue. No one expects combatants to forgo their strategic, tactical, or technological advantages in the interests of fairness, and IHL provides wide latitude for combatants to exploit such advantages. Certainly IHL was never designed to shield political leaders from the consequences of war, nor are government or economic institutions that directly contribute the war effort immune from attack. At the same time, the employment of overwhelming force even against legal targets in populated areas is likely to produce significant civilian casualties when it is widespread, devastating, and directed at infrastructure and dual-use facilities that are necessary for the well-being of the civilian population. This pushes the boundaries of the laws of armed conflict by manipulating the collateral damage exemption to international humanitarian law.[57]

This problem is exacerbated with the use of precision or "smart" weapons. Unlike conventional bombs that use gravity to deliver their munitions, precision weaponry employs some type of guidance system to increase the accuracy of the target. In addition to the employment of land and sea-launched cruise missiles, Western militaries equip many of their aircraft with bombs that have an electronic sensor system, built-in computer, and a set of adjustable flight fins. Such smart bombs use either laser targeting or satellite guidance systems to deliver their payload with high accuracy, at least theoretically. Military officials argue that this allows them to attack targets deep in populated areas without inadvertently affecting civilians or civilian objects nearby. As a State Department spokesperson stated, "The precision capability that now exists allows us to keep civilian casualties to a lower number than we've seen in the past."[58] In fact, writing in 1999, Michael Schmitt bragged that "in the conflict of tomorrow, technologically-advanced states will be able to strike with near one hundred per cent accuracy using techniques in which significant collateral damage and incidental injury will be the exception, not the rule."[59]

The problem, of course, is that this encourages commanders to increase their target sets to include objects that are deeply embedded in civilian areas, greatly increasing the risk to noncombatants. According to a Pentagon official, the use of precision attacks and computer models that estimate civilian casualties can embolden military leaders to use more powerful bombs than they would have employed relying on less sophisticated modeling methods.[60] A sustained bombing campaign that targets objects located in populated areas requires a level of perfection that has never existed and will likely never exist even with the most sophisticated technology. As war journalist Michael Ignatieff suggests, "what separates a successful strike from a catastrophe is small—even tiny—requiring a prodigious faith in technological systems in aviators three miles up, who have to distinguish between a military and civilian target separated only be a dirt track."[61]

Regardless of how accurate a delivery system may appear, under these conditions, small miscalculations or mishaps can have great consequences for civilians. For example, Western militaries typically employ 500–2,000-pound bombs during aerial attacks, although the US military also has in its arsenal a 21,000-pound explosive known as GBU-43/B Massive Ordnance Air Blast Bomb. Generally, everything within 20 meters of a 500-pound bomb and 35 meters of a 2,000-pound munition will be severely damaged, destroyed, injured, or killed. The safe distance for unprotected individuals are approximately 1,000 meters for 2,000-pound bombs and 500 meters for 500-pound ones.[62] Moreover, the use of highly accurate rockets such as cruise missiles may be able to better pinpoint a particular target; however, they do not provide imagery of the attack and therefore cannot adjust to last minute changes in circumstances, such as the presence of civilians at the target point.[63] As a result, the use of such weapons—particularly in large numbers against infrastructure or targets near population centers—can cause large amounts of unintended damage. The strategy—although legal—is also reckless, at least from a civilian perspective, and is responsible for a fair amount of the collateral damage inflicted by Western armies.

Patricia Owens argues that the potential of high-tech warfare to produce regular "accidents" resulting in civilian deaths is increasingly known
in advance by military officials, and that as a result, "small massacres" of
civilian populations has become normalized in conflicts fought by the
United States since the September 11 attacks.[64] As the following pages
will demonstrate, this is not confined to the United States and has existed
as policy at least as far back as the end of the Cold War in 1989.

This problem is exacerbated by the practice of calculating expected collateral damage for each specific attack rather than making an assessment
of the likely cumulative effect of the entire campaign. Typically, military
lawyers evaluate the legality of targets on an individual basis. However,
compliance with both the spirit and intent of the proportionality principle requires the attacker to calculate not only the immediate loss of life or
probable injury caused by a specific attack, but also include the foreseeable overall effect on civilian objects and facilities vital to the survival of
the population. This includes the probability that such destruction could
lead to the creation of massive numbers of refugees, a condition that is
guaranteed to increase civilian death and misery. Michael Schmitt refers
to these as "reverberating effects," which he defines as "second, third,
fourth (and so on) tier-effects that result from an attack on a legitimate
target. They are not directly and immediately caused by the attack but
lie in the attack's chain of causation; in short terms, they would not have
occurred 'but for' the attack."[65] While Schmitt is correct that IHL only
protects civilians against potentially lethal attack, not inconvenience or
the mere diminishment in quality of life,[66] such protection does include
anticipated second-order effects that are harmful to their lives.

This interpretation is supported by the US-backed International
Criminal Tribunal for the former Yugoslavia, which ruled that "although
single attacks might not *per se* be illegal, their cumulative effect might
render them so . . . In case of repeated attacks, all or most of them fall-
ing within the grey area between indisputable legality and unlawfulness,
it might be warranted to conclude that the cumulative effect of such acts
entails that they may not be in keeping with international law. Indeed,
this pattern of military conduct may turn out to jeopardize excessively the
lives and assets of civilians, contrary to the demands of humanity."[67]

Perhaps in answer to this type of charge, Lieutenant Colonel (and
Judge Advocate) Joseph Holland argues that there are too many variables
to consider when calculating long-term or future collateral damage from

a particular attack because long-term effects are too remote and therefore not the attacker's responsibility.[68] Military lawyer Jefferson Reynolds goes further, objecting that the process of target review based on a "preoccupation to avoid collateral damage" could result in "cancelled targets, delayed engagements, failure to produce enough targets to adequately mass, and limited strikes producing inconsequential effects."[69]

Yet the principle of feasible precaution requires a reasonable effort to assess probable civilian losses and this has to include what are clearly anticipated long-term effects, effects that are not theoretical but probable. The issue is whether the long-term effects are foreseeable, and if so, whether the consequences from these effects on the population are excessive. For example, during the Gulf War of 1991, the US-led coalition targeted and destroyed or disabled most of Iraq's electrical power facilities throughout the country. Although the attacks were ostensibly designed to eliminate Iraq's military command and control capability, the destruction of these facilities also shut down most of the nation's water purification and sewage treatment plants. As a result, according to a study by Rand's Mathew Waxman, this led directly to epidemics of gastroenteritis, cholera, and typhoid, resulting in an estimated 100,000 civilian deaths and a doubling of the infant mortality rate.[70] This certainly paralyzed the Iraqi government and hastened victory, but it also destroyed most of the institutions necessary for the survival of the civilian population.

Exploiting Passive Precaution

Part of what makes it possible for Western states to pursue the strategy of employing overwhelming force in populated areas while still adhering to the laws of armed conflict is its exploitation of the principle of passive precaution. As mentioned earlier, this principle requires governments to separate their military and civilian facilities and not comingle combatants with noncombatants. However, in virtually all asymmetric conflicts (that is, those in which the resources of the warring parties are vastly uneven) most if not all of the combat occurs solely on the territory of the weaker side. This is not only true of unconventional conflicts involving nonstate organizations or militias, but it is also the cases where Western armies fight state forces, for example, Serbia or Iraq. This often places an almost insurmountable burden on the adversary to move its military facilities when they are located too close to civilian areas once hostilities break out.

It is not unusual for governments to locate military institutions in or near populated areas, since such facilities typically need to take advantage of infrastructure, access to workers, and support services. The interdependence of the civilian population with the infrastructure of a modern society makes the full implementation of passive precaution virtually impossible.[71] This issue is exacerbated when states broaden the definition of military targets, to include government buildings, economic installations, communications centers, bridges, and infrastructure, most of which are usually located in towns and cities that are densely populated by civilians. Once a conflict begins, it is not feasible to relocate such facilities. Clearly the adversary often cannot be expected to relocate these away from population centers even if they could.

At the same time, it has also become commonplace in asymmetric conflicts for the weaker party to deliberately comingle military and civilian objects for the purpose of discouraging their vastly stronger adversaries from launching attacks that could result in significant civilian casualties.[72] In doing so, they put their own populations at risk and violate international humanitarian law. Marine Corps Major W. Hays Parks argues that prohibiting attacks under these circumstances unfairly restricts the military from targeting economic, industrial, and political targets and encourages the defender to comingle civilian and military objects.[73] Stronger countries often take advantage of the difficulty or inability of a weaker adversary to clearly separate military from civilian objects by attacking both and then shifting the blame for collateral civilian deaths to that adversary. This enables vastly stronger attackers to avoid calculating expected collateral damage into their proportionality equation.

Thus by evoking the passive precaution principle, the Western powers often declare attacks on civilian areas to be legal, so long as there are military targets embedded within them. Certainly combatants who engage in concealment warfare bear some responsibility for deliberately putting civilians in harm's way; however, this does not relieve the attacker of its own obligation to minimize civilian casualties even if this means altering their attack strategy. While IHL was never designed to ensure a fair fight or level the playing field, the exploitation of passive precaution by an adversary does not release the parties to a conflict from their legal obligations with respect to the civilian population and civilians, including the obligation to take the precautionary measures to avoid civilian casualties.[74]

In fact, the responsibility to avoid civilian casualties is actually greater for the stronger side, since the condition of asymmetry provides it with a far wider set of target choices and an opportunity to deliberate prior to launching attacks. Although all belligerents have identical responsibilities and obligations in terms of the laws of armed conflict, the principle of feasible precaution differs for each party depending on their assets and resources.[75] This is particularly relevant for the Western powers, since in every conflict it has fought since World War II, its forces have completely controlled the airspace and therefore its ability to target any object at any time has been virtually uncontested. Moreover, since the entire conflicts have been fought on the territory of its adversaries, the dominant combatants have not had to defend their own population or facilities, thereby giving them the luxury of greater deliberation in determining where and when it will attack. These factors increase their responsibility to adhere to the legal principle articulated in the First Protocol that "when a choice is possible between several military objectives for obtaining a similar military advantage, the objective to be selected shall be that the attack on which may be expected to cause the least danger to civilian lives and to civilian objects."[76] Quite simply, the spirit (if not the letter) of IHL would strongly suggest that under conditions of asymmetric conflict, a dominant state has an obligation to be highly selective and judicious in choosing targets that could adversely affect the civilian population, even if it is not the military commanders' first choice. Military convenience is not the same as military necessity.

Risk Transfer and Collateral Damage

Risk transfer is an important component to the Western way of war inasmuch as it enables states to initiate military action without fear of incurring politically damaging casualties among their soldiers. As Malcom Shaw and Yagil Levy demonstrate, the protection of US and Israeli soldiers at the expense of foreign civilians has become a staple of Western efforts to wage war while shielding their own forces from its consequences.[77] This is known as "force protection." The laws and customs of armed conflict do not prescribe the level of risk combatants are required to assume in order to avoid killing or injuring civilians. Certainly soldiers are expected to minimize their own risk when engaging with other combatants; however, the principles of distinction and proportionality clearly prohibit them from trading the lives of soldiers for those of civilians except in extreme circumstances. Risk-transfer inverts the rights of civilians vis-à-vis those of soldiers, thereby violating the basic norm that combatants are to assume greater risks than noncombatants.[78]

The heavy use of strategic air attacks is an important tool in implementing risk-transfer. Air wars minimize the risks to the attacking force while increasing the dangers to noncombatants on the ground. The desire to avoid casualties among their soldiers by increasing the use of air power was a major factor in the war plans of all four conflicts studied in the following chapters. Although pilots and their aircraft may face substantial risks during a conflict with another major power possessing sophisticated air defenses, Western countries have not fought against such adversaries since World War II and are not likely to do so in the conceivable future. The risk of executing air attacks is therefore minimal. Even medium-size powers like Iraq and Serbia are virtually defenseless against an advanced air force such as the United States, Britain, France, or Israel. For example, in the first few weeks of the two wars against Iraq (1991 and 2003) and NATO's 1999 air campaign against Serbia, coalition air strikes eliminated most of their adversaries' air defenses and anti-aircraft systems, giving them virtual freedom of the skies. For that reason, NATO did not lose a single pilot over Serbia (although one of its planes were shot down), and the combined air forces of the United States, United Kingdom, Italy, Kuwait, and Saudi Arabia lost only 38 members of their air crews during the entire Gulf War of 1991.[79]

Although Western air forces cite a variety of strategic reasons for flying aircraft at higher altitudes, the primary purpose for launching attacks from aircraft flying 15,000 to 30,000 feet above their targets is to protect the pilots.[80] However, this inevitably creates significant risks for those living in the target areas, regardless of how precise the weapons may be or how sophisticated the ground operation. As I will demonstrate in the following empirical chapters, a fair amount of collateral casualties were the result of reckless air attacks launched from high altitudes. For example, as I discuss in chapter 4, a missile fired from a high-flying NATO aircraft aimed at the Luzane bridge in Serbia in 1999 inadvertently hit a passenger bus that was beyond the sight of the pilot, killing at least 23 civilians.

NATO had decided to fly at that altitude to shield their pilots from hostile ground fire, even though they knew that they would create a grave risk for civilians on the ground.

General Dunlap offers a political rationale for risk-transfer by arguing that "Americans do not instinctively draw a distinction that finds its soldiers' lives less precious than those of citizens of an enemy state. This is traceable to the American concept of who composes its military: citizens with just as much right to life as enemy citizens."[81] This turns military tradition and the principle of civilian immunity on its head. General Dunlap may not instinctively draw this distinction, but international law and several centuries of customary practice certainly does; combatants are agents of their states or organizations and principles in armed conflict, while civilians are not.

General Rogers acknowledges that "in taking care to protect civilians, soldiers must accept some element of risk to themselves."[82] However, he also argues that "the rule (of proportionality) is unclear as to what degree of care is required of a soldier and what degree of risk he must take. Everything depends on the target, the urgency of the moment, the available technology and so on." This, of course, provides just enough of a loophole to justify most types of risk transfer. However, the First Protocol mandates that attackers shall at all times choose the course of action which may be expected to cause the least danger to civilian lives and civilian objects. Clearly a policy that promotes zero-casualty warfare for its soldiers stretches this principle to the limit. Once again, whether or not this practice is legal is not my primary concern; rather, I simply observe that a risk-transfer policy is one of the factors that explains the level of collateral damage produced by Western armies.

Another form of risk-transfer occurs when political leaders and military officials relabel civilians and civilian objects as combatants and military objectives. This is often done in asymmetric conflicts where the adversary consists of insurgents, guerrilla forces, or other nonconventional armies. Unlike conventional military forces, insurgents often do not possess the types of tangible assets and resources that can be targeted according to the strategies promoted by the Western way of war. Moreover, although most guerrilla forces operate as a coherent military force under a central command, they are not as easily identifiable as national armies inasmuch as they do not always wear distinctive insignia when they are not engaged in battle and operate within the communities in which they live. In addition, insurgents usually rely on civilian allies and supporters to provide food, shelter, and cover.

All of this makes it difficult for superior conventional military forces to know definitively who is and who is not a combatant during times when there is no battle raging. This provides an incentive to military commanders to expand the definition of combatant so as to reduce the risk to their own soldiers when operating in an area where there is widespread sympathy for the insurgents. They do so by expanding their target set to include neighborhoods or communities where insurgents live, thereby killing or injuring them before they can engage in battle. For example, according to an unnamed high-ranking Israeli military officer, the Israeli Defense Force changed its policy that had previously required its soldiers to limit its attacks on individuals to those who had "both a weapon and a visible intent to use it." The new force protection policy told soldiers, "first you take him down, then you look into it."[83] This increases the probability of inadvertent casualties.

According to the International Committee of the Red Cross (ICRC), all persons who are not members of the armed forces of a party to a conflict are civilians and therefore entitled to protection against direct attack "unless and for such time as they take a direct part in hostilities."[84] Michael Gross argues that this participation is determined by the threat the civilian poses to the opposing military force, the harm she or he causes, and the contribution she or he makes to the war effort.[85] In order to qualify as direct participation in hostilities, a specific act must be likely to adversely affect the military operations, personal security, or military capacity of a party to an armed conflict. For the ICRC, there must be a direct causal link between the act and the harm likely to result either from that act, or from a coordinated military operation of which that act constitutes an integral part. The act must be specifically designed to directly cause the required threshold of harm in support of a party to the conflict and to the detriment of the adversary.[86] While this could include civilians who transport weapons, it would exclude those who support or sympathize with the insurgents as well as those who provide them with medical assistance, shelter, or food.

Some military officials argue that this protects "part-time combatants," who may alternate between civilian and fighter over different periods of time (the so-called farmer by day, soldier by night). Richard Rosen further posits that this provides "absolute sanctuary from attack to any person affiliated with insurgent or terrorist groups except when they are actually engaged in hostilities" and offers "respites from violence not enjoyed by any other soldiers on the battlefield."[87] This concern is a misplaced, since the laws and customs of war do not allow for a third category of "part-time soldier." So long as a person is actively engaged in the conflict in support of one of the belligerents, they remain a legitimate target even during those periods when they are not in the fight. As such they forfeit their immunity, although they retain their status as civilians. The issue of civilian immunity is not relevant for this category of individuals, but is aimed at protecting civilian supporters who do not directly participate in hostilities.

Mitigating Collateral Damage

Western militaries have certainly been sensitive to public concerns about collateral damage; however, there is little evidence that this concern has caused them to rethink their basic approach toward armed conflict. The US Army tried to address the issues of inadvertent civilian casualties by introducing the Civilian Casualty Mitigation manual in 2012. The 57-page document advanced a method for reducing civilian casualties (known as CIVCAS in military lingo) through what they term a six-stage mitigation cycle: prepare, plan, employ, assess, respond, and learn. While it discusses some concrete steps, for example, having commanders reduce the risk of civilian casualties by ensuring that their units have the necessary capabilities, training, leadership, and attitudes, it neither evaluates nor assesses the fundamental practices that are most likely to produce collateral damages, as discussed earlier.[88] Rather, most of the document advises caution, accurate information gathering, and increased awareness concerning the presence of civilians during operations, and as such is directed at individual soldiers and lower level commanders, not at the overall strategy the underlies the Western approach to warfare.[89] In short, the document couches civilian casualties in terms of accident and tragedy, while still placing military necessity at the top of the list of principles of humanitarian law.

In the following chapters, I will show how the level of collateral damage produced by Western military operations in four different conflicts is a function of its military strategy that defines the Western way of war.

3

The Persian Gulf War, 1991

Operation Desert Storm, the moniker for the 1991 war between the United Nations-sponsored coalition and the Republic of Iraq, provided the first opportunity for the advanced Western powers to apply their new war-fighting doctrines and technology to a major conflict. As military historian and consultant Williamson Murray described it, Desert Storm represented a "watershed in the conduct of air war. For much of the conflict, the fighting consisted of the application of air power to the economic and bureaucratic infrastructure of Iraq," for which Iraq had no effective defense.[1] Although the primary goal of the coalition's campaign was to expel the Iraq army from neighboring Kuwait, much of the war focused on executing massive aerial attacks on political and economic targets in Iraq's largest cities, far from what would have traditionally been considered to be the battlefield. Desert Storm was unprecedented in the amount of destruction inflicted on a country with conventional weapons in such a short period of time, at least since World War II. It was the strategic bombing of Iraq's major cities that produced the overwhelming majority of coalition-induced civilian casualties and the almost complete shutdown of Iraq's civilian utilities and communications systems.

In practice, there were actually two different conflicts fought in Desert Storm: a strategic air war waged by the Coalition against institutions, facilities, and infrastructure within Iraq's major towns and cities; and an air and ground war, fought against Iraq's troops in Kuwait and the Iraqi desert. Although the majority of bombing missions were targeted at military equipment and Iraqi troops outside of populated areas, the strategic bombing campaign became the focus of war, characterized by 38 days of continuous around-the-clock air strikes involving 2,695 attack missions into Iraq's heartland.[2]

The ground war, which most analysts had originally considered would be the principle means for driving the Iraqi army out of Kuwait, ended up being a sideshow. It lasted only four days with few coalition casualties, and was characterized by a complete rout of Iraqis forces. Despite having large numbers of soldiers deployed in Kuwait and southern Iraq, the Iraqi army barely put up a fight and was easily defeated. Even the Republican Guard, which fought much more effectively than the regular army units, was badly crushed. In fact, Iraq's military strategy and technology were more reminiscent of World War I than of a modern armed conflict. Most of their troops remained holed up in bunkers and trenches for much of January and early February, and their tanks and heavy artillery sat in the open desert, easy targets for incessant attacks by coalition aircraft. Iraq's soldiers in the Kuwait were so disconnected from the actions in their country's heartland, they scarcely knew that the strategic bombing campaign was even underway.

Iraq was only able to launch one feeble offensive, a small-scale attack against the Saudi town of Khafji, which it was not able to hold for more than two days. In fact, Iraq's only substantive effort to counter the Coalition's military campaign was sporadic attacks by medium-range SCUD missiles against Saudi Arabia and Israel. These inaccurate, low-yield rockets were designed more to terrorize than to inflict military damage. Few, if any, were fired from Iraqi population centers and the damage inflicted was limited, killing in total 28 US soldiers and 3 Israeli civilians.[3] In the end, although the large majority of Iraqi military casualties were in Kuwait and the Iraqi desert, very few of the civilian deaths and injuries occurred as a result of the ground war.

According to military and political leaders, the Coalition made significant efforts to minimize civilian casualties and avoid collateral damage. In their public statements and postwar analyses, they argued that the means and methods of attack that they employed in urban areas demonstrated that any noncombatant casualties were unintended and unavoidable.[4] Specifically, they cited the use of precision guided munitions to destroy key targets in the heart of downtown Baghdad while leaving untouched civilian buildings in the vicinity.[5] They also point to the operation plan that included a 10-page "no fire" list prohibiting "attacks on cultural sites, hospitals, mosques, civilian population centers, and other non-military structures." Toward this end, the planners argue that they took unprecedented precautions to avoid destroying Iraq's basic infrastructure and making it too difficult to rebuild the country after the war.[6] Indeed, "the strategic air campaign had not only been precise, efficient and legal but had resulted in very few civilian casualties."[7] Studies by Middle East Watch (part of Human Rights Watch) and Greenpeace confirm that there was no evidence that the Coalition deliberately targeted civilians, nor does it appear that they engaged in indiscriminant attacks in civilian areas.

Yet contrary to the public portrait of an antiseptic war fought with flaw-less precision, coalition attacks killed between 2,278 and 3,500 civilians and injured approximately 5,976, most of them far from the battlefield in southern Iraq and Kuwait.[8] In addition, coalition bombing destroyed sig-nificant parts of Iraq's urban infrastructure, in particular the electrical grid, healthcare facilities, roadways, bridges, and the sewage system.[9] Analysts estimate that as many as 100,000 civilians died over the months follow-ing the end of the war from the second-order effects produced by these attacks.[10] Moreover, the destruction of civilian houses and businesses was widespread throughout the country. On the other hand, coalition losses were very light in comparison. Approximately 340 coalition soldiers were killed in combat and 776 wounded. Of these, approximately a quarter of the deaths were due to "friendly fire," that is, accidental attacks against their own soldiers.[11] Thus, approximately 8–10 civilians died for every Coalition soldier killed.

How and why a one-sided conflict of short duration produced this level of collateral damage is the focus of this chapter. In the following pages, I will demonstrate that the overwhelming number of civilian casualties and damage to civilian objects were the result of three factors: (1) attacks on dual-use infrastructure; (2) the decision to target political, leadership, and economic targets within population centers that were unrelated to defeating Iraq's military forces; and (3) the failure of the Coalition to take feasible precaution when launching these attacks.

Historical Context

The Gulf War was the outcome of the political conditions and systemic changes that arose in the aftermath of the Iran–Iraq conflict and the end of the Cold War. The eight-year war between Iraq and Iran ended in 1988, and had virtually bankrupted both countries. Iraq's public debt was esti-mated to be $500 billion and its unemployment rate was so high that the government decided that it could not afford to demobilize its armed forces. On top of this, the truce ending the war had provided no tangible benefits that could justify the eight years of sacrifices by the Iraqi population and nation. As a result, the Iraqi regime feared widespread domestic instability.[12]

Compounding these internal conditions was a growing tension between Iraq and the other Persian Gulf countries, particularly Kuwait. Iraqi President Saddam Hussein accused the other Arab states of failing to recognize or compensate his country's sacrifices in checking Iran's power in the region, and charged that Kuwait was cheating on Organization of Petroleum Exporting Countries (OPEC) agreements and stealing Iraq's underground petroleum through lateral (slant) drilling into its territory. On the other hand, states such as Saudi Arabia were suspicious of Iraq's growing military power in the region. Tensions increased when crude oil prices dropped in July 1990 from $18 to $12 per barrel. Iraq blamed Kuwait and the United Arab Emirates for the price decline, claiming that these countries sparked the drop by overproducing crude oil in disregard of the national production quota set by the OPEC. Iraq had counted on high oil prices to pull itself out of its postwar economic depression.

On August 2, 1990, more than 100,000 Iraqi soldiers backed up by 700 tanks invaded Kuwait and within a few hours, overthrew the al-Sabah monarchy and established a provisional occupation government. On August 8, the government shocked Arab and world leaders by announcing the annexation of Kuwait to Iraq, in essence abolishing it as a sovereign state. This caught the major powers and Arab states by surprise. During the summer of 1990—as tension was building in the region—US analysts had concluded that even if Iraq were to attack Kuwait, it would be a limited invasion with narrow objectives. Many thought, for example, that Iraq was only looking to seize the Warba and Bubiyan islands and perhaps the Rumalia oilfield. Iraqi leaders, in turn, believed that the Western powers would view the entire enterprise as an internal Arab affair and remain neutral, so long as Iraq did not threaten Saudi Arabia. Until the invasion, the United States and Iraq had relatively good relations despite Iraq's traditional alliance with the Soviet Union. Although many Western powers viewed Saddam Hussein and the rise of the Ba'ath Party with suspicion, his military challenge to Iran shortly after the Iranian revolution and hostage crisis brought the United States and Iraq closer. American policymakers saw Iraq as a regional balancer to the rising power of Iran and fundamentalist Islam.

Following the 1990 invasion, the main concern for American and British policymakers was not Kuwait, but Saudi Arabia, a country with whom the Western powers had a quiet economic alliance since the early post-World War II era. Iraq sought to soothe this fear in an August 6 meeting with US Chargé d'affaires Joseph Wilson, proposing that Iraq would respect the US interest in the Middle East, establish diplomatic relations, and guarantee the free flow of oil from the Gulf.[13] The United States rejected the offer and accepted an invitation by Saudi King Fahd Abdul Aziz-al Saud to deploy what would eventually become 120,000 US and 32,00 Arab troops in Saudi Arabia, an operation labeled Desert Shield. Over the next few months, the United States and the United Kingdom worked through the UN Security Council to build the political foundation for what was to become the largest, most massively armed coalition of states since World War II.

These events occurred in the wake of the most significant systemic change since World War II, the end of the 40-year Cold War between the North Atlantic Treaty Organization and the Warsaw Pact, a conclusion that was officially declared at the Malta Summit in 1989. The end of this East–West conflict allowed the UN Security Council to function as it was designed for the first time since its founding, and enabled the United States and Britain to build an international coalition to forcibly expel Iraq from that country without facing a challenge from the Soviet Union. The conflict also provided an opportunity for the United States to demonstrate its power and influence in the wake of the Soviet Union's withdrawal from global leadership.

As part of the effort, the 34-member coalition would eventually deploy 956,600 troops, most of which were from the United States, with the United Kingdom and France providing the other major resources.[14]

Coalition Goals and Strategy

On November 29, 1990, the UN Security Council authorized its member states to use "all necessary means" (a UN euphemism for military force) to compel Iraq to withdraw "immediately and unconditionally all its forces" from Kuwait.[15] This relatively narrow mandate provided the framework through which an international coalition led by the United States, Britain, and France could deploy troops under UN auspices. Two months earlier, US President George Bush had offered a similar if somewhat more expansive set of goals before a joint session of the US Congress. He stipulated US objectives to include Iraq's complete and unconditional withdrawal from Kuwait; the restoration of "Kuwait's legitimate government"; assurance of the "security and stability of the Persian Gulf"; and the protection of American citizens abroad.[16]

Yet despite denials by Coalition officials, the unspoken goal of Operation Desert Storm were much broader: to effect regime change by assassinating Saddam Hussein and other top officials and sparking a military coup or popular uprising against the Ba'ath-led government.[17] Toward this end, the Coalition planned to engage in sustained and massive attacks against leadership and infrastructure targets in Baghdad. The aims of these attacks were several. First, military planners wished to shock the civilian population into turning against the Ba'ath regime, in particular, Saddam Hussein. For example, in its postwar analysis of the war, the US Air Force-commissioned *Gulf War Air Power Survey (GWAPS)* found that military planners hoped to "inflict disruption and a feeling of helplessness on the Iraqi public without bringing about severe suffering." Similarly, *Washington Post* reporter Molly Moore found that "a major objective of the allied raids—in addition to undermining the Iraqi military capability—was to shatter normal life . . . The systematic bombardment of public facilities confirmed that the objective was to destroy the country's infrastructure."[18]

At the same time, planners also hoped that the destruction of large government buildings would have a significant psychological effect on both the regime and the population, and that by incessantly bombing Iraq's intelligence, secret police, and other government agencies they could pave the way for a coup or insurrection.[19] Journalist Martin Woollacott concluded that the bombing of ministries in Baghdad that were unrelated to the war effort were designed to send the message that "there will be no Iraq left to govern and no means by which to govern it unless Saddam is removed soon."[20] Military officials acknowledged that the attacks on the electrical grid were designed to send a message to the Iraqi people, specifically, "we are not going to tolerate Saddam Hussein or his regime. Fix that and we'll fix your electricity."[21] As air war planner Col. John A. Warden put it, "Saddam Hussein cannot restore his own electricity. He needs help. If there are political objectives that the U.N. coalition has, it can say 'Saddam, when you agree to do these things, we will allow people to come in and fix your electricity. It gives us long-term leverage.'"[22]

The degree to which the Coalition war plan reflected these goals was confirmed by the US Air Force's postwar self-study, which stated that the intention of the planners in targeting electrical power was at least in part to "depress the morale of the Iraqi people in ways that might serve to loosen Saddam Hussein's political grip on the country."[23] This was echoed by Lt. General Charles Horner, who asserted that middle-of-the-night bombing in Baghdad was designed to remind Iraqis that a war was going on and that Saddam Hussein was vulnerable and unable to stop it.[24]

Although the air war was technically commanded by General Horner, the plan for the strategic bombing attacks reflected the theories and approach of Col. Warden, who headed up the Checkmate planning division. Initially the Commander in Chief of Desert Storm, General Norman Schwarzkopf, asked Warden to develop a strategic bombing campaign as a contingency if Iraq were to employ chemical weapons or invade Saudi Arabia, neither of which occurred. However, within days of being given this task, Warden's Checkmate group sketched out a plan to prosecute the war through a series of around-the-clock massive air attacks against targets deep within Iraq's major urban centers. In the words of the *GWAPS*, the Checkmate plan was to attack, disable, and destroy elements of the Iraqi state and armed forces.[25] Warden dubbed the plan Instant Thunder, a reference to the US Rolling Thunder bombing campaign in Vietnam from 1965 to 1968. Unlike Rolling Thunder, however, the campaign's stepchild would askew the application of gradual, escalating attacks in favor of massive, focused bombing against a wide variety of targets within Iraq.

The goal of the campaign would be to damage or destroy Iraq's "centers of gravity," in particular, leadership and government facilities, symbols of the regime, the national electrical system, and communication nodes in downtown Baghdad, as well as factories, oil refineries, railroads, bridges, and highways.[26] This would "cripple production" and "complicate movement of goods and services."[27] In addition, the air campaign would target communications facilities such as radio and television transmitters, relay stations, and telephone and telegraph installation, not specifically to disrupt the Iraqi military, but to prevent the Ba'ath regime from communicating with the Iraqi population or "propagandize" against the United States and its allies.[28] As Air Force Chief of Staff, Gen. Michael J. Dugan put it, "if push comes to shove, the cutting edge would be downtown Baghdad, where Iraq's centers of gravity are located."[29] Of course it was also where the country's largest concentration of civilians was located as well.

In developing these plans, Warden gathered dozens of his officers and drew his now-famous five concentric circles on a blackboard to designate the priorities and locations of these centers. In the inner circle was Iraq's leadership, including government buildings, bunkers, and economic assets. The next circle included Iraq's petroleum industry and electrical grid, followed by the country's physical infrastructure, the population, and finally Iraq's fielded army, which Warden said they should ignore.[30] From the perspective of the Checkmate group, the war would not be fought against Iraq's military forces in Kuwait but against its political and economic institutions in Iraq's population centers.

Not all coalition military officials agreed with this plan. While Checkmate favored a campaign focused primarily on air attacks on Baghdad and other centers of gravity, General Schwarzkopf preferred focusing on a ground assault against Iraq's Republican Guard (not sur-prising for an Army officer). There was also considerable resistance from the Army brass and some Air Force officers such as Lieutenant General Buster C. Glosson and General Horner to the dominance of air power, its relationship to the ground forces, and whether the focus should be on the Kuwaiti theater rather than the centers of gravity. They offered an alternative to Instant Thunder: a series of demonstration strikes on sev-eral key installations and sustained attacks on Iraqi armed forces in the field, providing for a possible diplomatic solution. However, ultimately both General Schwarzkopf and Chair of the Joint Chiefs of Staff General Colin Powell backed Warden's plan. General Powell did not actually want Saddam to withdraw the invasion force from Kuwait (this was known in political circles as the "nightmare scenario"). He wanted the Iraqi army destroyed, leaving "smoking tanks as kilometer fence posts all the way to Baghdad."[31] To this end, Schwarzkopf and Warden advocated that the strategic air campaign run its entire course, even if Saddam surrendered.

Targets for Strategic Bombing

The strategic air campaign was divided into two major target sets: (1) military assets such air defense installations, airfields, SCUD missile launchers, tanks and artillery, nuclear and chemical weapons facilities, and command and control facilities; and (2) Iraq's political and economic centers of gravity including transportation, energy, communications, government and leadership facilities, and basic infrastructure. The military targets were largely destroyed within the first two weeks of the campaign with few civilian casualties (only the mobile SCUD launches remained elusive), while the latter remained key priorities for several weeks after, producing the large percentage of collateral damage.[32]

The original strategic air war plan proposed by Instant Thunder called for targeting 57 strategic sites, not including airfields, military equipment, or Iraqi forces in the field. By the time Desert Storm began the list grew to 400, and ultimately approximately 700 strategic targets were placed on the attack list. Many of them were only peripherally—if at all—related to defeating Iraq's military forces in Kuwait.[33] The main foci were Baghdad, which was bombed for 39 consecutive days, and Basra, Iraq's largest city in the south and a military communications and supply center.

The first set of attacks set the stage for what was to become the mode of operation, striking leadership targets such as a presidential palace, the Ba'ath Party Headquarters, a government conference center, the Ministry of Industry and Military Production, TV transmitters, the Auto Exchange, the national power grid, the Directorate of Military Intelligence, the Ministry of Defense, and the Republican Guard headquarters, all in central Baghdad. After the first day of massive air attacks on Baghdad, it became clear to American military leaders that Iraq was doomed and would not be able to wage much of a fight. By sunrise, Saddam's command and control network no longer existed, and his ability to mount a coherent military response was gone.[34] By the third day, the coalition achieved air superiority and was able to fly at will anywhere in Iraq.[35] This gave the coalition the luxury of choosing the time and place of each engagement, and greatly reduced Iraq's ability to launch any type of coherent attack. By the end of the campaign, bombers had attacked 260 leadership targets, most of which were located in central Baghdad.[36]

In addition to leadership targets, the Coalition focused on other centers of gravity such as electrical generation plants, oil and petroleum facilities, and economic infrastructure.

The attacks on the electrical system and oil production/distribution had the greatest impact on the civilian population. The Coalition executed approximately 890 air strikes on electrical power and oil facilities. Thirteen of the country's 20 electrical plants were struck in the first few hours of the war, and eventually Coalition attacks damaged or destroyed 88% of the electrical system.[37] Four of the five dams used for harnessing hydroelectric power were also attacked, destroying 75 to 100% of the facilities.[38] In addition, the Coalition launched 518 sorties against 28 oil targets, including storage tanks, distilling towers at the heart of the refineries, and the pipeline for oil exports to Turkey. Many of the oil facilities were attacked late in the war after victory was all but assured, raising speculation that the purpose was primarily to create postwar leverage over Iraq rather than influence the course of the conflict.

The other main infrastructure target was transportation, particularly bridges and highways. Bridges had long been a major target during military campaigns, aimed primarily at stopping the flow of enemy troops and supplies to combat zones. Thus, at a March 1991 news briefing, Air Force Chief of Staff General Merrill McPeak said that the Coalition targeted bridges to prevent reinforcement of Iraq's deployed field army in southern Iraq and Kuwait.[39] As such, the Coalition bombed and destroyed 42 of Iraq's major bridges, most spanning the Euphrates River.[40] However, according to the *GWAPS*, virtually all of Iraq's ground forces were already well-entrenched in the Kuwaiti theater by the start of the air campaign, and therefore the need to block reinforcements was limited. Very little material was moved once the war began and at any rate it became obvious early in the campaign that the ground war would not last very long, making resupply a nonfactor. Rather, the analysts contend, the attacks against the bridges were designed to prevent the troops from *retreating* back to Iraq before they could be destroyed by coalition attacks.[41] In addition, some attacks on bridges were simply targets of opportunity; many were listed as backup targets in the event that pilots were unable to strike their primary ones and needed to dispose of their ordnance before returning to their bases.

Finally, an extensive on-site investigation by Human Rights Watch found that a number of economic targets that directly impacted civilians were also struck, including government food processing plants and feed storage warehouses, a government-owned textile factory, a dairy factory near Basra, flour-milling facilities, and a domestic heating plant.[42] These were government assets but were unrelated to either the war effort or the support of Iraq's army.

Casualty Analysis

Coalition military and political leaders argued that civilian losses were light and collateral damage was kept to a bare minimum. They attributed those civilian losses that did occur to Iraq's strategy of comingling civilian and military objects, placing the responsibility for such losses on their adversaries. As military leaders stated in their report to the United States Congress:

> Despite conducting the most discriminate military campaign in history, to include extraordinary measures by U.S. and Coalition aircrews to minimize collateral civilian casualties, some collateral damage and injury did occur. The Government of Iraq located military assets (personnel, weapons, and equipment) in populated areas and adjacent to protected objects (mosques, medical facilities, historical/cultural sites) in an effort to obtain protection for its military forces.[43]

The report also cited Iraq's failure to evacuate Baghdad's five million residents prior to the war, leaving them vulnerable in a combat zone.

An analysis of the civilian casualties produced by coalition attacks rejects this explanation as even a minor cause of collateral damage during the Gulf War. Few civilians were killed or injured as the result of attacks on military equipment or troops that were deliberately located in or near populated areas, nor was the use of civilians used as human shields by the Iraqi government a factor. Those facilities that were adjacent to civilians (such as command and control communication centers) had been there long before the war began. According to the *Washington Post* report, senior military officers acknowledged that the worst civilian suffering was not the result of errant bombs but from precision-guided weapons that hit exactly where they aimed: electrical plants, oil refineries, and transportation networks.[44]

There were two major sources of civilian casualties and destruction of civilian objects: (1) those that were the direct result of coalition attacks by aircraft and cruise missiles against political and economic targets in Iraq's towns and cities; and (2) the postwar secondary effects of the destruction of Iraq's infrastructure.

Most of collateral damage occurred in the cities of Baghdad and Basra, Iraq's two largest population centers. The following breakdown of known casualties offers an insight into how and why collateral damage did occur. Much of the information was gathered from three extensive on-site examinations of Iraq in the immediate aftermath of the war by Human Rights Watch, the Harvard Medical Team, and military analyst William Arkin, who was working on behalf of Greenpeace. None of the casualty figures drawn from these examinations include the deaths from UN economic sanctions or the brutal Iraqi government response to the aborted uprisings by Kurdish and Shiite rebels after the war. Only incidental deaths and damage from coalition attacks are cited.

The most extensive collateral damage (in which the targets are known) was from attacks on bridges; more than 500 confirmed civilian deaths can be traced to strikes on these objects. For example, a daytime attack on a bridge near Nasiruiya killed 100 civilians who were crossing and injured 80 more. Similarly, a British attack on a highway bridge over the Euphrates River in Falluja killed approximately 130 civilians who were nearby. Approximately 100 people were killed in a Samawa when an attack against a nearby bridge produced an explosion near a crowded market.[45]

Attacks on oil installations also caused a large number of casualties. An afternoon strike on an oil storage tank near a gas distribution point killed or injured approximately 200 civilians lined up to purchase cooking oil and heating gas. Multiple attacks on Jordanian fuel trucks and oil tankers killed dozens if not hundreds more.[46] All of the trucks were privately owned by citizens of a state (Jordon) that was not a party to the conflict and who were not supplying military forces.

Attacks on leadership targets accounted for the next largest number of known civilian casualties. A bombing in the Bataween Quarter of Baghdad, for example, killed 30 to 40 civilians and destroyed dozens of houses. Although journalists could not identify a specific military target in the area, witnesses told Middle East Watch that it was rumored that Saddam Hussein had been hiding in a building nearby.[47] An aerial strike on the five-story Ministry of Affairs and Ministry of Justice building destroyed the structure, killing at least six civilians and wounding seventeen.[48] The largest single civilian casualty incident involved an attack on the al Firdos bunker in the middle class suburb of Amariyah in Southwest Baghdad. The US Central Intelligence Agency believed that it might be used to shield members of Iraq's General Intelligence Department and other government officials, although as they later discovered, it was a civilian air raid shelter. Between 200 and 400 civilians were killed, including about 100 children.[49] The bombing occurred on February 13, long after it was clear that Iraq would soon be defeated, leading many to conclude that the purpose was to kill large numbers of officials in the Iraqi government rather than affect the course of the conflict.

This raises two disturbing issues that relate to the level of collateral damage produced by Coalition air attacks. First, the Coalition failed to take feasible precaution when targeting a facility that they should have known could have resulted in significant civilian casualties. Witnesses interviewed by Middle East Watch stated that civilians had been consistently using the Ameriyya shelter since the first days of the air war.[50] Although US intelligence agencies thought that the bunker may have been used as a command and control center, and that government officials may have been inside, there were enough questions about the presence of civilians to have required military planners to postpone the attack until its use could be verified. General Glosson, for example, said that the evidence purporting to show that the bunker was being used by Iraqi intelligence was purely circumstantial.[51]

The apparent failure to carefully check intelligence data for the presence of civilians has been noted as one of the fatal flaws in the bombing of the Ameriyya shelter. Yet it is not simply a case of intelligence failure, but of a failure to take the required feasible precaution when considering launching devastating attacks in a major city. Second, even if the bunker had been used by Iraqi government officials, they would have been noncombatants, and therefore not legitimate military targets. Here the political objectives merged with military ones, stretching the meaning of military necessity beyond any reasonable interpretation and leading to avoidable civilian casualties.

Hundreds of other casualties were attributed to attacks where the target was unclear. For example, up to 150 civilians were killed in on February 5 in a market in al-Kat after numerous bombs fell in an open yard next to the market.[52] A hundred and twenty-five more lost their lives as the result of Coalition bombing in the Ma'gil neighborhood of Baghdad. In addition to deaths and injuries, hundreds of houses and civilian buildings were damaged or destroyed in these types of attacks, for example in Najaf and Al Dour and the General Teaching Hospital in Basra.[53] Additionally, several schools, hospitals, and water tanks were also destroyed by Coalition bombing, particularly in Basra.

The civilian toll became so great that on February 6, Colin Powell ordered the Air Force to stop bombing bridges altogether and by February 13 (following the attack on the al Firdos bunker) he placed all of Baghdad off limits (this order was later reversed by Secretary of Defense Dick Cheney, and attacks on leadership targets resumed).[54]

At the same time, investigators found few confirmed civilians casualties produced by the Coalition during the ground war or during the air attacks against Iraqi troops in the desert. It was the strategic air campaign conducted well outside the theater of battle that produced most of the direct collateral damage.

The greatest level of collateral damage was caused, however, not by direct effects of the bombing, but by the secondary effects produced by the systematic destruction of much of Iraq's infrastructure. By 1988 Iraq has become a primarily urbanized society, with 73% of its population living in cities.[55] As such, the population was highly dependent on its transportation systems for moving food, goods, and medical supplies, as well as electrical power for water purification and distribution, sewage treatment, refrigeration, and the functioning of hospitals and health centers. Attacks on bridges, roads, and electrical systems caused major secondary effects on the population, resulting in numerous deaths. This was documented by on-site investigations conducted by the Harvard Study Team, the United Nations, and military analyst William Arkin.[56]

Assaults on infrastructure were key parts of the Coalition's strategic air campaign, starting from the first set of strikes undertaken at the beginning of the war. Food shortages began almost immediately, affecting thousands of Iraqi civilians.[57] By the end of the bombing campaign, only two of the 20 generating plants remained operational, producing less than 4% of the prewar output. In Baghdad, Basra, and other parts of Iraq, the bombing left civilians without electricity, water, sewers, telephones, or any functioning communications or transportation system.[58] Chemicals used in the purification of water for drinking were unavailable because air attacks destroyed the plants where they were manufactured.[59]

The results of this damage were stark. According to former US Commerce Department Demographer Beth Osborne Daponte, an estimated 110,000 civilians died in the aftermath of the war due to health effects cause by damage to the electrical grid, healthcare facilities, roadways, the distribution system, and the sewage system.[60] A similar, if somewhat lower estimate of 70,000 to 90,000 deaths was cited in the GWAPS, which they attributed to the lack of electricity in Iraq for water purification and sewage treatment.[61]

Explaining Collateral Damage in the Gulf War

There is no evidence that the Coalition deliberately targeted civilians; on the contrary there are strong indications that military planners took a number of steps to minimize civilian casualties and avoid attacking cultural site, mosques, schools, and health facilities. At the same time, the evidence strongly suggests that most of the civilian casualties and damage to civilian property and objects was both foreseeable and preventable. The most compelling explanations for the level of collateral damage can be found in the Coalitions carefully calibrated war strategy and their failure to take feasible precaution when it was clear that this strategy would likely produce significant civilian losses.

Thirty-nine days of continuous bombing in Baghdad, Basra, and other major towns and cities were guaranteed to produce significant civilian casualties, particularly since many of the attacks were carried out by Stealth Bombers using 2,000-pound bombs. Experience and history would surely have suggested to military planners that large-scale collateral damage is an inevitable outcome of a massive strategic air campaign over populated cities, regardless of the degree to which the attackers adhere to international law and avoid deliberate attacks on civilians. At least some military officials anticipated the probability of this result. Air Force chief General Tony McPeak had warned President Bush prior to the start of Desert Storm that engaging in the type of war they had planned would kill "2000 people you're not mad at."[62] The Pentagon itself acknowledged that they recognized at the outset that destroying the electrical generating system would cause "unavoidable hardships" for the Iraqi populace.[63]

Military analysts argued that modern technology had reduced if not eliminated significant collateral damage during their operations. According to the Gulf War Air Power Survey, the Coalition "was able to attack high-value targets in urban areas like Baghdad time and again because, for the most part, damage could be largely confined to the targeted buildings or structures and civilian casualties avoided."[64] Similarly, Central Command Chief of Staff Major General Robert Johnson declared, "I quite truthfully cannot tell you of any reports that I know of that would show inaccurate bombing... I cannot tell you of any that I know that have grossly missed the target."[65]

These claims were suspect on their face. First, 90% of the munitions dropped by Coalition bombers during Desert Storm were not precision-guided missiles, but unguided gravity bombs.[66] While most of these "dumb bombs" were used against Iraqi troops in the field rather than in the cities, those that were employed against fixed targets in populated areas gravely threatened civilians. As Pulitzer Prize-winning military historian Rick Atkinson argues, if darkness or confusion caused an attacking pilot to fly 20 knots too slow, the first bomb would hit 60 feet short of the target. A dive angle that was five degrees too shallow would leave a bomb 130 too short.[67] Thus of the 82,000 tons of nonprecision bombs dropped, only 25% hit their targets as intended.[68] Sometimes the results were devastating. The *Washington Post*, for example, reported that an errant bomb in the town of al-Haswa killed 35 to 40 civilians and Human Rights Watch documented a bomb explosion at a bus station in central Baghdad that killed 40 to 50 people waiting for buses. They speculated that the intended target was an Iraqi government intelligence building that was 300 meters away.[69] This was not only predictable, but predicted. Air Force Vice Chief of Staff, General John Loh, admitted that "planners never expected more than half of the unguided bombs to fall within the established circular error probable. So the fact that a large number missed was consistent with expectations."[70] At least some of the collateral damage that military officials attribute to accidents are more accurately explained as the inevitable result of a strategy based on executing a massive bombing campaign over populated towns and cities. The deaths may have been inadvertent, but not unavoidable.

Second, even the attacks using precision-guided munitions fell well short of their promise. For example, the Navy fired 288 Tomahawk cruise missiles at various strategic sites, only about 50% of which accurately struck their targets.[71] On January 30, the Coalition dispatched three waves of Stealth Bombers—at the time, its most sophisticated aircraft—on strategic attack missions. The first wave targeted bridges, communications facilities, an airfield, and a telephone exchange report nine hits and five misses. The second wave reported 16 hits and 12 misses.[72]

This problem was exacerbated by the inevitable problems in any type of massive air campaign. As the *GWAPS* itself acknowledged, the decision to launch ordnance from 10,000 to 15,000 feet (to avoid anti-aircraft fire) decreased the accuracy of the gravity bombs and led to an increase in civilian casualties.[73] Moreover, in targeting military vehicles from this altitude, Air Force pilots could not make visual contact with them, relying instead on their Joint Surveillance Target Attack Radar Systems (JSTARS). JSTARS enabled pilots to locate moving targets but not identify them; rather, such attacks were often launched against vehicles that looked suspicious. Anti-SCUD patrols included teams of aircraft armed with laser-guided bombs, cluster munitions and gravity bombs. The aircrews used "targeting pods," which a Lieutenant Colonel described as being like "looking through a straw to locate targets."[74]

As are result, Coalition aircraft killed or injured hundreds of refugees while they were riding buses and cars on the Baghdad-Amman highway fleeing the bombing in vehicles that the Coalition mistook for military convoys and SCUD missile launchers.[75] For example, on February 9, coalition warplanes attacked a Jordanian bus carrying civilians fleeing Kuwait, killing 27 in the bus and another four in two cars traveling with it. The bus was hit by two separate rocket attacks, timed two minutes apart.[76] Similarly, on February 13, 30 more civilian refugees were killed by coalition attacks near the Jordanian border. Warplanes bombed several Bedouin encampments in western Iraq, killing scores of civilians. The Pentagon attributed these and other casualties to misidentification of targets and incidental damage during operations aimed at legitimate targets: "Some oil trucks were mistaken for SCUD launchers and other military vehicles during night attacks; others were struck collectively during attacks on nearby military targets."[77] A military official further explained that it was "impossible to tell which trucks were carrying civilian cargo and which were carrying military material," and that therefore collateral damage was unavoidable.[78] Of course under these circumstances, the principle of feasible precaution requires that attacks be postponed or canceled.

Evaluation and Conclusion

An examination of the Coalition's goals, targets, and strategies—along with an analysis of the civilians casualties caused by Coalition attacks—leads to the conclusion that while the Coalition did not engage in indiscriminant attacks or deliberately target civilians, the collateral damage was both predictable and preventable.

The Persian Gulf War involved two different fields of battle, one over the towns and cities of Iraq and the other in the deserts of Iraq and Kuwait. The main goals of the UN coalition were to drive all Iraq forces out of Kuwait and restore that country's sovereignty and government. This was accomplished with few civilian casualties or damage to civilian objects. Most of the collateral damage was inflicted by the Coalition's strategic air campaign, an effort that many analysts claim was unnecessary to securing either the liberation of Kuwait or the defeat of the Iraqi military. Nor were President Bush's other two goals (providing for security and stability of the Persian Gulf and protecting American citizens abroad) achieved through strategic bombing. If the military defined Iraq's military resources as a threat to the security of the region, it was virtually eliminated by the destruction of Iraqi forces and heavy weapons in the desert. It is difficult to see how bombing water and sewage treatment plants in northern Iraq on the eve of the rout of the Iraqi army contributed to liberating Kuwait, preserving the security and stability of the Persian Gulf, or protecting American citizens abroad.

In its report to Congress, the Pentagon argued that "disrupting the electricity supply to key Iraqi facilities degraded a wide variety of crucial capabilities" that aided the war effort.[79] However, military analyst William Arkin, upon his return from a postwar inspection of Iraq and Kuwait, concluded that that attacks on economic and infrastructure targets contributed little to hurting the Iraqi military, but caused significant hardships to the civilian population.[80] A two-year independent study commissioned by the Air Force found little evidence that the strategic attacks against Baghdad and other urban targets had been critical in the allies' success.[81] More specifically, attacks on Iraq's electrical systems had little to no effect on the military outcome and were irrelevant to the defeat of the Iraqi army.[82] As a result of the Iraq–Iran war, Iraq had developed an extensive system for supplying power to its military that was totally independent from its commercial electrical generating plants. The Coalition command was well aware of this, and therefore attacks on the civilian electrical power infrastructure was inconsistent with military necessity. Moreover, the Iraqi government anticipated which buildings would likely be targeted and moved their key strategic operations into other, more secure, locations. This included command, control, and communication facilities necessary for military action.[83]

Attacks on leadership targets were generally unsuccessful inasmuch as they failed to achieve the goals of disrupting governmental functioning, isolating the leadership, or forcing regime change, despite their ferocity and breadth. According to the *GWAPS*, UN inspection teams destroyed more of Iraq's nuclear missile programs than all of the air attacks combined.[84] All of this should have been known by the military planners from previous experience. For example, a comprehensive study on the use of strategic bombing in Vietnam commissioned by the US Senate Foreign Relations Committee concluded that while the bombing succeeded in making North Vietnam pay a high price for its support of the Viet Cong, the air war did not stop the flow of supplies to the South, break Hanoi's will, or force the North Vietnamese to negotiate an end to the war.[85]

Rather, the strategic war was initiated to secure political ends, none of which were consistent with the principle of military necessity: the overthrow of the Iraqi government, the assassination of government officials, creating leverage in the Middle East after the war, and demonstrating American and British power at the end of the Cold War.[86] As journalist Lamis Andoni observed while covering the conflict, "the systematic bombardment of public facilities confirmed that the objective was to destroy the country's infrastructure" for political, not military, purposes.[87] A legitimate military target must meet two tests: it must directly contribute to the enemy's military action and its destruction must offer a "definite military advantage" to the attacking party in the "circumstances ruling at the time." The military advantage to the attacker must be "concrete and perceptible," not hypothetical. Targeting government officials, buildings, and facilities that are unrelated to winning the war stretched the definition of military necessity; while the attacks may have been legal, they were reckless and unnecessary for securing victory. More importantly, they directly led to large numbers of civilian casualties and the destruction of civilian objects necessary to the survival of the population.

The practice of risk transfer was also evident in Coalition planning and helped to contribute to high levels of collateral damage. From the onset of the conflict with Iraq, the fear of heavy allied casualties was a major factor in decision-making among both political and military circles. Lt. General Horner, for example, argued that support for the war among the American people depended largely on the ability to operate with "less than anticipated losses among Coalition troops."[88] This partially explains the ferocity of the attacks on the Iraqi homeland (the hope that this would drive the government to surrender before the ground war) and the practices of flying aircraft much higher than their ability to verify the presence of civilians when launching attacks. As Secretary of Defense Dick Cheney said, "While you still want to be as discriminating as possible in terms of avoiding civilian casualties, your number one obligation is to accomplish your mission and to do it at the lowest possible cost in terms of American lives."[89] This may be reasonable from a commander's perspective, but it is a violation of centuries of law and custom in warfare; military officials may not trade civilian lives for those of their soldiers.

The level of collateral damage can also be at least partially attributed to the lack of concern demonstrated by the Coalition toward civilian casualties, and from this, their failure to take feasible precaution when launching many of their attacks. None of the many assessments conducted by the US and British military devoted more than a passing mention of civilian losses or the effect of their actions on the civilian population.[90] General Powell himself commented on civilian casualties by saying, "I don't have a clue and I don't really plan to undertake any real effort to find out."[91] Political and military officials were shielded from public pressure in this area by the tight controls on the media they imposed during the war, controls that bordered on censorship. The public was generally ignorant not only of collateral damage, but also of the extensive damage to Iraq's infrastructure and neighborhoods; at least they could not view it on television even though the military allowed the filming of air attacks from the cockpits of Coalition aircraft. This removed some of the public pressure that would normally influence the scale of collateral damage in a democracy.

4

NATO's Air War Against Serbia, 1999

The North Atlantic Treaty Organization's (NATO) air war against Serbia in 1999—dubbed Operation Allied Force by the alliance—offers a unique insight into how Western political and military strategy determines the scope of collateral damage during its armed conflicts.[1] Like the 1991 Gulf War, Operation Allied Force became a prototype for a form of combat that would further define the Western way of war. Secretary of Defense William Cohen emphasized this point when he declared that the campaign "illuminates in many ways how America and our allies and adversaries are going to approach the art of war in the next century."[2] By this he was referring to the sustained use of massive air power against political and economic targets as the primary, if not the sole, tool for coercing a weaker adversary; this would minimize risks to allied troops as well as financial cost to the treasury. At the same time, Allied Force was also consistent with what has become the standard for small-scale warfare waged by Western states against weaker adversaries: that it (1) be of short duration (78 days); (2) be fought in territories that are far removed from the Western heartlands (Eastern Europe, outside of NATO's region); and (3) result in few casualties among their own soldiers (zero).

As mentioned in the previous chapter, the use of aerial bombing has commanded a central role in the military strategies of the technologically advanced states since the early days of World War II. However, traditionally, aerial warfare had always been employed as part of a broader strategy that coordinated air attacks with the deployment of ground troops and sometimes naval fleets. Although states had occasionally launched independent air strikes as reprisals or responses to specific incidents, the practice of prosecuting an entire conflict from the air was new in the history of warfare. NATO had first employed this approach on a much smaller scale in Bosnia during Operation Deliberate Force in 1995, flying 3,500 sorties and attacking 338 targets in an effort to force Serbia to negotiate an end to the Balkan wars. Yet Deliberate Force paled in comparison to the intensity, scale, and target sets of Allied Force. The focus of the 1995 air attacks was limited to Serbian heavy weapons (such as artillery, mortar, and other combat systems), munitions storage sites, and air defense systems in the vicinity of the safe areas designated by the United Nations.[3] During this campaign, NATO expressly rejected targets that included military infrastructure (such as airfields and base-supply depots outside the safe area); civilian installations that provided support in the safe area (such as arms factories, electricity stations, and bridges); and command, control, and communications infrastructure.

Allied Force, on the other hand, involved 38,400 sorties, 10,484 of which were attack missions delivering 26,614 bombs.[4] In addition to traditional military objects such as anti-aircraft systems, tanks, troop concentrations, and airfields, the targets included political institutions, economic infrastructure, civilian bridges, media centers, and electrical generation plants, many of which were located deep within Serbia's largest cities. As a result, NATO attacks killed at least 500 civilians and wounded 820 others during the two-month campaign.[5]

Why a campaign with limited objectives and extremely low risk to the attacking forces produced this level of collateral damage is the focus of this chapter. In the following pages, I will demonstrate that the overwhelming number of civilian casualties and damage to civilian objects were the result of four factors, all of which relate to the Western approach toward warfare: (1) attacks on infrastructure and political/economic targets unrelated to defeating Serbia's military forces; (2) the use of overwhelming force under conditions likely to cause civilian casualties; (3) the decision by NATO governments to transfer risk from their soldiers to civilians by relying solely on aerial attacks and by flying at altitudes that protected their pilots but reduced their ability to take feasible precaution to avoid inflicting civilian casualties; and (4) the use of cluster bombs.

Conditions for Low Collateral Damage

The war was highly asymmetric in terms of military resources, level of threat, and depth of national interest—conditions that should predict a low level of civilian casualties inflicted by the stronger party. Serbia was a small power with a very limited ability to either inflict damage on NATO or resupply its own troops during the conflict. The NATO countries had a combined defense budget of approximately $450 billion, more than 300 times Serbia's $1.5 billion.[6] The US defense budget alone was 15 times the size of Serbia's entire Gross National Product.[7] Serbia's inability to project military power beyond its immediate borders made the alliance's member states invulnerable to counterattack or retaliation on either their home territories or their military facilities in central Europe. As journalist Michael Ignatieff (who supported the campaign) argued, NATO's absolute domination of Serbia's military forces encouraged it to develop a sense of "moral superiority" in developing Rules of Engagement that would limit collateral damage to civilians. "The contest was so unequal," Ignatieff suggests, "that NATO could only preserve its sense of moral advantage by observing strict rules."[8]

Actually, it might seem to be inaccurate to even characterize the campaign as an armed conflict, since only one side (NATO) was engaged in military action against the other. As Daalder and O'Hanlon argue, the conflict consisted of two separate but functionally unrelated wars, NATO's two-month air campaign against Serbia—for which Serbia had no effective response—and Serbia's ground war against Kosovo—which NATO chose not to directly challenge except in a few discreet incidents.[9] Since NATO had no ground forces in the theater of combat and Serbia had virtually no capability to challenge NATO's aircraft once its air defenses were destroyed,[10] the Western alliance not only held the initiative throughout the entire conflict, it could do so without having to defend its own positions. Moreover, Serbia had no military allies or source of military support and was surrounded on all sides by countries friendly to NATO (Russia had historic ties to the former Yugoslavia but remained uninvolved throughout the conflict).

All of this gave NATO the luxury of choosing the time, place and circumstances of each engagement. It also provided NATO with the ability to carefully select its targets and review each attack at various levels and by a range of political leaders, legal advisors, and military officials. Military decisions were therefore carefully calculated, divorced from the heat of battle. This should have provided for few nonmilitary deaths and injuries.

Another condition that should have predicted a low level of civilian casualties was the humanitarian rationale for the war—to end attacks against the ethnic Albanian population in Kosovo by the Serbian military and paramilitary forces. Since the formal reason for military action was to protect the civilian population, the minimization of collateral damage would have presumably been one of the primary factors in determining military strategy. Killing and injuring civilians in order to prevent deaths and injuries to civilians appears, at least on its face, to be contradictory. Moreover, the lack of either a security threat to NATO's territories or a challenge their economic interests should have skewed the proportionality equation decidedly in favor of minimizing civilian casualties at the expense of military advantage. This placed strong political pressure on NATO's to limit noncombatant damage, and as a result, the alliance was officially committed to taking extraordinary efforts to minimize collateral damage during Allied Force.

NATO also faced strong internal pressure. According to Benjamin Lambeth of RAND, political pressure within the alliance to avoid civilian casualties and unintended damage to nonmilitary structures were greater than any previous combat operation involving US forces.[11] The US Air Force sought considerably more leeway to pursue an air campaign without many of the restrictions imposed by some members of the alliance, but were stymied by other NATO countries, particularly Britain and France. As the Air Force lamented in its postconflict report to the US Congress, "not all members of the 19-nation alliance would have accepted the intensity and violence required to fight this war if military planning had followed optimum Air Force doctrine."[12] Instead, military officials argued that the range of targets were so constrained by individual member states that each exerted a virtual veto power over both the kind of targets that could be attacked and even the individual missions.[13] French President Jacques Chirac and Italy's Lamberto Deni in particular were highly critical of NATO's expanding target sets that included infrastructure, and both British and French officials expressed strong reservations about targeting facilities that housed civilians or were located near apartment buildings, hospitals, and schools.

NATO officials and sympathetic security analysts argue that as a result of these pressures, the alliance went to great lengths to review the range of possible collateral damage for each target and planned its strikes so that the weapons used, the angle of approach, and the aim point would minimize it.[14] According to the US Department of Defense, targets chosen by NATO command (particularly those in downtown Belgrade, Montenegro, or ones likely to involve high collateral damage) underwent legal reviews in the field. Target sets that met the criteria requiring approval of the National Command Authority were given additional scrutiny by the Joint Chiefs of Staff Legal Council and the Department of Defense General Council.[15] NATO pilots were themselves required to get authorization for striking field targets from the Combined Air Operations Center.[16] The result, in the words of two security analysts, was "the most precise and lowest collateral damage air operation ever conducted."[17]

Yet the statistical indicators suggest that these restrictions were insufficient for minimizing civilian casualties and damage to civilian objects. Civilians accounted for 46% of all combat deaths; approximately 576 Serbian soldiers and 500 civilians were killed by NATO attacks.[18] At the same time, the ratio of civilians to allied soldiers killed was 500–0; no one from NATO died during the conflict. [19] On its face, at least, the number of civilian dead was very high in relation to the number of casualties suffered by combatants on both sides. This occurred under conditions that should have predicted a low rate of noncombatant casualties. The explanation for this can be attributed to how NATO employed the Western way of war and the strategies that failed to take feasible precaution, as required by international humanitarian law and the restrictions imposed on NATO's military organizations by their own field manuals.

Historical Context

The conflict between NATO and Serbia was the second act of a drama that began with Western efforts to stem the political upheavals and violent clashes accompanying the breakup of Yugoslavia, from 1991 to 1995.[20] Yugoslavia was created in the aftermath of World War I as a union of six Slavic republics under the principle of pan-Slavism. In June 1991, Slovenia and Croatia declared their independence from the Slavic federation, sparking a violent conflict with Yugoslavia's central government, who responded with military force. At first the United States and its Western allies sought to prevent the dissolution of the federation, in part because they feared that it could lead to a similar breakup of the Soviet Union and in part because they wanted to avoid the first major war in central Europe since 1945. As such, the allies opposed Croatian and Slovenian secession, but remained neutral and avoided blaming on any of the parties for the unrest. The European Community's (EC) priority was to prevent the conflict from escalating or spreading, and toward that end, they imposed an arms embargo on all parties to the conflict in November 1991. The effect was to freeze the large advantage for the heavily armed Serbian forces at the expense of Croatia.

Germany broke from this consensus in July 1991 and declared its support for the independence of Croatia and Slovenia. The United States, Britain, and France, however, continued to oppose secession for several months. This changed after a ruling by the EC's Arbitration Commission of the Peace Conference on Yugoslavia (dubbed the Badinter Commission for its president, Robert Badinter) affirmed the legality of Yugoslavia's dissolution. At that point, the three countries shifted their positions and supported independence based on the principle of self-determination. This was the first step in a Western tilt against Serbia. While the wars in Croatia and Slovenia continued, Bosnia declared its independence in January 1992 sparking a military response from the Yugoslav People's Army (JNA) as well as an internal uprising from ethnic Serbian militias within Bosnia. The United States and EC countries initially refused to recognize Bosnia as an independent state but soon relented in April. Over the next few years, the EC, the United States, and the United Nations tried to resolve the Bosnian conflict by offering four different peace plans to mediate the Bosnia-Herzegovina War, all to no avail.

Although the war between Yugoslavia and Croatia was brutal on both sides, the conflict within Bosnia between the Bosniaks, Bosnian Serbs, and Bosnian Croats produced atrocities on a scale unseen in Europe since World War II.[21] In particular, the Bosnian Serb Army (Army of the Republika Srpska)—with support from the Yugoslavian central government—engaged in widespread ethnic cleansing, mass rape, and civilian massacres. In 1993, the UN Security Council sought to provide protection to the civilians in the war-torn areas by creating "humanitarian corridors" (also known as "safe areas") in which any military action was prohibited. These areas included the major cities of Srebrenica, Žepa, Gorzade, Tuzla, and Bihac, as well as the capital city of Sarajevo. This action, however, failed to contain the violence, and violations of the corridors by Serbian militias were routine. In July 1995, the safe areas fell to attacking Serbian forces. The blatant violation of these corridors—in particular, the indiscriminate mortar attacks on civilians in Sarajevo and the kidnapping of UN peacekeepers—led to a decision by NATO to initiate three weeks of air strikes against Serbian positions. After 21 days of attacks, Serbian President Slobadon Milošević relented and agreed to negotiate an end to the fighting. This led to Dayton Peace Accords.

Unlike the breakup of the Yugoslav federation, the crisis in Kosovo—which sparked the 1999 conflict—occurred solely within the sovereign territory of Serbia. The Serbian province of Kosovo was dominated by an ethnic Albanian majority, many of who sought independence—or at least substantial autonomy—from Serbia. Tensions between the Serbian and Albanian communities in Kosovo had erupted periodically throughout the twentieth century, particularly during the First Balkan War of 1912, World War I, and World War II. Although former Yugoslav President Josip Tito had provided extensive political autonomy to Kosovo in the 1970s, the political transformation of Yugoslavia that accompanied the 1989–1990 revolutions in Eastern Europe reignited that conflict between those calling for independence from Serbia and those advocating increasingly restrictive policies toward the province by the central Yugoslav authorities. In 1996, the ethnic Albanian Kosovar Liberation Army (KLA) began launching a series of violent attacks against Serbian government institutions, sparking a retaliatory military response by Serbian security forces. Fighting between the KLA and the military forces from the Federal Republic of Yugoslavia (which was at this point reduced to Serbia and Montenegro) escalated in 1998, leading to a massive movement of up to 250,000 internal refugees and a proliferation of diplomatic initiatives by the United Nations and NATO.[22] The failure of these initiatives and an increase in violent attacks against Kosovar Albanians by Serbian forces led the NATO governments to consider taking military action against Serbia.

NATO's Goals and Strategy

The refusal of Serbia to sign the Rambouillet Accords (which, among other things, would have allowed NATO forces unrestricted access to all of Serbia) provided the alliance with a justification for launching the planned attack. NATO leaders outlined a wide variety of objectives for the bombing campaign. At its April 12, 1999 meeting, the alliance presented the following goals: (1) an end to Serbian attacks against civilians in Kosovo; (2) the creation of an international military presence in the province; (3) a return of Kosovar refugees who had been displaced by

Serbian attacks and ethnic cleansing; and (4) the development of a political framework based on the Rambouillet Accords.

In its report to the US Congress, the Department of Defense also cited
as key goals (1) demonstrating the seriousness of NATO's opposition to
Serbia's aggression in Kosovo; (2) deterring the Serbian government from
continuing its attacks on civilians; and (3) damaging Serbia's capacity to
wage war against Kosovo.[23] To this, Secretary of Defense Cohen added
ensuring the stability of Eastern Europe, thwarting ethnic cleansing,
and ensuring NATO's credibility.[24] British Defense Secretary Roberson
posited a campaign that would "reduce the Serb's capacity to repress the
Albanian population and thus avert a humanitarian disaster," while US
President Bill Clinton phrased it as an effort to "seriously damage the
Serb military capacity to harm the people of Kosovo."[25] These statements
reveal a mix of humanitarian (protect the population of Kosovo), political (protect NATO's credibility and seriousness), and military (reduce
Serbia's capabilities) goals.

NATO's political leaders (in particular US President Bill Clinton)
decided from the outset that they would not introduce ground troops into
the theater of conflict, but would instead rely solely on the use of air attacks
to coerce the Milošević government into accepting the Rambouillet
accords. These leaders were largely responding to domestic pressures to
keep their own military casualties to a minimum, especially since their
countries were not directly threatened by the Balkan conflict. In particular, polls in the United States showed that public support for military
action was very soft and predicated on the understanding that American
casualties would be low.[26] Indeed, there was a widespread expectation
that the military would suffer few, if any, casualties.[27] As British Air Chief
Marshal Sir Richard Johns assured the public, modern air force technology is able to provide "pinpoint delivery accuracy to achieve maximum
strategic effect, with minimum collateral damage and minimum risk to
the weapon carrier and launcher."[28]

At the same time, the decision to rely solely on air power precluded
any direct confrontation with Serbian troops, thereby making it difficult,
if not impossible, for NATO to protect the civilian population of Kosovo
(NATO's humanitarian goal). There was no battlefield in Kosovo, and
Serbian security forces were highly disbursed, rarely emerging as easy
targets for planes flying 15,000 feet above ground. Thus, from the beginning, NATO had no clear plan to either stop the expulsion of Kosovar

Albanians from their homes or defeat the Yugoslav army in the field. Their military plan would instead focus mostly on targets that were either indirectly or tangentially related (or in some cases unrelated) to Serbia's military forces. As a result, NATO planners blurred the distinction between their political and military objectives in selecting targets, with significant implications in the way the NATO would come to define military necessity and military advantage, often to the detriment of civilians.

Most military and political officials within NATO assumed that a short, sustained wave of bombing would force the Milošević government to quickly capitulate without risking either their own troops or the cohesion of NATO; some even suggested that it could be accomplished in as few as two days. This belief was based, at least in part, on their experience from Operation Deliberate Force, where air strikes on Serbian military targets forced the government to negotiate and ultimately sign the Dayton Accords.[29] Assuming a short decisive air campaign, NATO officials initially declared that electrical plants, media facilities and dual-use industries would be off limits to the attacks. Indeed, they stipulated that its forces would avoid targets in Belgrade and other urban areas in order to minimize collateral damage and preserve Yugoslavia's infrastructure.[30] "Our targets are military and do not involve civilians," UK Defense Minister George Robertson explained. Action will only be taken "against only military targets with a very clear objective, not to bomb common sense or even self-interest into the mind of President Milošević, but to reduce the military capacity that is being used against a civilian population."[31]

At first NATO did limit its attacks to air defense systems and airfields, dubbed as Phase I targets by the alliance. Using a combination of cruise missiles and piloted aircraft, NATO quickly succeeded in all but eliminating or disabling both sets of objectives. However, over the next week it became clear that the Serbian government would not quickly capitulate, leading NATO to begin what they dubbed as Phase II, which focused on Serbian troops and military equipment in Kosovo. The Serbian government responded to this shift by dramatically escalating its campaign to drive the ethnic Albanians out of Kosovo; NATO could do little to prevent this.

After several weeks of heavy bombing, it became clear that NATO's effort to inflict damage to Serbian troops operating in Kosovo was completely ineffective; according to a number of reports, the NATO attacks in Kosovo did relatively little damage to the Serbian ground forces.[32] Even General Wesley Clark, NATO's chief commander, acknowledged that after six weeks of bombing there were more Serb forces inside Kosovo than when the bombing began.[33] In the absence of ground forces, NATO officials determined that forcing Serbia to capitulate would require destroying or at least disrupting objects of value to the civilian population and to the political and economic elites supporting the Milošević government. Moreover, after a month of nonstop bombing, the NATO command had begun to run out of targets that had a low risk of collateral damage. As a result, despite his initial reluctance to attack infrastructure and other dual-use facilities, General Clark began to pressure the alliance's political leaders to authorize a broader range of targets that involved higher risk to civilians.[34]

On April 23, alliance leaders met at a NATO summit in Washington, DC and decided to expand their target list to include a wide variety of objects deep inside Serbia, such as political party headquarters, bridges, industrial centers, oil refining plants, infrastructure, telephone exchanges, and media outlets.[35] This would involve striking Phase III targets that affected a large number of civilians by disrupting transportation, water, and electricity.[36] Such attacks would be launched around the clock and would continue until the Serbian government accepted all of NATO's conditions.[37] Between April 24 and May 9, NATO more than doubled the number of targets. Of these only 40% focused on the Serbian military or air defenses; the majority included factories, infrastructure, oil and petroleum refineries, roads, bridges, railways, and dual-use communications (70% of which were primarily civilian).[38] In an ironic twist, after justifying its attack on Serbia as necessary to halt ethnic cleansing, NATO found itself conducting air operations largely irrelevant to that purpose.

This decision reflected a shift in strategy from military to political objectives that included punishing Serbia's political and military elites, shocking the government leadership, disrupting the functioning of the state, and weakening President Milošević's "four pillars" of power: his political institutions, the communications media, the military and security forces, and the national economy.[39] Although NATO warplanes continued to launch some attacks on Serbian tanks, military vehicles and ground forces in Kosovo, the target list shifted mainly toward political and leadership sites that had little to do with the war effort, such as factories tied to government supporters that included automobile and construction equipment plants, a tobacco distribution center, and an appliance factory owned by his political supporters.[40] The idea, according to senior NATO and Pentagon officials, was to undermine the Milošević government by "chipping away at his system of political and economic patronage." In other words, the attacks were designed to turn loyal supporters against Milošević by destroying their own sources of wealth and power.[41] Thus the blurring of military and political objectives had now become alliance policy.

At the same time, NATO was also trying to disrupt the daily lives of the Serbian population in an effort to turn them against Milošević. Human Rights Watch concluded after its extensive postwar examination of Serbia that the around-the-clock bombing campaign was part of a psychological warfare strategy of harassment undertaken without regard to the greater risk to the civilian population.[42] The Defense Select Committee in the UK House of Commons concluded that attacks were launched for the purpose of influencing the perceptions of the population and that "there was a belief—or hope—in the UK and the wider Alliance that Serbian morale would 'crack' and the Serbian population would be encouraged by the air campaign to protest the policies of the Milosevic government."[43]

As NATO spokesperson Jamie Shea explained at a press briefing, "if President Milošević really wants all of his population to have water and electricity, all he has to do is accept NATO's five conditions."[44] This attitude was echoed by Allied Air Forces Southern Europe Commander, Lieutenant General Michael Short, who mused, "I felt that on the first night (of the attack) all of the power should have gone off, the major bridges around Belgrade should have gone into the Danube, and the water should be cut off so the next morning the leading citizens of Belgrade would have got up and asked, 'Why are we doing this?' "[45] This gross expansion of military objective came close to promoting unlawful "acts or threats of violence the primary purpose of which is to spread terror among the civilian population for the purpose of intimidation," as defined and prohibited by the 1977 First Protocol to the Geneva Conventions.[46]

Casualty Analysis

The connection between NATO's strategy and the scale of collateral damage is suggested by an analysis of civilian casualties produced by the

NATO bombing. According to the International Committee of the Red Cross (ICRC), during the first week or two of the bombings—when NATO was focused on Phase I and II targets—the number of civilian casualties appeared to be low. As the campaign intensified, however, the ICRC observed both a corresponding rise in the number of Serbian civilian victims and increased damage to civilian objects.[47] This observation was verified by an in-depth on-site examination of the damage caused by the air attacks, conducted by Human Rights Watch (HRW). HRW documented 90 separate incidents involving NATO attacks that killed or injured civilians. Of these, 33 occurred as a result of attacks on densely populated urban areas.[48] Six incidents occurred each in the major cities of Belgrade, Nis, and Vranje and two or three incidents each in Aleksinac, Cacak, Novi Sad, Surdulica, and Valjevo. Nine involved attacks on infrastructure and installations that HRW considered to be of questionable military value.[49] Only two incidents involved pilot error or intelligence failure and none as a verified result of Serbian authorities using civilians as human shields.[50] Almost all of the civilian deaths were produced as collateral damage rather than mishap.

Attacks on infrastructure and political/economic targets unrelated to defeating Serbia's military forces not only accounted for a large number of civilians deaths and injuries, but also for the destruction of numerous civilian objects necessary to the survival of the population. As Rebecca Grant of the Air Force Association's Aerospace Education Foundation observed, the air strikes knocked out roads, rail lines, and bridges across Yugoslavia, halting the normal flow of the civilian economy.[51] By the time Allied Force had reached its halfway point, the bombing of infrastructure targets had halved Yugoslavia's economic output and deprived more than 100,000 civilians of jobs. This produced an "economic catastrophe" in which its "industrial base (was) destroyed and the size of the economy cut in half."[52] Two-thirds of the main industrial plants were destroyed.[53]

Probably the most devastating effects were produced by the systematic attacks on Serbia's electrical grid and component generation plants. According to former US Army Judge Advocate James A. Burger, NATO took great care to distinguish the military from the civilian aspects of dual-use targets, by limiting the effects that attacks on such facilities would have on the latter.[54] In the early days of the campaign, the initial attacks on the grid were designed to cause only temporary outages using CBU102 munitions (which disable rather than destroy the facilities). In late May, however, NATO began launching more direct attacks against Serbia's five major power stations, long distance power lines, transformers and distribution nodes using high-explosive bombs. This not only eliminated electrical power to 80% of the country; it cut power to water pumps, leaving 60% of Belgrade without any water service at all and shutting down most hospitals, schools, and other public facilities for extended periods of time.[55]

The other main aspect of NATO's civilian infrastructure targeting was the systematic destruction of Serbia's main bridges, most of which were in urban areas far from the fighting. NATO justified these attacks by arguing that the destruction of the bridges prevented the Serbian military from resupplying its forces in Kosovo; however, the chronology of the attacks belie this assertion. If this were in fact the primary goal of the attacks, NATO would have launched them early on in the campaign, before Serbia's troop buildup in Kosovo was complete. Instead, the airstrikes on urban bridges began more than a month and a half into the conflict. By the time these bridges were attacked in May, Serbian troops were already well entrenched in Kosovo and the campaign of ethnic cleansing had been almost complete. As Human Rights Watch concluded, "the risk in terms of civilian casualties in attacking urban bridges . . . was excessive in relation to the concrete and direct military advantage."[56]

At least 50 civilians were killed and 62 wounded as a result of attacks on seven bridges, all of which were primarily civilian thoroughfares within urban settings, and none of which were major routes of communication.[57] A missile strike on a bridge over the Južna Morava River at the Grdelica Gorge destroyed a passenger train that was crossing the river, killing 14 people and wounding 16 others. At least 23 civilians died when a NATO missile aimed at the Luzane Bridge hit a passenger bus that was crossing over. Additionally, at least 11 civilians were killed and 40 injured when NATO bombers mounted a daylight raid on a bridge in Varvarin in south-central Serbia.[58]

Most of the civilian dead during the 78-day campaign can be attributed to NATO's failure to take feasible precaution when attacking political and military targets. For example, during an attack intended for an ammunition dump in Surdulica, a missile struck the Special Hospital for Lung Diseases, killing 23 and injuring twenty-six.[59] On April 5 fighter jets launched 20 missiles on the Aleksinac military barracks, killing 10 civilians and injuring 30; 16 private houses and more than 400 apartments were damaged or destroyed.[60] An attack on a refugee convoy over a 12-mile stretch of road in Djakovica in western Kosovo killed 73 civilians and injured thirty-six. NATO initially claimed that this was caused by a single pilot error; however, they later acknowledged that about a dozen planes had been involved in numerous attacks on the convoy over a period of several hours. Although one may assume that the pilots mistook the refugees for a Serbian convoy, there were no military vehicles present on the scene, raising the question of why a long sustained attack failed to detect the presence of civilians.[61]

The largest single collateral damage incident occurred on May 14, when NATO aircraft dropped 10 bombs on the village of Korisa, killing 87 civilians, mostly refugees.[62] During the same set of attacks, 19 civilians were killed in Dubrava prison by NATO bombs (others were subsequently executed by Serbian security forces).[63] Although NATO insisted that the attack was directed at a military command post and that the pilots did not know that there were civilians in the area, HRW concluded that these casualties occurred because NATO failed to take sufficient measures to verify that the military facilities did not have concentrations of civilians nearby.[64]

What these incidents have in common is they were the result of a strategy that made it extremely difficult for the pilots' to take feasible precaution to avoid civilian casualties. President Clinton implicitly acknowledged that a strategy of employing massive air power around the clock would produce significant civilian casualties when he told a reporter that "there is no such thing as flying airplanes this fast, dropping weapons this powerful, dealing with an enemy this pervasive, who is willing to use people as human shields, and never have this sort of tragic thing (civilian casualties) happen."[65] RAND analyst Benjamin Lambert echoed this, explaining that "given the volume of ordnance that was expended over the course of the 78-day air war, it is most remarkable—even astonishing—that the incidence of unintended civilian fatalities was not higher.[66] This expectation—that NATO attacks would likely cause significant collateral damage—was also held by military planners. For example, prior to the attack on Serbia's Socialist Party Headquarters in downtown Belgrade the NATO command estimated that the strike would likely kill between 250 and 350 civilians.[67] Fortunately this potential tragedy was avoided; however, it demonstrates that NATO was pursuing a political strategy that it assumed in advance would produce considerable collateral damage.

The heavy use of precision weapons did improve the accuracy of NATO's attacks, and this in turn may have reduced the incidence of collateral damage. At the same time, with a massive bombing campaign that included 900 targets and 9,800 aim points, even small deviations from their targets had significant effects on the safety of civilians, as the Korisa incident (described earlier) demonstrated. Since NATO's weapons hit their aim points only approximately 58% of the time,[68] collateral damage was an inevitable outcome of the around-the-clock bombing strategy.

This problem was exacerbated by NATO's decision to transfer the risk from their pilots to the civilians on the ground by flying aircraft at 15,000 feet and attacking urban targets without warning (NATO officials told Amnesty International that they chose not to issue warnings to civilians for fear of endangering the crews of attacking aircraft).[69] These choices were sources of great controversy and debate between supporters and opponents of NATO's war over the next few years. Regardless of one's position on the issue, the practice strongly suggests that reducing the risk to their pilots was a higher priority for the alliance than protecting innocent civilian lives. At such an altitude, visual discrimination between civilian and military objects was difficult at best, resulting in multiple target identification errors. In reference to the Djakovica incident, for example, the International Court for the Former Yugoslavia report stated, while there is nothing unlawful about operating at the height above Yugoslav air defenses, it is difficult for any aircrew flying at several hundred miles an hour at a substantial height to distinguish between military and civilian vehicles in a convoy.[70] The same problem of visual identification led to the destruction of the passenger train during the attack on the railway bridge in Leskovac and the bus on the Luzane Bridge. NATO's political leaders implicitly acknowledged the perils of this risk transfer policy by eliminating the 15,000 foot rule following the April 14 Djakovica attack.

A number of civilian casualties were also caused by NATO's decision to attack political targets that had little if any military value, but which would strike at the Serbian government. One of the highest single incidents of civilian deaths, and certainly the worst in Belgrade, was the bombing of the state Serb Radio and Television (Radio Televisija Srbije or RTS) headquarters in the early morning of April 23. At the time of the attack, there were an estimated 120 civilians working in the building; at least 16 were killed and another16 wounded.[71] Beside the recklessness of attacking a building populated by civilians in downtown Belgrade, the legitimacy of striking the facility itself was questionable as a military target. NATO asserted that the radio relay control buildings and towers were targeted as part of the ongoing campaign to degrade the FRY's command, control, and communications network, and that the building housed a large multipurpose communications satellite antenna dish that could be used for issuing military instructions.[72] Yet in a statement issued two weeks earlier, NATO said that the TV stations would be targeted unless they broadcast six hours per day of Western media reports,[73] strongly implying that the attack was political rather than military.

Finally, between 90 and 150 civilians were killed as a result of seven to 12 separate cluster bomb attacks.[74] In one of the most lethal incidents, a mid-day attack on the Nis airfield (located inside the urban zone) sent bomb submunitions into the Nis Medical Center, the downtown area, the bus station, and the 12 February Health Center. Following this attack, the United States stopped using cluster bombs (although the British continued to do so), suggesting a recognition that such weapons were inherently threatening to civilian life. However, the collateral damage produced by the use of these weapons extended beyond the immediate effects. According to the British *Guardian* newspaper, between June 1999 and March 2000, 54 people were killed and 250 maimed in Kosovo by previously unexploded cluster munitions and landmines. Indeed, according to a study sponsored by the Norwegian Foreign Ministry, 2,500 unexploded munitions from cluster bombs remained 10 years after the war ended, placing thousands of Serbian civilians at risk.[75] This could have been avoided, or at least minimized; however, the United States command refused to permit their troops to remove the bomblets for fear of casualties to their forces.[76]

Learning from the Past? Libya, 2011

The extent to which military officials and security analysts used the experience of Kosovo to develop policies aimed at reducing collateral damage is mixed. On the one hand, Anthony Cordesman, analyst from the Center for Strategic and International Studies, reflects the widespread view within the US military that one of the main lessons of Kosovo is to avoid or minimize the kind of limitations that NATO placed on air power. Military effectiveness, Cordesman says, should be given greater weight even at the expense of civilian casualties.[77] This line of argument is based on the position that limiting military action in the short term can extend the overall length and intensity of the war, thereby increasing casualties in the long run. This is a common position taken by many military officials and security analysts dating back to the aftermath of the Vietnam War. The evidence from Kosovo, however, does not bear this out. As NATO expanded its attacks to include infrastructure and political targets in urban areas, the rate of collateral damage increased without having any significant effect on ethnic cleansing. The use of around-the-clock bombing from high altitudes resulted in a high number of casualties in Leskovac, Djakovica, Korisa, and Surdulica. By the time the Serbian government agreed to terms with NATO, the alliance had all but run out of targets and the ethnic cleansing operation had been completed; it is not clear what was left to bomb.

The best evidence of what NATO learned from its experience in Kosovo can be derived from it air campaign over Libya 12 years later. Like the 1999 campaign, NATO decided to prosecute the war using air power alone, although this time the operation was endorsed by the UN Security Council.[78] Once again NATO's political leaders offered a humanitarian justification—protecting civilians from indiscriminant attacks by forces loyal to the government of long-time authoritarian leader, Muammar al-Gaddafi during a civil war. Over a seven-month period in 2011, NATO launched 17,939 armed sorties, striking thousands of targets. An inquiry launched by the UN Human Rights Council concluded that NATO conducted "a high precise campaign with a demonstrable determination to avoid civilian casualties."[79] NATO itself said that it had establish a standard of "zero expectation" of deaths or injury to civilians and that no targets were struck if there was any reason to believe that civilians would be killed or injured in a strike.[80] Toward this end, they instituted two major changes from the Kosovo war: they did not attack electrical grids or any generation facilities, and they decided not to use cluster bombs or ordnance containing depleted uranium.[81] As a result, the number and ratio of civilian casualties were considerably lower in the Libyan campaign than Kosovo, suggesting that some changes had been made in alliance policy.

Yet NATO attacks killed at least 72 civilians and wounded fifty-five.[82] At the same time, investigators from human rights organizations, media outlets, and intergovernmental organizations point out that these figures are very likely to be much lower than the actual total, since the investigating bodies had limited access to sites in several cities and towns where the air campaign was active. Many concluded that there are a significant number of casualties uncounted.[83] Human Rights Watch, in particular, only counts casualties that they can attribute to specific individuals, with their home addresses. Moreover, none of these figures include the extensive destruction of civilian homes, businesses, and infrastructure vital to the survival of the civilian population that was produced as a direct result of the attacks by the protectors.

For example, *New York Times* investigators found significant damage to civilian infrastructure from attacks which risks to civilians were clear. They documented the remains of air attacks on food storage warehouses that were near businesses and houses that were destroyed, and other damage in areas where no military target could be identified.[84] Moreover, after accidentally striking a convoy of anti-government rebels, "the attack continued as civilians, including ambulance crews, tried to converge on the craters and flames to aid the wounded."[85] The single largest case of civilian casualties from a NATO airstrike took place in the town of Majer on August 8, where the UN Commission found NATO bombs killed 34 civilians and injured thirty-eight. After the initial airstrike killed 16, a group of rescuers arrived and were hit by a subsequent attack, killing eighteen.[86]

Although it is clear that NATO took significant steps to minimize civilian casualties during the campaign, its strategy and political goals undermined these efforts. The UN Security Council resolution approved the use of force solely to protect Libyan civilians.[87] As long as NATO was targeting tanks, mortars, helicopters, and other military objects directly involved in attacking civilians it was able to maintain low civilian casualty rates. However, it soon became clear that NATO was also targeting government installations that helped Gaddafi maintain power rather than participated in repressing civilians. For many political observers, NATO was pursuing regime change more than civilian protection. This resulted in targeting facilities that were located within populated towns and cities, thereby increasing the risk to civilians. For example, warplanes attacked houses where government officials lived and were thought to be meeting, as well as businesses and economic assets tied to close supporters of Qaddafi. This included the home owned by Major General El-Khweldi el-Hamedi, an attack that left approximately 13 civilians dead.[88]

These attacks continued even long after Qadaffi's forces had lost the initiative and were actually in retreat, making it unlikely that they were any longer a threat to civilian populations. In fact, the largest civilian casualty toll inflicted by NATO bombing occurred on August 8, after Qadaffi's forces were all but defeated; at least 35 civilians were killed and scores wounded in a series of NATO attacks on private residences.[89] By the second month of the campaign NATO leaders were publicly calling for Qadaffi's over-throw, and its targeting choices made it clear that the alliance was focused far more on pursuing regime change and providing military support to the rebel militias than they were trying to protect civilians from attack.[90]

The approximately 72-plus civilians killed is perhaps the least lethal outcome of NATO's campaign. Having succeeded in destroying most of Libya's government institutions and infrastructure, including its security forces and basic services vital to the survival of the population, NATO left the country without a government or any other type of authority that could stabilize the chaotic environment. Indeed, as of late 2015, govern-ment has been replaced by roving bands of competing militias that not only continue to kill and injure thousands of civilians, but also fail to pro-vide for the basic necessities of life. These deaths, injuries, and destruction can be counted as another form of collateral damage from NATO's war.

Once again, NATO made it difficult for its leaders to learn from these incidents. Faced with credible allegations that it killed civilians, the alli-ance said it had neither the capacity for nor intention of investigating, and often repeated that disputed strikes were sound.[91] As NATO Secretary General Anders Fogh Rasmussen stated, "We have carried out this opera-tion very carefully *without confirmed civilian casualties.*"[92]

Conclusion

The extraordinary fact about the air war against Serbia, journalist Michael Ignatieff observed, was that it was more effective against civilian infra-structure than against military forces in the field.[93] This, in a nutshell, summarizes NATO's 1999 air war against Serbia. Once it was clear that NATO could not protect the Kosovar Albanians, the alliance prosecuted a war of coercion that was primarily focused on pressuring the Serbian government to sign the Rambouillet Accords by undermining its polit-ical and economic power. This led to an expansive definition of military objective that facilitated attacks against infrastructure and dual-use facili-ties resulting in disproportionate civilian casualties.

The principle of proportionality balances civilian casualties against the expected military advantage from particular attacks. Determining a formula for measuring these disparate values is extremely difficult; however, the concept of military advantage is contextual and cannot be established by simply declaring entire categories of targets to be militarily necessary. In the case of the Kosovo bombing, there was a major disconnect between the stated goals of the campaign and the targets chosen for attack, targets that increased the risk to the civilian population. Cutting off electricity and water to the civilian population and destroying government and leadership institutions furthered the alliance's political goals but it is a stretch to consider them consistent with a definition of *military* necessity. As argued in chapter 2, military convenience is not the same as military necessity. Perhaps one could overlook this legal distinction if it was accomplished without causing collateral casualties; however, the evidence clearly demonstrates that many civilians paid the price.

At the same time, the use of overwhelming force through around-the-clock air strikes, cluster munitions, and high-altitude sorties made it difficult if not impossible for the pilots to exercise feasible precaution in preventing civilian casualties, as required by international law. The alliance did indeed take extraordinary measures to minimize collateral damage; however, these measures were undermined by the very strategy that NATO employed in its air attacks.

This was not helped by NATO's refusal to investigate or even acknowledge civilian casualties. Aside from continually assuring the media and public that this was the most careful operation ever conducted, NATO did not even officially keep track of the scale of collateral damage they caused. Ultimately, NATO officials accepted the figure of approximately 500 civilian deaths, possibly because this is the lowest estimate offered by any mainstream body. The number of dead and wounded was undoubtedly higher; Human Rights Watch only counted as dead, individuals who could be identified by name and age. In their report, they indicated that there were many more potential casualties that were not verified and therefore not counted. For example, they report that on April 27, an attack on the Jovana Jovanovica Zmija street army barracks in Surdulica killed 11 children; however, they added that "there are widespread reports of sixteen dead ... other reports stated some twenty dead."[94]

5

Israeli–Hezbollah War, 2006

The 34-day war between Israel and Hezbollah in 2006 represents the type of armed conflict that has become increasingly common over the past few decades, an asymmetrical fight between a sovereign state and a nonstate organization that lacks formal governing authority over a territory and population. Traditionally these types of conflicts have tended to be internal, a struggle between the ruling authorities and armed insurgents fighting over the composition of the government and state. This conflict, however, was not a typical guerilla war. The nonstate actor, Hezbollah, was not an insurgent organization vying for state power (at least not in Israel), but was rather an external political and military force based in a foreign country. The issues that defined the dispute were those that more typically characterize an international armed conflict between two states, and in fact Israel had itself labeled the war as such. According to Israeli Prime Minister Ehud Olmert, "The events of this morning (Hezbollah's attack on Israeli border guards that precipitated the conflict) cannot be considered a terrorist strike; they are the acts of a sovereign state that has attacked Israel without cause . . . Lebanon is responsible and Lebanon will bear the consequences of its actions."[1] This was echoed the Ministry of Foreign Affairs, who stated that "Israel views the sovereign Lebanese Government as responsible for the action that originated on its soil and for the return of the abducted soldiers to Israel."[2]

Yet the conflict doesn't fit the model of a typical interstate war either, since Hezbollah did not represent the Lebanese government and both the Lebanese Prime Minister and his Council of Ministers had disavowed and condemned the attack by Hezbollah that set into motion the series of events that led to the war.[3] In letters sent to the UN Secretary General and Security Council President on July 13, Lebanon's representative stated that "the Lebanese Government was not aware of the events that occurred and are occurring on the international Lebanese border" and are "not responsible for these events and does not endorse them."[4] The Lebanese national army did not participate in the war at all and the Lebanese government did not sponsor any military operations, even after Israel launched attacks throughout the country. Although Hezbollah held seats in the Lebanese Parliament (as well as two positions in the Cabinet), the organization itself had no legal or practical affiliation with the Lebanese state.

At the same time, Israel's definition of the war as an international armed conflict with Lebanon as its adversary enabled its military to engage in the types of widespread attacks against Lebanese infrastructure, leadership, public institutions, and economic assets that have come to characterized the Western way of war, as defined in chapter 2. Moreover, by characterizing anyone having any affiliation with Hezbollah as a military target, Israel expanded the definition of combatant well beyond those who are actually engaged in combat or military action. Israel's decision to characterize the conflict and belligerents in this way was a primary explanation for many of the civilian casualties suffered by the Lebanese.

Ironically, Israel and Hezbollah did not directly engage each other's military forces in any significant way until the last few days of the conflict. Israel launched its first large-scale ground foray into Lebanon near Maroun al-Ras on July 17, and continued to conduct small battalion-size raids into southern Lebanon, but it never initiated a major ground invasion until the last three days of the conflict, after the UN Security Council had already approved a ceasefire. The Israeli Defense Force (IDF) was never able to penetrate more than four miles into southern Lebanon.[5] Rather, most of the war involved an exchange of air and missile attacks against each other's territory. The IDF launched 7,000 air strikes using 500 to 2,000-pound bombs, and fired 173,000 artillery shells and battlefield rocket rounds at Lebanese targets, more than were expended during the much higher-intensity Yom Kippur War of 1973.[6] Hezbollah, in turn, fired approximately 4,000 unguided Katyusha rockets into Israel, 900 of which fell on populated areas, the rest in open fields.

According to military analyst, William Arkin, Israel had entered the war committed to avoiding large numbers of civilian casualties.[7] Indeed, Israel's own military manuals adopted virtually all of the provisions of the four Geneva Conventions (which Israel signed) and the two protocols (which it did not) regarding the protection of civilians and the inviolability of civilian objects.[8] Israeli political and military leaders told Arkin that the Israeli Cabinet decided not to attack infrastructure and to spare the civilian population the secondary effects of the loss of modern life-support systems.[9] As such, Israel did not seek to destroy Lebanon's power grid, unlike NATO in Kosovo and the US-led coalition in Iraq. Moreover, prior to its attacks on Lebanon's towns and cities, Israel issued warnings through leaflets, radio broadcasts, and loudspeakers, ordering civilians to leave the area.

Yet Israeli attacks killed approximately 1,200 Lebanese civilians, injured 4,000 others, and destroyed about 130,000 Lebanese homes and numerous businesses and public buildings.[10] According to the United Nations Children's Fund (UNICEF), approximately 30% of the civilian casualties were children.[11] In addition, its widespread attacks on large population centers led to the displacement of approximately 975,000 civilians, representing one quarter of Lebanon's entire population.[12] Conversely, Hezbollah attacks killed 43 Israeli civilians—including 13 in Haifa and eight in Akko—wounded 190, and damaged or destroyed 6,000 housing units.[13] All of these figures dwarfed the military casualties, which stood at 118 Israeli soldiers and an estimated 500 Hezbollah fighters killed.[14] As such, the civilian casualty ratio between Lebanese civilians and Israeli soldiers was approximately 10–1, and the ratio of Lebanese civilians to Hezbollah fighters was at least 3 to one.

This chapter will examine why a war between a state and a nonstate militia based primarily in the southern part of Lebanon produced such high numbers of civilian casualties throughout the country. It will argue that the level of collateral damage can be explained by the strategy pursued by the Israeli political leadership, in particular, its determination to punish Lebanon and the Lebanese government for the aggressive actions of Hezbollah. Although Israel continued to publicly label Hezbollah as a terrorist organization, it developed a war strategy that treated them as if they were the government of Lebanon. As such, they engaged in widespread attacks against Lebanon's political, social, and economic resources, as well as the neighborhoods where Hezbollah supporters lived. All of this was consistent with the Western way of warfare: determination to keep casualties among their own soldiers low, pursue a decisive victory over a negotiated settlement, and keep the conflict short, in this case by means of devastating attacks on Lebanese infrastructure. What differs is the fact that Israel was fighting an adversary that was a border state, something that NATO and the United States did not have to be concerned with in their conflicts.

Since the overwhelming majority of civilian casualties were inflicted by Israel attacks—and Israel's civilian casualty ratios were heavily weighted toward civilians—this chapter will focus on the collateral damage produced by the policies and practices of the Israeli military and political leadership. At the same time, although Hezbollah lacked the sophisticated military resources of a state, its attacks did killed civilians, mostly through rocket strikes against Israeli towns and cities. Hezbollah's rockets were crude and low-yield (holding approximately 22–66 pounds of explosives), inflicting far less damage than the more sophisticated missiles used by advanced military powers such as Israel. However, since they did not contain any type of guidance system, they were inaccurate and incapable of distinguishing between military and civilian targets. Hezbollah forces could direct a rocket at a general target but without precision, and as a result its fighters did not know precisely where they would land. Moreover, many of the rockets that hit the most densely populated coastal areas—the city of Haifa and the string of its suburbs to the north and east known as HaKrayot—were packed with thousands of six-millimeter steel ball bearings that sprayed out upon impact. Therefore, as a matter of international law, Hezbollah's rocket strikes are considered to be indiscriminant attacks, and as such a serious violation.[15]

Historical Context

The 2006 war was the latest chapter in an ongoing conflict between Israel and Hezbollah that dated back to the Israeli invasion and occupation of Lebanon in 1982. The 1982 invasion was designed to drive the Palestine Liberation Organization out of Lebanon (which it successfully accomplished) and install a friendly government in Beirut (which it did not), but ended up leading to an 18-year occupation of the southern part of the country by Israel. With the help of Iran's Revolutionary Guard, Shiite activists in Lebanon formed Hezbollah as a militia to fight the occupation. Over the next few years, its fighters attacked and harassed Israeli soldiers stationed throughout Lebanon. Its forces also occasionally struck US targets in the region and kidnapped Westerners living in Lebanon.

In 1985, Israel redeployed its forces to what it termed a "security zone" in southern Lebanon, located north of its border with Israel. For the next 15 years Hezbollah was the primary military force challenging Israel's presence in the zone, launching frequent guerilla attacks against both Israeli soldiers and those of the Israeli-allied South Lebanon Army. At the same time, Israel and Hezbollah struck an informal agreement that Israel would not attack civilian targets in Lebanon, and Hezbollah would limit its attacks to Israeli soldiers in the security zone.[16] In general the agreement was honored by both sides, although Hezbollah would occasionally fire rockets into northern Israel and Israel would respond by launching air strike into southern Lebanon.[17] This led to several conflicts between Hezbollah forces and Israeli troops, including two major Israeli operations against the organization in 1993 (Operation Accountability) and 1996 (Operation Grapes of Wrath).

In 2000, Israel ended its occupation and unilaterally withdrew from most of the zone, although it continued to maintain a military presence on Lebanese territory in a border area known as Shebaa Farms. Without the support of Israeli troops, South Lebanon Army collapsed, leaving Hezbollah as the only military force in the region.

Hezbollah took advantage of its presence in southern Lebanon to establish an extensive network of social, political, and economic institutions, operating schools, hospitals, and social welfare programs for Shiite Muslim communities, which had been its base of support. At the same time, its military wing continued to attack Israeli forces stationed in the Shebaa Farms region and occasionally across the border. In addition to building up their stock of small arms, the organization amassed a significant arsenal of short and medium-range rockets, some of which they would occasionally fire into northern Israel. Over this period of time, Hezbollah received military assistance and funding from Iran (the only majority Shiite state in the world) and to a lesser extent Syria, although most political analysts agree that Hezbollah has operated with a significant amount of autonomy over their own affairs. By 2006 they had 2,000 to 3,000 fighters and thousands of short-, medium-, and long-range rockets.[18]

Hezbollah's role in Lebanese politics was complex. The country has long been badly divided by ethnic and religious rivalries; the Lebanese constitution recognizes 18 distinct religions, and Lebanon has long struggled to find a national identity that encompasses all of these groups. After the bloody Lebanese civil war (1975–1990), the country established an intricate system of governance that attempted to carefully balance the various religious interests by dividing political power among them. As the most prominent Shiite organization within a highly sectarian-divided Lebanon, Hezbollah had retained a significant degree of popularity among Lebanon's Shiite population (about 25–30% of the country), although they were opposed by the Sunni Muslim, Christian, and Druz populations. By the time the 2006 war began, Hezbollah had approximately 100,000 supporters, half of whom were party members.[19]

Over time, Hezbollah had become a multifaceted organization. Its political wing operated as a regular political party at the national level, and in southern Lebanon it assumed governance functions within the Shiite communities. During the 1990s the organization became deeply involved in Lebanese electoral politics, winning a significant number of seats in the Parliament, and it remained a significant political force since. Its military wing, the Islamic Resistance, was well-armed and organized as both a regular army and a guerrilla force. Although they did not possess tanks, heavy artillery, or aircraft, they had an arsenal of smaller arms such as mortars, rocket-propelled grenades, and anti-tank weapons, in addition to their supply of rockets. At the same time, its political and social activities were mostly segregated from their military ones, and most of their members and supporters remained uninvolved in military affairs.

On July 12, 2006, Hezbollah fighters attacked two Israeli armored vehicles patrolling on the Israeli side of the border fence. The ambush killed three soldiers, and during the operation the fighters seized two IDF soldiers and brought them into Lebanon. Hezbollah's leader, Hassan Nasrallah, said the men were taken in order to set up an exchange for Lebanese prisoners being held in Israel. Israel refused to trade for the soldiers, and its army unsuccessfully attempted to rescue the captives. During the operation, five more Israeli soldiers were killed. Israel responded by launching more than 100 attacks, mainly against Hezbollah bases in south Lebanon, including their regional headquarters in Ya'tar. They also destroyed bridges across the Litani and Zahrani rivers, and targeted and destroyed 59 medium-range Fair rocket launchers positioned throughout southern Lebanon. Israeli analysts estimated that this attack eliminated between half and two-thirds of Hezbollah medium-range rocket capability and most of its long-range Zilzal missiles.[20] Hezbollah retaliated by firing dozens of rockets into northern Israel.

Over the next few days, Israel launched missile and bomb attacks from the air and sea, expanding their scope to include Hezbollah's headquarters in the southern suburbs of Beirut and the offices and homes of the organization's leadership. Hezbollah responded by firing medium-range rockets into the Israeli city of Haifa. The "second Lebanon war" of 2006 had begun.

Israel's Goals and Strategy

Initially, neither Hezbollah nor the Israeli government expected the conflict to escalate into all-out war, but events and political considerations overtook expectations. Israeli leaders were divided over the type of action they should take in response to Hezbollah's border attack. Some advocated a limited retaliatory strike against Hezbollah positions in southern Lebanon, with a possible limited ground assault south of the Litani River. Such a proposed attack would not include the use of tanks or other heavy armor, and the troops would avoid entering houses or populated areas.[21] One Israeli officer cautioned that any broader conflict would be a "war of choice . . . the enemy is not about to wipe us off the map . . . it is not the Yom Kippur war."[22] However, Israeli Prime Minister Olmert was under significant political pressure to take aggressive action against Hezbollah. He had only been recently elected to office and his government's approval ratings were low, particularly on the issue of security. He was not only afraid of looking weak personally; the Israeli military believed that it had lost its deterrent power to prevent attacks on its borders. The northern border had been relatively quiet over the past few years, but Hezbollah's attack had come during a period of unrest among Palestinians in Gaza and the West Bank, including rocket attacks by Hamas into southern Israel. Most importantly, the recent seizure of Israeli soldier Gilead Shalit by Hamas in Gaza weighed on the Israeli government.[23]

At the same time, the Prime Minister wanted to avoid a ground war of any kind. Israel's senior leaders believed that an invasion of Lebanon would produce heavy casualties among their soldiers and that Israel would become bogged down in an unpopular and unwinnable war.[24] Memories of the 18-year occupation of Lebanon, and the 1,000 Israeli troops who died during that period, were still fresh in the memories of the officials. As a result, the cabinet decided to avoid engaging Hezbollah directly except

in a series of small skirmishes, relying instead on an extensive and massive air and naval campaign waged throughout Lebanon. In this effort, the
Israeli military adopted the US effects-based operations approach.

Initially Israel had cited four basic goals for the operation: (1) gain
the return of their two soldiers; (2) impose a new order in Lebanon;
(3) strengthen Israel's deterrent against future attacks; and (4) weaken
and potentially crush Hezbollah.[25] By "new order" the Israeli leadership
meant convincing the Lebanese government to deploy its national army
in the south to displace Hezbollah's forces and evict them from southern Lebanon.[26] Some officials also wanted the Lebanese army to disarm Hezbollah, a goal that was extremely unlikely given the nature of
Lebanon's badly fractured political system and the strength of Hezbollah.
Thus, several Israeli political and military leaders proposed a campaign
aimed at punishing Lebanon for allowing Hezbollah to continue operating in the south by wreaking such havoc on the country that the population and government would turn against the organization.[27]

As Israeli Chief of Staff Lt. General Dan Halutz stated, Israel would
deliver a "clear message to both greater Beiruit and Lebanon that they've
swallowed a cancer and have to vomit it up because if they don't their
country will pay a high price."[28] He said that massive bombing would
turn back the Lebanese clock 20 years and that "nothing was safe in
the country."[29] General Yitzak Harel emphasized this point, stating that
"Lebanon is at the high point of the tourist season. This is where we have
to hit them . . . Shut down the airport in Beiruit and signal to the [Prime
Minister] Siniora government that its days are numbered."[30]

Early on, punishment, deterrence, and the destruction of Hezbollah
had become the primarily aims of the war and by mid-July Israeli leaders made it clear that the release of its soldiers was no longer their main
objective.[31] Their war aims would be accomplished by unleashing massive
attacks of such ferocity that it would discourage any future threats to its
northern border and destroy Hezbollah's political standing in the country.
The political and military leadership decided on a two-pronged approach,
both of which relied almost exclusively on air, naval, and artillery attacks.
The first prong was to target Hezbollah's military, economic, social, and
human resources, many of which were located in populated areas. This
included striking military targets such as weapons storage facilities and
rocket launchers, as well as political ones, including the businesses,
homes, and neighborhoods where Hezbollah supporters lived. The

second prong involved extending their attacks throughout Lebanon, targeting the nation's infrastructure, economy, and transportation systems.

Hezbollah's greatest military threat was its short-range Katyusha rockets, all of which were located (by necessity, given their reach) in the south, close to the Israeli border. This was the threat that the Israeli military was ultimately unable to successfully counter. Despite numerous attacks on the Katyusha launch sites, Hezbollah was able to continue launching these rockets until the end of the war. Hezbollah's long-range rockets potentially posed a greater threat to Israel inasmuch as they could reach deep into the country, however, as mentioned earlier, Israel had destroyed most of this arsenal during its July 13 attack, and at any rate, Hezbollah never employed them against Israel during the war.[32] Hezbollah's most effective weapon was its medium-range rockets, which (though far fewer in number) could reach deeper into Israel to the city of Haifa.

In addition to targeting Hezbollah's military arsenals and supporters in the south, Israel expanded the attacks to include Hezbollah assets and supporters, and political, social, and economic institutions in the suburbs of South Beirut and the Bakka Valley (where Hezbollah had a strong base of support), as well as northern and central Lebanon, which was outside of Hezbollah's operating area but where much of the country's infrastructure lay.[33] The political targets included the main offices, homes, and businesses of Hezbollah's public officials as well as their party headquarters in Beruit and its suburbs. In addition, warplanes attacked other political objects such as welfare agencies, schools, banks, shops, media centers, charitable organizations, and residential buildings of Hezbollah supporters, party members, and those considered sympathetic to the organization.[34]

General Halutz argued that the key to destroying Hezbollah was to target Lebanon's civilian infrastructure and force the Lebanese government, Sunni Muslims, and Lebanese Christians to turn against the Shiite organization.[35] In pursuit of this goal, the target list expanded to include water pumping stations, electrical power plants, water and sewage treatment facilities, and industrial enterprises. This resulted in the damage or destruction of 330 water distribution facilities, 159 sewage treatment plants, 142 industrial enterprises and factories, 900 medium enterprises, and 2,800 small businesses. In all, about two-thirds of the industrial sector was damaged.[36] The transportation infrastructure was also targeted, resulting in damage or destruction to 80 bridges, 94 roads, and 25 fuel stations.[37]

The Israeli Foreign Ministry defended its strategy arguing that "the guiding principle adopted by IDF was to target only infrastructure that was making a significant contribution to the operational capabilities of the Hezbollah terrorists."[38] Moreover, "the roads in Lebanon are used to transport terrorists and weapons," and are therefore legitimate targets.[39] As discussed in chapter 2, this represented an expansion of military object from those that directly contributed to military action to those that were "war sustaining," and accounted for much of the collateral damage.

Ultimately, most analysts agreed that the attacks on Beirut, the suburbs, and the Bakka Valley had little effect on suppressing rocket fire from Hezbollah, by far the biggest threat to Israel during the war. In fact most of Israel's attacks on Lebanon's infrastructure, and even its strikes against political and economic targets related to supporters and leaders of the organization, were militarily ineffective, and had little discernable effect on the campaign's outcome.[40]

Casualty Analysis

One of the main controversies in determining how and why civilians were killed in this conflict centers on who counts as a civilian, and the conditions under which those designated as such could be considered to be legitimate targets. As mentioned in chapter 2, any member of or participant in the armed forces of a party to a conflict is a combatant and is not only permitted to attack other combatants, but is him or herself a legitimate target for attack by the adversary. This includes those who are members of guerrilla forces, insurgents, and other types of unconventional armies. All others are civilians and they retain this status for the duration of the war. However, civilians may lose their protected status at "such time as they take a direct part in hostilities," at which point they became legitimate targets.[41]

In order to qualify as directly participating in hostilities, a specific act must be likely to adversely affect the military operations, personal security, or military capacity of a party to an armed conflict. More specifically, there must be a direct causal link between the act and the harm likely to result either from that act, or from a coordinated military operation of which that act constitutes an integral part. Finally, the act must be specifically designed to directly cause the required threshold of harm in support of a party to the conflict and to the detriment of the adversary.[42]

The status of Lebanese civilians was probably the main controversy of the conflict, at least from the Israeli perspective. As mentioned earlier, Hezbollah is a multifaceted organization that includes legislative, political, economic, service, and military components. Their military force was separated from their political and governance arms, and those who were part of this force would be automatically considered as combatants, even when they were not engaged in any fighting. As demonstrated in the following section, Israel adopted a very broad definition of what constituted membership in the military wing of Hezbollah, including party members, supporters, political allies, and individuals providing shelter and sustenance to the fighters. They extended this definition to Hezbollah-related civilian objects, such as housing units, businesses, transport vehicles, and other civilian institutions owned or inhabited by members or supporters of Hezbollah. By expanding this definition of combatant, the Israeli Defense Force was not only able to target a wider range of facilities and objects than one would conventionally consider to be a legitimate military objectives, but it also enabled them to reduce the risk to Israeli forces inasmuch as they would simply attack anyone or any facility they deemed suspicious.[43] This was a form of risk-transfer.

For the purposes of this analysis, I accept the characterizations of "civilian" and "combatant" adopted by the nongovernmental organizations, human rights groups, and outside investigators that conducted on-site investigations after the conflict ended. These investigators are probably the most reliable sources, since they were not a party to nor allied with any of the belligerents in the conflict. Moreover, each of them have a long record and experience in investigating civilian casualties in a broad range of conflicts involving a wide variety of belligerents. While government and nonstate military organizations routinely attack their findings, particularly when they are the objects of the reports, their investigations are clearly the most comprehensive and nonpartisan available. Most importantly (from a social science perspective), organizations such as Human Rights Watch have established a standard method of counting civilians in each conflict, using markers that apply across conflicts regardless of the identity of the belligerents.[44]

There was no evidence that Israel engaged in deliberate attacks on hospitals, mosques, or schools, or that they deliberately targeted civilians, at least those that they designated as civilians. At the same time, the connection between Israel's military strategy and the scale of collateral damage is demonstrated by an analysis of civilian casualties produced by the aerial attacks.

Most of the civilians killed during the war died either inside residential homes or while riding in civilian vehicles or convoys trying to flee the fighting.[45] At least a third of the civilian deaths in Lebanon occurred as a result of attacks on residential buildings.[46] Half of the housing units and buildings that were damaged were in the northern part of Lebanon, far from the original battlefield in southern Lebanon.[47] For example, the northern town of Yater was heavily bombed, destroying 230 homes and damaging 620 others on July 12. The town had been used as a base for Hezbollah fighters. Similarly, in the town of Bent J'beil, which was known as the "capital of the resistance," 800 homes were destroyed, killing 15 fighters and 27 civilians. Another 100 to 200 others were injured, mostly civilians.[48] According to journalist Mark Parker, who toured one of the sites, "The scale of the destruction was truly incredible. One bunker buster seemed to have wiped out at least four nine-story blocks in a high-use estate. Only a 30-foot pile of smoking concrete remained with layers of furniture, clothes, belongings squashed between collapsed floors."[49]

A few specific examples can illustrate the level of collateral damage from these types of attacks: 39 civilians were killed in an August 7 attack on three multilevel apartment buildings in the Chiah neighborhood of South Beiruit. A week later, 36 civilians and four members of Hezbollah lost their lives in an air attack on the Imam Hassan Building Complex in Riveiss, in southern Beiruit.[50] An attack on the home of Shaikh Adil Muhammad Akash not only killed him, but also his wife and 10 children. Akash was a strong supporter of Hezbollah, but he was a religious leader, not a combatant. Twenty-eight more civilians, including 17 children, died and 22 were wounded in an attack on an apartment complex in Qana.[51] Israel claimed that the entire town was a combat zone because Hezbollah missile crews were hiding there and that rockets had been launched from within the village. However, this action dramatically turned international sympathies away from Israel, causing Israel's Arab allies and even the UN Security Council (including the United States and Britain) to condemn its attacks.[52]

The southeast Beiruit suburbs were also heavily attacked by warplanes. This region was a center for Hezbollah's political activities including their party headquarters and television station, and home to many of their family members. It was also a densely populated commercial center of 220,000 people. Most of the residential homes in the city were destroyed. During one bombing raid in the town of Dehiyeh, 35 civilians were killed and another 41 lost their lives in the town of Chizah. In all, about 110 civilians were killed and 300 injured in the region.[53]

The other major cause of collateral damage was attacks on residential buildings, food warehouses, transportation infrastructure, and vehicle convoys in the south. Israel had attempted to undercut Hezbollah's position and base of support in southern Lebanon by trying to depopulate the territory south of the Litani River.[54] Thousands of civilian structures were damaged or destroyed in more than 100 towns in southern Lebanon.[55] To justify this, Israel argued that anyone who supported or was affiliated with Hezbollah was a legitimate target, regardless of whether they were armed. As Israel's Deputy Ambassador to the United Nations, Daniel Carmon stated, "There is hardly any distinction between Hezbollah and the civilian population" in southern Lebanon.[56] The IDF began distributing warnings through leaflets and radio broadcasts ordering everyone to leave all areas controlled by Hezbollah, which essentially included the entire southern part of the country. On July 27, Justice Minister Haim Raimon declared, "all those now in South Lebanon are terrorists who are related in some way to Hezbollah."[57] This redefinition of what constitutes a combatant was one of the main reasons for the high level of civilian casualties in south Lebanon.

Israeli warnings to evacuate towns in southern Lebanon led to large numbers of civilians fleeing to the north. The Israeli government told Human Rights Watch that "the IDF took pains to ensure that sufficient routes remained open to enable civilians to leave combat zones ... Efforts were also made to ensure that damage to civilian vehicles was minimized.[58] However, warplanes continually attacked roads and bridges that provided escape routes, and helicopters and aircraft frequently attacked civilian convoys on the suspicion that they were carrying weapons to Hezbollah fighters. Moreover, the government charged that since Hezbollah used ambulances and other rescue vehicles for cover of its movements and to transport weapons and personnel, they were also legitimate targets.[59] On August 7 the IDF distributed a leaflet that declared, "any vehicle of any kind traveling south of the Litani River will be bombarded on suspicion of transporting rockets, military, equipment, and terrorists."[60] This led to frequent attacks on emergency and medical vehicles, attacks which killed or injured the occupants. Obviously fighter pilots and helicopter crews could not know what was inside an ambulance or rescue vehicle; however, by banning all traffic from southern Lebanon, the IDF operated on the assumption that all vehicles were legitimate targets.

This created two contradictory problems that led to civilian casualties. First, according to Human Rights Watch, many of the IDF warnings either gave an unrealistically short time frame for civilians to leave the area or were too vague for residents to know exactly where they should go. On the other hand, after Israel had decided that there were no more civilians in a particular area, they continually bombed roads and vehicles, making evaluation dangerous for those who chose to heed the warnings.[61] In addition, warplanes launched extensive attacks on Lebanon's transportation infrastructure, particularly bridges across the Litani River and in the north. Approximately 109 bridges and overpasses were destroyed in these attacks, including those in the north, too far to be useful for resupplying Hezbollah.[62] As a result, attacks on road traffic produced numerous civilian casualties.

For example, on July 15, warplanes attacked a convoy of vehicles fleeing the village of Marshin, killing 23 people, most of whom were civilians.[63] After the first missile attack, fleeing civilians were tracked by a helicopter and all were killed. On August 7 Israeli airstrikes killed five civilians in Insan as they were leaving home.[64] A July 18 attack on the Rmeileh Bridge killed 12 civilians riding in a van. A similar strike on the al-Hayssa Bridge on August 11 killed 11 more.[65]

Both sides used cluster bombs during the conflict, although Hezbollah's arsenal was relatively small and did not result any confirmed civilian casualties. According to the head of an IDF rocket unit in Lebanon, Israel's military fired about 1,800 cluster bombs, containing over 1.2 million cluster bomblets, sometimes covering entire towns in munitions.[66] Beyond the immediate casualties produced by the attacks, military experts estimate that between 500,000 and one million unexploded munitions remained on the ground in Lebanon after the war, killing or maiming between 192 and 239 civilians over the following years.[67] Moreover, the large number of submunitions used and the high dud rates severely damaged the economy by turning agricultural land into de facto minefields and interfering with the harvesting of tobacco, citrus, banana, and olive crops.

One question that was raised by Israel and pursued by investigators was the degree to which civilian casualties were the result of Hezbollah's use of populated areas to store weapons and fire rockets. As mentioned in chapter 2, concealment warfare is illegal and a mitigating factor in civilian deaths. According to the IDF, Hezbollah had the advantage of civilian cover against attack and an urban setting from which to ambush IDF forces and conduct guerrilla warfare once Israeli ground forces advanced.[68] They further argued that Hezbollah offices were surrounded by civilian institutions and densely populated civilian residential building.[69] "The Hizbullah terrorists in Lebanon have purposely hidden themselves and stockpiled their missiles in residential areas . . . wishing to shield their actions behind civilians in order to thwart Israel's response," explained the Israeli Ministry of Foreign Affairs.[70]

Human Rights Watch investigators found that Hezbollah did indeed store some weapons in or near civilian homes, sometimes comingled their fighters with the civilian population, and occasionally placed rocket launchers within populated areas. At the same time, they concluded that there was no evidence that this practice was systematic or widespread. "In the 94 incidents involving civilian deaths that Human Rights Watch investigated, we found evidence of only one case involving civilian deaths that Hezbollah weapons were stored in the building. Rather, it appeared from our interviews and a review of publicly available reports on Hezbollah's military strategy that Hezbollah had stored most of its weapons and ammunition, notably rockets, in bunkers and weapon storage facilities in the fields and the valleys surrounding villages."[71] Hezbollah offices and its other institutions, or course, were located in towns and cities because that is where organizations, political parties, public officials and residences are almost always based.

Conclusion

An examination of the Israel's goals, targets, and strategies—along with an analysis of the civilians casualties caused by IDF attacks—leads to the conclusion that while Israel did not deliberately target civilians, their strategic war plan and redefinition of combatancy made a high level of collateral damage inevitable. Israel had not faced a military threat from a nation-state since it overwhelmingly defeated the coalition of Arab states in the 1973 Yom Kippur War, its fourth such victory in 25 years. Rather, its primary threats came from nonstate militias such as the

Palestine Liberation Organization (until the 1992 Oslo agreement), Hamas, Hezbollah, and small-scale violence initiated by terrorist cells and individuals based primarily in Gaza and the West Bank. Yet its military resources and war strategies remained designed for major conflicts with heavily armed nation-states.

As a result, the IDF fought its war with Hezbollah as it would against a nation-state's military, employing the strategies that have come to define modern warfare waged by advanced states. Yet since Hezbollah was not a government and did not have the assets and authority of a state, there was a mismatch between war strategy and opponent. By expanding the war beyond southern Lebanon and broadening its target list to include facilities and objects that do not make an effective contribution to military action, the Israeli military dramatically increased the potential for collateral damage. As seen in the other contemporary cases, massive aerial attacks on populated towns and cities are almost inevitably going to result in significant civilian casualties, regardless of how precise and accurate the weapons.

The other cause of collateral damage by Israel can be traced to how it defined a legitimate target during the conflict. The primary goal of Israel's campaign was to severely damage or destroy Hezbollah, and as such Israel considered anyone with any type of affiliation with the organization to be a combatant. As a result, businesses, private vehicles and houses, economic resources, and even entire neighborhoods were attacked. Yet this approach to war contradicts the rulings of Israel's own high court (not to mention its own military manuals) concerning the definition of a combatant. Quoting from the interpretations by the International Committee of the Red Cross of customary international law, Israel's High Court of Justice stated that "civilians are protected against attack unless and for such time as they take a direct part in hostilities."[72] Attacking civilian supporters of Hezbollah—even vocal and active members of the political party—violates this principle. One's sympathies in a conflict are irrelevant to their status in wartime. The only criteria for determining the status of a target is whether it provides a direct contribution to military action.

Fear of incurring casualties among Israeli soldiers drove much of the government's decision-making. Rather than confront Hezbollah directly through a major ground invasion of southern Lebanon, Israel—like other advanced military powers—chose to employ massive air and artillery strikes against towns and cities in Lebanon. They did this knowing that these types of attacks would likely result in significant civilian casualties.[73] This practice constitutes risk transfer by trading the lives of civilians for one's own soldiers, and was a major cause of collateral damage. Indeed, the ground war between IDF and Hezbollah troops killed far fewer civilians than the air, artillery, and naval attacks in both northern and southern Lebanon. In fact, ground combat produced little collateral damage.

Ultimately, the principle of proportionality allows analysts to determine the degree to which civilian casualties are justified. According to Protocol I, "an attack which may be expected to cause incidental loss of civilian life, injury to civilians, damage to civilian objects, or a combination thereof, which would be excessive in relation to the concrete and direct military advantage anticipated."[74] Israel argued that proportionality is measured not by the military advantage of a specific attack, but by the military operation as a whole.[75] This is consistent with the position taken by other Western militaries like the United States and Britain. This interpretation, which is not shared by most legal analysts, also accounts for the relatively high level of collateral damage during the 2006 war between Israel and Hezbollah. It allows for attacks against targets that are known in advance to likely cause civilian casualties, justified by primarily political rather than military considerations.

Finally, like the experiences with NATO in Kosovo and the US-led coalition in Iraq, it is difficult for Israel's political and military officials to learn from their experiences inasmuch as they refused to investigate or even acknowledge civilian casualties beyond blaming them on their adversaries. For example, the Israeli government appointed the Winograd Commission to evaluate the circumstances that led to the war, the performance of the IDF, and the decision-making process within the government of Prime Minister, Ehud Olmert and the military under Minister of Defense, Ehud Barak. The final report was highly critical of both the government and military, labeling the war as a "missed opportunity" and chastising the leadership for poor decisions, poor planning, and poor performance.[76] Yet the report did not mention Lebanese civilian casualties at all, although it did discuss the effect of the war on Israeli civilians. While the commission was not tasked with conducting such an analysis, it is troubling that its in-depth study of Israel's military strategy and performance did not even make a passing reference to the effect of its operations on Lebanese civilians.

6

The US War Against al Qaeda, 2002–2017

From 2002 until at least 2017, the United States has been engaged in a conflict with al Qaeda and those referred to by US political leaders as "associated forces." Unlike the empirical cases discussed in the previous chapters, this conflict has not involved easily identified belligerents organized into established fighting units operating within a defined battle-space. In fact even the US adversary itself is not a single entity. Al Qaeda is a transnational network of fundamentalist Sunni Muslims dedicated to overthrowing secular nationalist governments in Muslim countries, replacing them with theocracies governed by Sharia Law, and eliminating external Western influences from the Middle East and North Africa.[1] Although it had operated, at least in part, through a central command until the early 2000s, its primary activities have been generally organized through its local organizations and affiliates in various countries, including Egypt, the Sudan, Saudi Arabia, Yemen, Somalia, Eritrea, Djibouti, Afghanistan, Pakistan, Bosnia, Croatia, Albania, Algeria, Tunisia, Lebanon, the Philippines, Tajikistan, Azerbaijan, and the Kashmiri region of India and the Chechnyan region of Russia.[2] Some of these affiliates are formally organized groups fighting under an official name and resembling regular armed forces, while others consist of loosely structured associations that mobilize along ethnic, clan, religious, or tribal lines.[3]

Although many political leaders and security officials have conceptualized al Qaeda's activity as simply "international terrorism," it is the prevailing view of many current US policymakers that it is more accurate to view the al Qaeda network as a "global insurgency," which Lt. Colonel David Kilcullen defines as a transnational "popular movement that seeks

to change the status quo through violence and subversion, while terrorism may be just one of its tactics."[4] In this sense the dispute between al
Qaeda and its Western adversaries is multidimensional, involving both
armed conflict and other forms of political violence.

Unlike most armed conflicts, however, the war against al Qaeda and
associated forces has not had any geographic or temporal boundaries.
US officials never defined the limits of where its forces would operate
nor specified the conditions under which the conflict would end. Rather,
the US government has claimed the right to pursue al Qaeda and their
unnamed state sponsors anywhere in the world. As President Bush
stated, "our war on terror will be much broader than the battlefields and
beachheads of the past. The war will be fought wherever terrorists hide,
or run, or plan," and it "will not end until *every* terrorist group of global
reach has been found, stopped, and defeated."[5] Similarly, the Obama
administration took the position that once a state is engaged in an armed
conflict with an armed nonstate organization, the conflict follows the
members of that group wherever they go, as long as the group's members
continue to engage in hostilities against that state.[6] In pursuing this strategy, American military forces have operated in such diverse territories
as Afghanistan, Pakistan, the Philippines, Indonesia, Sudan, Yemen, and
Somalia.

This chapter will focus only on that part of the confrontation that can
be characterized as an armed conflict between the United States and al
Qaeda and its associated forces, as defined by international law. The focus
will therefore be limited to the targeted killing campaign in Pakistan and
Yemen. It will not include Afghanistan, which is the site of a more traditional type of guerrilla war between the Taliban and the US-based Afghan
government. In particular, it will examine how and why a strategy aimed
at targeting individuals with technological precision produces such high
levels of civilian casualties.

The primary strategy employed by the United States for fighting this
conflict has been targeted killings, defined as an intentional, premedi-
tated, and deliberate use of lethal force against specific individuals who
are designated as belligerents in the conflict.[7] Unlike more traditional
methods of warfare, targeted killings do not seek to disable, degrade, or
destroy military assets, weapons systems, equipment, or supporting infrastructure. Rather, the purpose is to eliminate specifically named individuals, or in many cases, individuals who are unidentified but behaving in a

manner considered by military and government officials to resemble the actions of combatants.

As a tactic of war, targeted killings are not in and of themselves unique, and their use does not challenge the traditional laws and customs of warfare so long as those targeted are combatants in an armed conflict. Even in traditional conventional conflicts, it has not been unusual for militaries to target specific commanders or operatives by attacking facilities or compounds where they were thought to be residing. What is unusual in this case is that targeted killings are not a tactic in the war, but the primary approach employed by one of the belligerents. Moreover, the means through which these targeted attacks are conducted—unmanned aerial vehicles—created more of a "virtual war" than an armed confrontation, inasmuch as at least one of the belligerents does not even have a physical presence in the theater of operations or battlespace.

The US strategy of targeted killings has been shrouded in secrecy and controversy ever since it was employed in Pakistan in 2004.[8] Much of this controversy has revolved around the means through which the United States has employed the strategy. Although targeted killings can be executed through sniper fire, helicopter attacks, car bombs, or actions by special forces, the United States has relied almost exclusively on the use of Unmanned Aerial Vehicles (UAV), more commonly known as drones. UAVs are jet-powered, pilotless aircraft usually directed by an operator at a ground control station. Over the past decade, more than 40 countries and nonstate militias have developed various types of UAVs, although those possessed by the United States, Israel, and Russia are by far the most advanced and lethal.[9] In their most sophisticated form, drones are capable of a wide variety of missions—surveillance, reconnaissance, intelligence-gathering, and air attacks—and can be controlled remotely via satellite from thousands of miles away.

Drones are a particularly effective tool for implementing the Western approach to warfare. They are relatively cheap to build and deploy, employ the latest advances in military technology, enable the United States to fight in territories that are far removed from the Western heartlands, risk few if any casualties among their own soldiers, and seek to produce a decisive outcome through the use of overwhelming force. UAVs can fly for up to 24 hours at altitudes greater than 60,000 feet, and can hover indefinitely over a target. Moreover, unlike pilots, drones do not get hungry, scared, or tired.[10] Yet like the other tools used by Western militaries in prosecuting the Western way of war, they have produced a significant amount of collateral damage, both in terms of civilian casualties and the fear and terror they cause in the areas where they have been employed. Despite the notion of "targeted killing" as a precise operation to eliminate specific individuals, the attacks have been anything but precise.

According to the Bureau of Investigative Journalism (TBIJ), the United States launched at least 527–551 drone strikes in Pakistan, Yemen, and Somalia between June 2004 and July 2015, killing a total of 2,950 to 4,762 people and injuring 1,252 to 1,969 others. Of this number, at least 488 to 1,067 of the dead were civilians, creating a civilian casualty ratio of 10 to 23% on the low end and 36% on the high end.[11] These figures do not include the collateral effect of terrorizing entire communities by keeping thousands of civilians living in a state of constant anxiety and fear. The civilian casualty rate reached its peak in 2010, and declined between 2013 and 2015, due primarily to the dramatic reduction in drone strikes in 2014 and the commitment by US President Obama to reduce civilian casualties.

At the same time, these estimates likely undercount the actual total of noncombatant deaths, since the military's definition of who constitutes a combatant—and thus a legitimate target—is hotly contested by legal scholars, human rights organizations, and journalists.[12] Moreover, in many cases, there is little information available about whom the drones are killing beyond the small number of specifically named targets; indeed the military command and political leadership probably know less about this than the nongovernmental organizations and research groups who investigate them.[13]

The Nature of the Conflict

Since the rise of al Qaeda as an adversary of Western states in the mid-1990s, government leaders differed on how to characterize and address the conflict between themselves and al Qaeda and its associated groups. Both political and military leaders have commonly referred to attacks against their states' interests and citizens as terrorism and labeled those who perpetrated these attacks as terrorists. Traditionally, terrorism has been treated by governments and international organizations as criminal activity under both domestic and international law. As such, the means and methods used to fight it have been comparable to those that are used against any other criminal activity: investigation, arrest, interrogation, indictment, trial, and, if found guilty, incarceration or execution.

In the past, the United States and other governments arrested and charged those they considered to be terrorists with either the specific acts they committed—for example, sabotage, murder, piracy, or kidnapping—or with the more general crimes of racketeering and conspiracy. Under this paradigm, governments were regulated in their pursuit of individual suspects by the principle of due process and, in the case of foreign attacks, sovereignty. In the absence of permission from the host government, law enforcement agents and security forces are prohibited from pursuing a criminal suspect outside of the state's territorial jurisdiction. Moreover, the use of lethal force against suspects accused of crimes against the state is only permitted in cases of self-defense, where the target poses a credible and *imminent* security threat to the state or its citizens, and where there is no opportunity for deliberation or alternative choice of means.[14] Many legal scholars and political leaders therefore argue that under a law enforcement paradigm, targeted killings would be considered "summary execution," and thus illegal, since the targets are almost always attacked at a time when they pose no immediate threat.[15]

At the same time, the form of political violence employed by al Qaeda and its associates has been far more organized and sophisticated than the sporadic acts of violence that traditionally defined terrorism, and its transnational nature and level of organization have many characteristics of an armed conflict. The designation of transnational insurgents as combatants in an armed conflict has provided greater leeway for security forces from Western states to pursue them than it would for law enforcement agents, although this raises other types of legal restrictions. The laws of war permit official agents of the state (soldiers) to target, attack, kill, or injure designated combatant targets at any time—balanced by the principles of proportionality and feasible precaution—whether they are armed, unarmed, awake, or asleep, as long as they remain active combatants. Unlike the pursuit of a criminal suspect, the pursuers are not required to ask for their surrender or provide due process to the target.[16]

The conflict between the United States and al Qaeda does not fit neatly within either paradigm and as a result there has been a debate among political leaders and legal scholars over how it should be characterized. Under international law, an armed conflict exists whenever there is "a resort to armed force between states or protracted armed violence between government authorities and organized armed groups or between such groups within states."[17] This standard applies to both international armed conflicts, which are those between states, and "armed conflicts not of an international character," which until recently was a term typically applied to internal conflicts such as civil wars and insurgencies.

Since the early 1990s, al Qaeda operated internationally and has labeled specific states as among its adversaries, even though it never itself represented a defined territory or population. The network was headquartered in the Sudan from 1991 until approximately 1996, but maintained offices in various parts of the world. In 1996 its symbolic leader, Osama Bin Laden, and other members of al Qaeda's central leadership relocated to Afghanistan, where they remained until driven out by NATO forces following the battle of Tora Bora in late 2001. At its height, al Qaeda maintained a command and control structure which included a consultation council (*majlis al shura*) charged with discussing and approving major undertakings, including terrorist operations. Al Qaeda also had a military committee, which considered and authorized those they defined as military matters. Local insurgency organizations affiliated with the network by pledging an oath of allegiance (called a *bayat*).

Al Qaeda operatives have engage in both conventional military action and acts of terrorism, and although it had functioned as a fairly coherent entity from the mid-1990s until the early part of the twenty-first century, over the past decade it acted more as a confederacy of affiliated organizations around the world that it inspires, leads, and supports, than as an organized force operating through its own cells.[18] For this reason, Human Rights Watch does not consider the hostilities between al Qaeda and Western states to have reached the level of an armed conflict, nor do they consider al Qaeda operatives to be combatants.[19]

At the same time, since both the US government and the leadership of al Qaeda consider their hostilities to constitute a state of war, in practice the question of whether the confrontation has risen to the level of an armed conflict is less problematic. According to President Barack Obama's State Department legal advisor Harold Koh, for example, "as a matter of international law, the United States is in an armed conflict with al-Qaeda, as well as the Taliban and associated forces, in response to the horrific 9/11 attacks . . . As recent events have shown, al-Qaeda has not abandoned its intent to attack the United States, and indeed continues to attack us. Thus, this [is an] ongoing armed conflict."[20] This view was echoed by President Obama himself in a 2013 speech at the National Defense University, when he stated that "under domestic law, and international law, the United States is at war with al Qaeda, the Taliban, and their associated forces."[21]

The conditions for triggering a noninternational armed conflict occurring beyond the territory of a single state were articulated by the International Criminal Tribunal for the Former Yugoslavia (ICTFY), and many legal advisers believe that it has become part of customary international law: (1) that the hostilities reach a minimal threshold of intensity and duration to be considered "protracted," sustained, and ongoing; and (2) that they are carried out by groups possessing a command structure and have the ability to carry out military operations in an organized manner. In addition, a dispute can be raised to the level of an armed conflict if that the UN Security Council places the conflict on its agenda and considers resolutions on the issue.[22]

This interpretation has been supported by courts in both the United States and Israel, holding that that when the minimal conditions are met, hostilities between a state and a nonstate actor operating across state borders can be considered to be an armed conflict, covered by international humanitarian law. Specifically, in 2006 the US Supreme Court classified the US dispute with al Qaeda as noninternational armed conflict.[23] As a matter of diplomatic practice, the UN Security Council also recognized the existence of an armed conflict in several resolutions, declaring al Qaeda attacks and other acts of international terrorism to constitute "a threat to international peace and security" under Chapter VII, triggering language for declaring an act of military aggression.[24] At the same time, al Qaeda also indicated that it considers itself at war with the United States and its allies, as articulated by two fatwas issued by its leadership in 1996 and 1998, as well as several other official pronouncements in the early twenty-first century.[25]

Strategy and Goals

Following al Qaeda's attacks on US territory on September 11, 2001, US President George W. Bush sought to avoid characterizing the conflict with al Qaeda as either a criminal enterprise or an armed conflict.

Despite of his frequent rhetorical use of the word "war" in public forums, President Bush's legal advisors argued that since international networks such as al Qaeda are not nation-states and its operatives are not members of national armies, they are not entitled to the protections guaranteed to combatants under the four Geneva Conventions.[26] Neither, however, are they entitled to due process protections under the US constitution or review by US courts, since they are enemy soldiers. In pursuing this approach, President Bush authorized the creation of military tribunals that would operate independently of US criminal law, denying detainees the rights of habeas corpus, legal counsel, or prisoner-of-war status.[27] At the same time, President Bush pursued a strategy that focused on large deployments of US troops in Afghanistan and Iraq, as well as smaller clandestine deployments throughout the Middle East and North Africa, and small-scale targeted killings through UAVs.

Upon assuming office in 2009, President Obama pledged to follow international law in its conflict with al Qaeda, and shifted its strategy for confronting al Qaeda and its associated groups from the traditional uses of force favored by the Bush administration—large military deployments— to a more focused approach based on targeted killings.[28] He described his strategy as a "series of persistent, targeted efforts to dismantle specific networks of violent extremists that threaten America" that would "take al Qaeda commanders, trainers, bomb makers and operatives" off the battlefield.[29] While part of his rationale was the difficulty in deploying American forces in areas of Pakistan, Yemen, and Somalia where the government only had a tenuous reach into their own territory, his primary motivation was to avoid risking the lives of US soldiers that would mean "more U.S. deaths, more Black Hawks down, and more confrontations with local populations."[30] Moreover, the US administration did not want to take prisoners, in large part because he had no place to put them. President Obama did not want to add more detainees to the Guantanamo detention camp, but at the same time, as a legal matter, since he considered his targets to be combatants, they would have to be treated as prisoners of war under international law.[31]

Since al Qaeda and its associated forces neither controlled territory nor possessed the institutions and infrastructure necessary to execute governance functions, the Obama administration sought to degrade other types of assets that supported its operations: individual fighters, community supporters, safe houses, weapons caches, and transportation. The primary goal of the drone campaign, according to President Obama, has been to "dismantle networks that pose a direct danger to the United States, and to make it less likely for new groups to gain a foothold."[32] This led to an ongoing discussion within political and military circles over who was to count as being part of these networks.

According to Obama legal advisor Harold Koh, the determination of "whether an individual joined with or became part of al-Qaeda or Taliban forces or associated forces [and is therefore a legitimate target] . . . can be demonstrated by relevant evidence of formal or functional membership, which may include an oath of loyalty, training with al-Qaeda, or taking positions with enemy forces."[33] According to the Jeh Johnson, General Counsel of the Department of Defense from 2009 to 2012, in order to qualify as an associated force, a party had to have two characteristics: (1) be an organized, armed group that has entered the fight alongside al Qaeda; and (2) be a cobelligerent with al Qaeda in hostilities against the United States or its coalition partners.[34] In other words, the group must not only be aligned with al Qaeda ideologically or rhetorically, it must also have joined the conflict against the United States or its coalition partners.

The main focus of the targeted killings campaign has been in the Federally Administered Tribal Areas (FATA) of Pakistan, although attacks have also been launched in Somalia and Yemen. FATA includes six Frontier Regions bordering Afghanistan that are populated almost entirely by members of the Pashtun tribe, which is deeply rooted in both countries. This is also known as Pakistan's autonomous regions inasmuch as the national government has little control or authority over the territory or population. Within this region the primary targets are in North Waziristan, a large territory that houses 840,000 people, most of whom are unaffiliated with any of the associated forces and only a very small percentage of whom are armed fighters.[35] Several armed networks operate in the area: Afghan Taliban (which is involved in supporting the Afghan insurgency), Pakistani Taliban (which is fighting the Pakistani government), and al Qaeda-linked insurgents (which have an international reach). As a result, in addition to the drone wars orchestrated by the United States, the region is also plagued by indiscriminate air and ground attacks by Pakistani security forces on insurgents and civilians alike, as well as brutal attacks by insurgents on both government forces and civilians.[36]

Another, albeit smaller, war has also been waged by the United States against al Qaeda in the Arabian Peninsula (AQAP), located in Yemen.

AQAP formed in 2009 through the merger of the Yemeni and Saudi Arabian affiliates. Although most of AQAP's attacks in Yemen have been directed against government, police, and military targets, they have orchestrated some attacks on Western targets in the Arabian Peninsula and were responsible for the 1998 attack on the American naval warship the USS *Cole*, in which killed 17 sailors.[37]

The targeted killing campaign is built upon the development of lists of al Qaeda operatives marked for death, as well monitoring patterns of activity in the regions for people suspected of being part of or supporting al Qaeda. Both the creation of the lists and the attacks on "patterns of life" activities have been developed in accordance with the doctrine of effects-based targeting, as discussed in chapter 2.[38] Under the Obama administration, the designation of a specific individual as an al Qaeda fighter or member of an associated group was determined through a long process involving dozens of analysts from various agencies. Analysts drew up lists of potential targets and developed a "resume" for each one, including their affiliations, past activities, and any other intelligence information available.[39] The names were then put through a process of vetting, validation, and evaluation and prepared for presentation to a committee of national security officials headed by the president. This committee met weekly at the White House and through teleconference to evaluate and discuss the resumes of suspected al Qaeda and associated group members and then voted on who, where, and when to attack them.[40]

One of the biggest controversies, with implication for at least a fair number of civilian victims, was deciding who can be legally targeted.[41] While both international law scholars and government officials would agree that senior officials and operatives of al Qaeda can be legitimately designated as combatants based on their positions within the network, it is less clear who counts as a cobelligerent.

According to the laws of armed conflict, all persons who are members of a military force that is a party to the conflict are automatically combatants. In addition, targeted killings may be employed against those who have a "continuous combat function" and are likely to contribute effectively to "the achievement of a concrete and direct military advantage without their being an equivalent non-lethal alternative."[42] This includes those involved in the preparation, execution, or command of acts or operations.[43] In the context of al Qaeda and its associated groups, this would also involve anyone who swears an oath to the network and engages in violent action against their Western adversaries on behalf of an al Qaeda affiliate. Everyone else, including supporters, friends, neighbors, and sympathizers, is a civilian and therefore entitled to protection against direct attack "unless and for such time as they take a direct part in hostilities."[44]

At the same time, the US strategy of employing targeted killings to dismantle al Qaeda networks have not been limited to attacks on named individuals. In 2008, President Bush approved a policy that drone operators no longer had to conform to the identification of the target before attacking. Rather, they would be authorized to strike convoys of vehicles that bore the characteristics of al Qaeda or Taliban leaders.[45] This was later expanded to include public gatherings. These types of attacks—based on a pattern of activity rather than an identification—are known as "signature strikes," meaning that they are based on a particular "signature" that is common to al Qaeda and its associated groups.[46] This policy was continued by the Obama Administration.

The criteria for launching signature strikes are not entirely clear. To some degree, the determination is made by commanders, analysts, and drone pilots located thousands of miles from the attack site using standards that are at least partially subjective. Journalist David Sanger observed that the move toward signature strikes lowered threshold for targeting from identifiable "high-value targets" to what he called the "reasonable man" standard.[47] This is inherently risky to civilians, since patterns of activity among civilians and combatants within communities outside of a battlefield are often similar. Men loading a truck could be bomb makers, but they also might be farmers, and the drone pilots located thousands of miles away who have never been to the country and never been subject to the risks and rigors of combat might not be able to definitively know the difference. For example, US General Stanley McChrystal recounted one incident in Afghanistan when his headquarters ordered a strike against a man they had been tracking by a surveillance drone; he was observed digging near the side of a road used for coalition convoys. This was deemed to be characteristic of an insurgent planting a roadside bomb, and the order was given to kill him in an airstrike. As it later turned out—too late—he was a farmer rerouting the flow of water from an irrigation ditch.[48]

The majority of targeted attacks in Pakistan have been signature strikes, and these account for a large percentage of the collateral damage.[49] Although President Obama announced a dramatic reduction in such strikes in 2013, subsequent attacks revealed that in practice they had continued almost unabated at least into mid-2015.[50]

Drone Warfare and the Risk to Civilians

As mentioned earlier, the delivery system for executing the targeted killing campaign has been UAVs. Unlike targeted killings that employ the use of snipers or assassins, UAV attacks are guided by a combination of computer software, cameras, and listening devices, deploying missiles or other high explosive munitions to destroy their targets. Their "pilots" are located on bases in the United States thousands of miles away from the battlefield, directing operations through video screens and remote audio feed. This makes it difficult for the attacker to evaluate the environment and context through which a particular attack is ordered, prior to authorizing fire. As one legal analyst argues, "Looking through a Predator's camera is somewhat like looking through a soda straw . . . Your field of view tends to be distorted . . . You might be able to tell a Saudi headdress from and Afghan one . . . but it'd be pretty hard to do."[51] This problem is exacerbated by the lack of clarity that is often characteristic of a live video feed using satellite transmission, making it difficult to make the kinds of distinctions necessary for evaluating the surrounding environment. Moreover, the several second delay caused by the time it takes to bounce a signal off a satellite in space makes it difficult to accurately hit a moving target and to make adjustments if civilians enter the vicinity of the attack.[52]

The detachment of the pilots from the battlefield allows those attacked to be faceless and the collateral damage from the attacks to remain hidden. For example, recounting his first attack mission in Iraq, Predator drone pilot Lt. Colonel Matt Martin (who was operating in Nevada at the time) explained, "I also felt electrified, adrenalized. My team had won. We had shot the technical college full of holes, destroying large portions of it and killing God knew how many people . . . Sometimes I felt like God hurling thunderbolts from afar."[53] In this context, it is difficult to accurately conduct an evaluation of the balance between military necessity and expected collateral damage, and as I will discuss later, has had the effect of increasing civilian casualties. This problem is further exacerbated by the use of the CIA as the agency overseeing virtually all of the targeted killings in Pakistan. Unlike members of the armed forces, intelligence agents do not generally operate within a framework of, and are not usually well-trained in, the laws and customs of war and are therefore less likely to take the same feasible precautions required by international humanitarian law.[54]

Since the program is shrouded in secrecy and the strikes occur in areas that are not easily accessible by outside investigators, the number of combatants and civilians killed in these attacks are not precise. Part of the problem in acquiring accurate statistics on civilian casualties is that even US military officials are often not sure who they hit much less who they kill. Their practice is to label all of the dead as "militants" or "terrorists"— neither of which has any meaning under the laws of armed conflict— without actually verifying their identity.[55] This accounts for at least some of the civilian casualties produced by drone attacks. While "direct participation in hostilities" would include those who build or deploy explosives and plan or command operations, it does not include associates, supporters, or those who shelter, feed, fund, or travel with combatants. However, it has at times been US policy to count all "military-age men" in a strike zone as combatants even if they are not identified prior to the attack.[56] This has enabled political and military leaders to exclude such individuals from their proportionality calculations when assessing the level of collateral damage.

The amount of lethal force employed in trying to kill an individual also raises questions of proportionality. Although high-level targets increase its military value, proportionality must also consider the means used to eliminate a single individual, particularly when it takes multiple efforts to do so. For example, US attempts to kill a Taliban leader in Pakistan, Baitullah Mehsud, required 16 separate missile strikes, resulting in between 207 and 321 deaths before he was eventually killed.[57] One strike alone killed nine civilians, while another resulted in at least 45 civilian deaths.[58] The reason so many civilians were killed was because the United States employed bombs instead of bullets to attack Mehsud, making it difficult if not impossible to limit the strike to Mehsud alone.

The issue of proportionality is also a factor when considering who the targeted killings campaigns have actually killed. The label "militant" is not only ambiguous in terms of identifying the degree to which an individual is a combatant with al Qaeda or its associated groups, it also obscures the distinction between (1) high-level targets who hold a leadership role in armed nonstate organizations; (2) armed insurgents involved in a military conflict with local Pakistani or Yemani authorities but not the United

States; and (3) low-level insurgents who pose no immediate threat to the United States or its citizens. Of the 500 militants the CIA believes it has killed between 2008 and 2010, for example, 14 were labeled as top-tier leaders, 25 as mid- to high-level targets, and the rest either low-level insurgents, associates of al Qaeda operatives, or civilians.[59] While in the course of battle there is no legal distinction between commanders and foot soldiers, proportionality is based at least in part on the value of the target, and an assessment of whether collateral damage is excessive in relation to the military advantage must certainly consider this.

Based on their stated mission—targeting and killing individuals deemed to be associated with al Qaeda—drones employ a level of force that is arguably excessive, particularly as it relates to collateral damage. The United States uses two types of UAVs, MQ-1 Predator and MQ-9 Reaper drones. The Predator is smaller, slower, and carries a smaller explosive payload than the Reaper. It is equipped with two weapon stations and can carry a combination of two Hellfire missiles (originally designed as anti-tank weapons), four small Stinger missiles, and six Griffin air-to-air missiles. The Reaper is a weapons system that consists of several units. Each Reaper system consists of four individual drones operated by four different flight teams. Each drone can carry as many as four Hellfire missiles, two GBU-12 Paveway II laser-guided bombs, or two 500-pound GBU-38 Joint Direct Attack Munitions (JDAMs).[60] In both cases, the lethal blast range and effective casualty radius of the munitions extend well beyond the individual target. As devices aimed at eliminating individuals, one could easily argue that they employ overwhelming force that is susceptible to the same issues regarding collateral damage as other types of aerial attacks.

Casualty Analysis

The US government has long argued that their operators take extraordinary safeguards to limit collateral damage. During the planning and execution of personality strikes, US forces identify expected risks to civilians by developing what they label a "collateral hazard area" around a target based on the expected effects radius of a weapon. Weapon effects include blast, fragmentation, and debris, each of which can be mitigated in different ways.[61] From this, analysts can develop a "collateral damage estimate." The surveillance capabilities of drones provide an opportunity to continually evaluate the likely effects of an attack prior to authorization to launch. The degree to which this guides the decision to strike a target is hotly debated, and this type of deliberation and evaluation is often missing during signature strikes.

US intelligence officials have labeled the drone program as the most precise and humane targeting program in the history of warfare, a characterization that government officials seem to apply to every conflict.[62] Some US officials argue that they often cancel attacks when the target is located near civilians.[63] National Security Agency adviser John Brennan claimed in 2011 that there were no noncombatant casualties killed in a year of drone attacks. President Obama was a bit less categorical, initially stating that the number of civilians killed in drone strikes during the first term of his presidency was in the single digits.[64] At his request, the Office of the Director of National Intelligence later revised this figure to between 64 and one hundred and sixteen.[65] An unnamed CIA official told a *New York Times* reporter that between May 2010 and August 2011, drone strikes killed more than 600 militants and not a single civilian.[66]

Yet a Pentagon-funded study of classified Afghanistan airstrike data found that drone strikes were of "an order or magnitude more likely to result in civilian casualties per engagement than manned aircraft."[67] And a senior legal advisor to the US Army Special Forces acknowledged that "for one bad guy you kill (in a drone attack), you'd expect 1.5 civilian deaths."[68] The data in fact does reveal a considerable number of civilian casualties produced during drone attacks during the US targeted killing campaign. Based on on-site investigations and interviews conducted by various research groups and journalists, there appear to be four main sources of collateral damage: (1) spillover effects of the explosions on civilians who were in the vicinity of the target; (2) family members, friends, or neighbors who were with the target at the time of the attack; (3) civilians who were simply mistaken for terrorists/combatants by drone operators sitting thousands of miles away; and (4) rescuers who were killed while trying to help the injured from an initial strike, when the drone returned for a second attack on the same target. Moreover, we can group the types of targets into four categories: houses and housing compounds, moving vehicles, public gatherings, and "second-strike" attacks launched minutes after a first attack (known as "double-tap" attacks).

In most of these cases, targets were attacked while in the presence of others. While the US government officials tended to label all of them as militants, their presence in a car or house alongside the target often has as much to do with culture than political affiliation or sympathy. The legal and moral code of Pashtuns, *Pashtunwali*, includes the principle of *melmastia* (asylum) which requires members of the community to protect both strangers and friends. This includes armed insurgents, making it a common practice for civilians to provide food and shelter.[69] Similarly, in cases where armed fighters share rides with civilians, their vehicles do not lose its civilian character, although the combatant remains a legitimate target. This does not automatically make the targets immune from attack, but it does require a thorough proportionality analysis that distinguishes between the armed fighters and the civilian passengers.

By far the largest number of attacks, at least in Pakistan, has been on buildings; this accounts for approximately 60% of all strikes and at least 222 of the civilian casualties.[70] Of these, religious structures (mosques and madrassas) account for both the highest number of attacks and the highest civilian death rate; at least eight strikes have hit such targets, killing on average over 17 people per attack. At least 99 civilians have reportedly been killed in total.[71] Attacks on residential compounds in Pakistan continue through the present, even though drone strikes on buildings were banned by the US government in neighboring Afghanistan in all but the most urgent situations.[72] This is particularly problematic inasmuch as in North Waziristan, extended families often live in compounds that contain several homes, including those of the intended targets. One compound is used by many families, such as siblings and cousins, although every family has their own space in the compound. Normally there are 20 to 25 people living in one compound, and in some cases there are more than fifty.

Within these compounds, the *hujra* (gathering room, which is often the target of the attack) is usually in close proximity to buildings housing women and children. As a result, a missile strike on a *hujra* often kills and injures numbers of unnamed civilians.[73] For example, on January 23, 2009, drones attacked two houses, one in Zeraki and one in Wana, both of which were suspected hideouts for al Qaeda fighters. Although the *Washington Post* initially reported that the attack killed 10 insurgents, a subsequent investigation revealed that seven of the 10 were actually civilians.[74] In a similar attack in North Waziristan on November 5, 2005, a failed strike against al Qaeda operative Abu Hamza Rabia destroyed his house, killing eight people, including Rabia's wife and three children.[75]

Attacks on moving vehicles were another major source of civilian casualties. Vehicles are popular targets for both personality and signature strikes. For personality attacks, the target can be easily tracked and often has no place to escape. For signature strikes, a CIA spokesperson asserted, analysts poring over drone footage and other surveillance have become adept at detecting patterns—such as the composition and movement of a security detail—associated with senior al Qaeda operatives.[76] Problems develop, however, when cars or conveys are mistook for al Qaeda assets or when fighters share rides with members of their community, most of whom are civilians. For example, a drone attack in Walad Rabei, Yemen in 2012 killed 12 civilians and two fighters in a truck that was driving from a market where most of the occupants had been selling their wares. The target was apparently a local al Qaeda leader who was riding in the vehicle.[77] Similarly, in June 2011, a drone fired two missiles at a car traveling in North Waziristan, killing five people, none of whom were Taliban or al Qaeda fighters.[78] In December 2013, a drone-fired missile struck a wedding procession in Yemen that was presumably mistaken for an al Qaeda convoy, killing 12 civilians and injuring 15 others.[79]

Spillover effects on vehicle attacks also produced significant collateral damage. A drone strike in central Yemen in 2014 targeting a truck carrying al Qaeda fighters also destroyed a vehicle carrying laborers from the al-Sawina'ah district. The missile hit the truck approximately 20 to 30 meters away from the car, indicating that the pilot took some care to isolate the target. However, shrapnel from the explosion hit the car, killing four of the passengers and injuring five. None of the car passengers were al Qaeda members.[80]

Some collateral deaths and injuries were the result of attacks on public gatherings. In March 2011, for example, a drone fired two missiles at a large gathering near a bus depot in Datta Khel, Pakistan. Forty-two people were killed and 14 injured, most of whom were civilians. The gathering was a *Jirga* (meeting of leaders) called to settle a local dispute. At least four members of the group were Taliban, but the gathering was also attended by tribal leaders and community members.[81] Similarly, in August 2012, a drone launched four missiles at a group of men standing outside a mosque, killing five. Three of the men were suspected members of AQAP, while the others were well-known community leaders.[82] Some of the gatherings were funerals. These are likely to be attractive targets inasmuch as funerals of fighters can bring large numbers of fellow fighters

into the open. However, funerals are also attended by friends and neighbors who are not combatants. In June 2009, for example, an attack on a
funeral in Miram Shah killed 83 people, 18 to 45 of whom were civilians
with no ties to armed fighters.[83]

The practice of double-tap attacks also results in significant civilian
casualties. Residents and rescuers who come to the scene of a strike are
often the victims of follow-up attacks, most likely on the assumption that
they were part of the group being targeted.[84] Such attacks often do in fact
kill fighters coming to the rescue, but they also kill and injure many civilians from the community who were simply trying to help the injured.
Statistics compiled by the Bureau of Investigative Journalism suggest
that of 74 people killed in double-tap attacks between May 16, 2009 and
July 12, 2011, 48 were civilians (65%).[85] Similar figures were reported
by Amnesty International.[86] Besides the immediate toll on the rescuers,
such practices discourage responders from coming to the aid of those
injured in attacks, thereby increasing the likelihood that at least some of
the wounded will die for lack of treatment.

Conclusion

The precision targeting of individuals in an unconventional conflict with
a nonstate actor could in theory be an effective and humane approach
toward prosecuting a war with a minimum of collateral damage. Following
the murder of 11 Israeli athletes during the 1972 Olympic Games, for
example, Israel embarked on a campaign of targeted killings to eliminate
the major leaders and operatives from the Black September organization
that perpetrated the attack. The operation (dubbed "Wrath of God") was
able to execute the operation with a bare minimum of collateral damage,
primarily because it was implemented by assassins targeting individual
targets primarily with small arms.[87] Certainly it was far less lethal to noncombatants than a bombing campaign or ground invasion.

The US targeting campaign, however, has not been precise, nor has it
avoided large numbers of civilian casualties. Employing the main components of the Western way of warfare, the military used the latest advances
in military technology and employed overwhelming force in an effort
to minimize (or in this case, eliminate) the risk to their own forces. By
engaging in a remote-control war, the campaign has often been reckless

and indifferent to the collateral damage, aside from the political consequences that likely limited the effects. Drones have many advantages, but their very nature makes their use threatening both to the civilian population and to the communities in which they reside.

In addition to the direct collateral damage (deaths and injuries to civilians), the drone war has produced a collateral effect similar to a campaign of terrorism, even if the intent to terrorize was absent. The seemingly arbitrary nature of drone attacks (striking houses, cars, caravans, and gatherings outside of battle zones) causes widespread fear among the populations. In large areas of Pakistan and Yemen drones are always present, striking unannounced without any public understanding of who is the target. This is particularly true of signature strikes. As US General Stanley McChrystal observed in Afghanistan, drone strikes create "a perception of helpless people in an area being shot at like thunderbolts from the sky by an entity that is acting as though they have omniscience and omnipotence.[88] Similarly, according to a Yemani sheikh interviewed by *The Economist*, "people are afraid to go to weddings because whenever large groups of men gather they are afraid a drone will hit them."[89]

At the same time, the statistics do show a significant decline in both the number of strikes and the number of civilian casualties in recent years. For example, in 2014, the United States only conducted 13 attacks in Pakistan, down from 25 in 2013, and significantly reduced from its height of 128 in 2010. The percentage of civilian casualties also dropped significantly in the past year and a half.[90] This is attributable in part to the dramatic scaling back of the program, but also to the commitment by President Obama to reduce collateral damage during the drone campaign.

In 2013, President Obama issued a Presidential Policy Guidance, outlining new criteria governing drone strikes. Although the document itself remains confidential, the White House released a fact sheet summarizing the main points. The three key points listed were that there must be near certainty that noncombatants will not be killed or injured; near certainty that the target is present (although this would not affect signature strikes); and an assessment that no other reasonable alternatives exist to effectively address the threats to the United States.[91] Obama reiterated this position in a speech later that day.[92]

In addition, the US has adapted the drone-mounted versions of the Hellfire Missile to reduce its spillover effects by lowering the explosive yield, resulting in a smaller lethal blast range and presumably fewer collateral casualties. At the same time, however, the United States is also phasing out the Predator in favor of the far more lethal Reaper drone, which also carries 500-pound GBU-38 Joint Direct Attack Munitions similar to those used by conventional bombers. It is not clear that this trend of lower civilian casualties will hold for future operations in the coming years.

In the end, drone wars are still wars, and the effort by government officials to sell them as near-perfect precision tools against "bad guys" (their term) obscures the fact that like all weapons of war, they do, have, and will continue to produce significant collateral damage during their operations.

Assessing Collateral Damage

Civilian casualties and the destruction of civilian property are a fact of life in wartime. Whether killed or injured by barrel bombs, missile strikes, or marauding bands of soldiers, civilians have long been victimized during armed conflicts. As General William T. Sherman is purported to have declared, "war is hell," reflecting a common view that in armed conflict brutality and violence are unavoidable, even against those who are not engaged in battle. For many people in government and the military, this often serves as an all-purpose justification for both atrocities and collateral damage.

At the same time, over the past century, states have steadily developed more complex rules and procedures for reducing the effects of the violence on noncombatants, while at the same time expanding their reach to include all types of armed conflicts regardless of the identities of the combatants, the locus of the fighting, and the nature of the cause. Toward this end governments, international institutions, and nongovernmental organizations have agreed that the civilian population is entitled to general protection against dangers arising from military operations. Thus, in the conduct of military operations, combatants are required to take constant care to spare the civilian population and civilian objects from attack, and must take all feasible precautions in the choice of means and methods to avoid, or at least minimize, incidental loss of civilian life, injury to civilians, and damage to civilian objects.[1] This is the foundation of international humanitarian law (IHL), and its principles have been incorporated into diplomatic practice and the rules of engagement adopted by many military organizations.

The preceding chapters have been concerned with those states who have adopted these rules as national policy yet continue to produce

significant numbers of civilian casualties and damage to facilities necessary for the well-being and survival of the civilian population. As such the
focus has been on the United States, NATO, and Israel after the end of
the Cold War and the beginning of the Geneva Protocol regime in 1989.
While it is no mystery why those who blatantly violate the most basic
principles of IHL kill and injure many civilians, it is puzzling why those
who adhere to its precepts do so as well.

This final chapter will discuss the degree to which the various theories developed in chapter 2 are supported by the empirical evidence in
chapters 3 through 6, and suggest why the progressive development of
international humanitarian law and the rising intolerance for collateral
damage within the international community has not had a greater impact
on significantly reducing the harm inflicted on noncombatants by states
who adhere to its principles. It will then discuss the implications of these
findings and offer suggestions for the future protection of civilians.

Evaluating the Evidence

As a rule, we should expect civilian casualty rates to be highest when
states are embroiled in protracted wars of attrition, civil wars, or counterinsurgency campaigns.[2] Wars of attrition are usually fought between
relatively evenly matched armies, and create situations that make combatants increasingly desperate to break the stalemate and reduce their losses.
Under these conditions, the military may believe that they have fewer
options and decide to take stronger action to ensure that the conflict ends
quickly and decisively in their favor. This encourages them to relax the
laws of armed conflict in order to continue fighting, limit their own casualties, and win the war by coercing the adversary into surrender.[3] Civil
wars are battles for survival, certainly for the government and to a large
extent also for the rebels. The stakes are not only unusually high, but the
battlegrounds are usually centered in towns, villages, and cities that are
inhabited mostly by civilians. Counterinsurgency campaigns tend to be
brutal, and government security forces are usually less concerned about
civilian casualties than in obliterating the opposition and its supporters.[4]

None of the cases studied in this book involved any of these types of
conflicts. All but one the wars lasted less than three months, and during the
fighting the Western armies lost few soldiers. In every conflict examined,

the Western states fought against adversaries who were considerably weaker and could not pose a threat to their survival, territorial integrity, sovereignty, or even their fundamental security. In fact, the adversaries could not even wage an effective defense against Western attacks.

Moreover, in four of the five cases the entire conflict was fought solely on the territory of the weaker party, and therefore the stronger states could threaten, damage, or even obliterate their institutions, infrastructure, and population without fear of retaliation. Quite simply, there was an extreme asymmetry of threat, with the Western states facing minimal risk to both their military forces and territories. Even in the war between Israel and Hezbollah, the threat posed by the latter was minimal and their ability to inflict harm on the Israeli population was very limited compared to Israel's capacity to destroy large parts of Lebanon.

As a result, we should have expected low levels of civilian casualties and damage to civilian objects produced by the dominant Western states in all of the conflicts examined in this book. As the case studies demonstrate, however, this is not what occurred.

It has been my central argument that the level of collateral damage produced by states committed to the principle of civilian immunity is the result of the reckless war-fighting strategies that they employ during their military operations. These strategies reflect the Western way of war, as described in chapter 2. In applying these theories to the practice of Western countries since 1989, I investigated four different types of conflicts fought by these states, focusing primarily on the strategies pursued, the level of civilian harm produced by their military organizations, and the reasons for the collateral damage.

In chapter 1, I cited two alternative explanations advanced by political leaders and military officials for the level of collateral damage produced by their armies: 1) the behavior of their adversaries, who comingle their military forces with civilians and civilian objects; and 2) the unavoidable accidents and spillover effects that are the inevitable byproduct of any type of military action. The empirical chapters considered these explanations and found them to be vastly inadequate.

According to the Pentagon's final report to Congress following the Gulf War, for example, Iraqi authorities "elected not to move civilians away from objects they knew were legitimate military targets" and "failed to evacuate civilians in any significant numbers from Baghdad," thereby placing those civilians at risk of injury incidental to Coalition attacks against these targets.[5] Similarly, the government of Israel argued that the primary cause of collateral damage in their 2006 war was "Hizbullah's deliberate placing of missile launchers and stockpiles of weapons in the heart of civilian centers, frequently inside and beneath populated apartment blocks," putting the civilian population at risk from Israel when they attacked legitimate military targets.[6] This was a similar argument made by some NATO officials in the wake of their war against Serbia in 1999.

The evidence shows that these explanations do not account for more than a small fraction of the collateral damage caused by attacks by the Western powers. During the 1991 Gulf War, the use of civilians as human shields by the Iraqi government was not a factor in accounting for any civilian casualties. Prior to the war, the Iraqi government did hold more than 800 Western, Japanese, and Kuwaiti nationals as involuntary human shields at strategic installations in Iraq and Kuwait to deter attack by the international Coalition. However, all of the foreigners were released by the end of 1990, prior to the initiation of hostilities.[7] There was no evidence in the other conflicts that the adversaries forcibly relocated civilians to shield military targets.

There is also little evidence of any significant effort by Iraq, Serbia, Libya, or Hezbollah to relocate their military assets to civilian areas in an effort to prevent attacks against these legitimate targets. Most of the targets in Baghdad, Basra, Belgrade, Nis, Novi Sad, and the Beirut suburbs were political and economic institutions and dual-use facilities that were part of the fabric of the towns and cities in which they were located. These institutions (such as government buildings, command and control communication centers, economic and social enterprises affiliated with the adversary's leadership or supporters, and transportation and economic infrastructure) had been there long before the wars began; they were not moved into civilian areas to create human shields. Rather, the casualties that resulted from the colocation of military objects within civilian areas were the result of decisions by Western forces to define the battle space to include areas within populated towns and cities and the designation of dual-use facilities, political and economic institutions, and infrastructure as military targets. It was the attackers that defined such spaces as battlefields, thereby creating the very situation that they condemn as concealment warfare.

Hezbollah did sometimes hide military equipment in civilian neighborhoods, and their fighters often did not wear insignia designating them as combatants until they were engaged in battle. However, as the Human Rights Watch report discussed in chapter 5 concluded, there was no evidence that this practice was systematic or widespread nor did it account for any significant civilian casualties. Israeli attacks on Hezbollah rocket launchers (the only substantive threat to Israel) occurred almost exclusively outside of populated areas and killed few civilians. Rather, as Human Rights Watch observed, most of the Israeli targets in populated neighborhoods were Hezbollah-run civilian institutions such as schools, welfare agencies, banks, shops and political offices, which Israel labeled as military objects because of their relationship to the organization rather than because they made an effective contribution to hostilities.[8]

In all of these cases, the comingling of combatants with civilians was less a matter of strategy than a consequence of the asymmetry of position enjoyed by the United States, NATO, and Israel. That is, since the fighting occurred primarily if not solely on the territory of the weaker adversary—often in densely populated settings—there were few opportunities for the weaker party to mobilize or protect themselves from aerial attacks. In many cases, the combatants from the weaker party—whether they were Hezbollah or al Qaeda—operated from these towns because it is where they and their supporters lived. Moreover, since the Western states maintained virtually complete control of the airspace, they were able to detect and attack their adversaries at will. This not only provided an advantage against which the weaker party could not defend or retaliate, but also offered the opportunity to exercise a higher level of feasible precaution in avoiding collateral damage, something that they often failed to do.

At the same time, in all of the cases studied in the book, most of the collateral damage inflicted by the Western powers occurred not during heated battles or under conditions of uncertainty brought about by the fog of war, but rather after careful deliberation and planning, under circumstances that were highly favorable to the attackers. Few of the civilian casualties in Iraq, Serbia, Libya, Lebanon, Pakistan, and Yemen were the result of stray missiles or missed targets, but rather the product of deliberate attacks on facilities, institutions, infrastructure, and individuals located in populated areas as part of a general effects-based war strategy. The targets themselves may have been legal, but the decision to strike them with overwhelming force was reckless in light of the circumstances. Given the intensity and persistence of the attacks, high civilian losses were almost a certainty, even if the attackers did not know precisely which ones would result in collateral damage.

Civilian Casualties and the Western Approach to Warfare

While it is impossible to prosecute a war without at least some level of civilian casualties, the cases demonstrate that the amount of damage inflicted by Western states in Iraq, Serbia, Libya, Lebanon, Pakistan, and Yemen was both excessive and the predictable result of the strategies pursued by the military organizations employing the Western way of war: that conflicts be of short duration, fought exclusively in territories that are far removed from the Western heartlands, result in few casualties among their own soldiers, and result in a decisive outcome (as opposed to a negotiated settlement). The cases demonstrate that this approach inevitably leads to significant numbers of civilian casualties. In most of the cases, these factors overlapped; for example, political officials and military leaders chose strategies and targets that simultaneously reduced the risk to their soldiers, increased the probability for decisive victory, and facilitated the achievement of political goals.

Risk Transfer

The preceding cases confirm that the policy of risk transfer accounts for at least a fair number of civilian casualties. From the onset of Gulf War, the fear of heavy allied casualties was a major factor in decision-making among both political and military circles. As mentioned in chapter 3, Lt. General Horner argued that support for the war among the American people depended largely on the ability to operate with "less than anticipated losses among Coalition troops."[9] Partly for this reason, the effort to evict Iraqi troops from Kuwait was preceded by ferocious attacks on Iraq's major cities, far from the battlefield with little direct effect on expelling Iraqi forces from Kuwait. The destruction of Iraqi society, its infrastructure, and its political and economic institutions was designed, at least in part, to reduce the likelihood of engaging in a protracted ground war with Iraqi soldiers in Kuwait and southern Iraq. These attacks accounted for the overwhelming majority of collateral damage inflicted by the Coalition during the war.

The coalition also increased this risk to civilians on the ground by flying their aircraft at altitudes that were beyond their ability to verify the presence of noncombatants and civilian objects when launching attacks. This was done, in large part, in an effort to avoid potential anti-aircraft fire, even though the coalition had destroyed most of Iraq's integrated anti-aircraft system in the first days of the war. This resulted in a fair number of targeting errors that cost many civilians their lives.

A similar dynamic was present in NATO's war with Serbia, Israel's conflict with Hezbollah, and the US targeted killing campaign against al Qaeda operatives. In all three cases, political leaders were very concerned that the prospect of casualties among their soldiers would spark significant domestic opposition to military action. Although NATO's stated purpose of the war was to protect the Kosovar Albanians from Serbian attacks, they refused to deploy ground forces, which virtually all analysts agreed would be the only way to effectively do so. By prosecuting the entire war from the air—and flying at heights designed to protect the pilots but also make it much more difficult to verify targets—NATO transferred the risk to Serbia's civilians, resulting in significant numbers of noncombatant deaths and injuries.

This also partly explains Israel's preference for engaging in massive air attacks on Beirut and its suburban neighborhoods rather than confronting Hezbollah directly with ground forces in southern Lebanon. As discussed in chapter 5, a ground war would have likely produced at least a fair number of Israeli military casualties, something that would have been extremely unpopular domestically. Since Hezbollah had no anti-aircraft capabilities, the massive bombing raids over Lebanese towns, cities, highways, and public facilities were virtually risk free, at least for the Israeli pilots.

The use of drones to execute the US policy of targeted killings in its conflict with al Qaeda has been the ultimate in risk transfer. Despite the documented problems with verifying targets and confirming the presence of civilians in the area of the attacks through video feeds from thousands of miles away, the entire campaign has been prosecuted remotely through unmanned aircraft. President Obama was determined not to employ ground forces to seek out and kill or capture al

Qaeda operatives and saw mechanical assassins as a workable alternative. Certainly the use of ground troops would have likely been dangerous and may have proven to be unwise for a variety of reasons; however, rather than consider other types of strategies to confront al Qaeda, the United States engaged in an equally risky approach, albeit one that was borne exclusively by civilians.

Overwhelming Force

Most of the collateral damage in four of the five cases occurred in the course of massive air attacks against political and economic institutions, dual-use facilities, transportation, and military objectives located in densely populated towns and cities. The fifth case, the US targeted killing campaign, also exhibited a use of overwhelming force, considering that they employed 500-pound bombs to kill individuals. All of these attacks were the means toward implementing an effects-based approach to warfare. Such an approach required a targeting strategy focusing on institutions and infrastructure that constituted the adversary's centers of gravity, which were usually located in populated areas (sometimes a segment of the population itself). In essence, effects-based warfare requires the destruction of at least some part or parts of the adversary's society. Although many of the attacks were executed using precision-guided bombs and missiles, the strikes were anything but surgical, as demonstrated by the level of collateral damage they produced.

As discussed in chapter 2, an effects-based strategy was been made possible by technological advancements in aeronautics, rocket propulsion, and sophisticated guidance systems. Early theorists of strategic air power, such as Guilio Douhet, HughTrenchard, and Billy Mitchell, foresaw the military advantage of using aircraft (and later guided missiles) to attack deep within the homeland of the adversary. Such attacks would enable them to strike the enemy's vital centers—such as their industrial facilities, population, government buildings, and infrastructure—without having to fight through fixed lines of defense.[10] The revolution in military technology enabled the advanced military powers to expand the delivery of such power from slow moving propeller aircraft to highly maneuverable supersonic fighter jets, helicopters, and extremely accurate and powerfully destructive missiles and unmanned aerial vehicles.

The case studies not only confirm the role of massive air power in promoting the Western way of war, but also as the primary cause of collateral damage. A rough estimate from the figures compiled in chapters 3 through 6 places aerial attacks as producing 90 to 95% of the civilian casualties.[11] In the cases of NATO's war against Serbia and the US campaign of the targeted killings, the figure is 100%. The virtually unchallenged control of the airspace in these conflicts enabled the Western militaries to launch devastating attacks on targets located within populated towns and cities with minimal risk to their soldiers. This, in turn, allowed them to largely focus their attacks on legal targets, and then define any resulting civilian casualties as inadvertent and unintentional.

At the same time, the targeted killings case demonstrates how a different strategy could reduce collateral damage, at least under some circumstances. The switch in tactics employed by the Obama administration in its targeted killing campaign after 2010 may offer some lessons on how reducing the use of overwhelming force and forgoing attacks on large facilities can reduce civilian casualties. Beginning in 2010 to 2011, the United States changed its preferred method of targeting individuals in Pakistan from compounds to vehicles. While attacking vehicles did continue to kill civilians, the collateral damage was much lower than attacks on residential compounds and public spaces, where the target's neighbors, friends, and family members were placed at grave risk.[12] This does not address the other issues associated with drone warfare (such as terrorizing entire regions of a country and violating a country's sovereignty), but it does suggest that a greater concern with civilian casualties can reduce their occurrence.

Decisive Victory

The employment of overwhelming force against political and economic targets in populated areas was also a means to secure decisive victories rather than negotiated settlements, another aspect of the Western approach to warfare. Partially for this reason, attacks on infrastructure, government, and other public facilities used by or located near the civilian population were designed to shock and awe their opponents into capitulation, a tactic Ward Thomas labels "duress bombing."[13] While there is nothing in and of itself wrong with trying to maximize one's advantage and achieve better terms of victory, this was often accomplished at the expense of noncombatant lives and the survival and well-being of the civilian population. This factor was present in five of the six cases.

During the Gulf War, the US-led coalition decided that it not only wanted to drive Iraq out of Kuwait (the only goal authorized by the UN resolution that created the international coalition), but also overthrow its government and destroy the country's military power and influence in the region. For this reason, once the war began it did not want a negotiated settlement or unilateral withdrawal by Iraq, but rather unconditional surrender. As observed in chapter 3, US leaders considered an Iraqi withdrawal from Kuwait with its military forces intact to be the "nightmare scenario."[14] The massive bombing of Iraqi's cities and civilian infrastructure was designed in part to further these goals, even though it contributed little to ending Iraq's occupation of Kuwait.[15]

NATO's decision to launch its air campaign against Serbia was sparked ostensibly by Serbia's refusal to sign the Rambouillet Accords, which would have, among other things, granted free and unrestricted access for NATO forces throughout the entirety of Yugoslavia and a referendum on Kosovo's secession from the federation. These were demands that no sovereign state would accept and NATO officials knew that it could not attain them through diplomacy. The alliance chose the military option largely because its leaders believed that massive destruction of Serbia's infrastructure and government facilities would force a surrender, and an air war was a relatively risk-free to its own troops and populations. Once it became clear that a few weeks of bombing would not succeed, the alliance still refused to settle for anything less than a decisive victory, and embarked on a significantly escalated campaign. Most of the collateral damage occurred during this period.

A similar dynamic was present during the Israeli–Hezbollah conflict. Throughout the war, the Israel government maintained it would refuse to negotiate any ceasefire that did not require the complete disarmament of Hezbollah and its expulsion from southern Lebanon, a condition that it knew would be unacceptable to the organization.[16] Although there were several attempts by the UN Security Council and Arab mediators to broker a ceasefire, Israel refused to participate until it became clear that the war was at a stalemate.[17] With the support of the United States, its leadership had hoped that the relentless bombing campaign would force the Lebanese government and population to turn against Hezbollah and expel them from the south. It was during this process that the large majority of civilian casualties occurred.[18]

Political Targets and Civilian Casualties

Some of the collateral damage can be attributed to attacks on targets aimed at achieving political objectives that were only indirectly related, or in some cases unrelated, to defeating the military forces of their adversaries, such as regime change (Gulf War, Libya), punishment (Lebanon), and intimidation (Serbia, Pakistan). While political objectives have always been a central part of warfare, they do not constitute a military advantage when calculating proportionality and evaluating the necessity of risking civilian lives. Political targets such as government buildings, business enterprises owned by associates of the adversaries' leaders, and the dwellings of political allies are almost always located primarily in heavily populated cities and therefore put civilians at risk.

In pursuing this approach, Western states attacked government and leadership facilities that did not directly contribute to military hostilities in Iraq, Serbia, Libya, and Lebanon. For example, NATO's decision to launch a cruise missile into the bedroom of Serbian President Milosevic (who is technically a civilian), and launching a missile attack on a nearby building housing his civilian presidential guard (killing 30 people) is symbolic of how NATO blurred the distinction between military objectives and political goals during its war against Serbia.[19] Similarly, attempts to assassinate Iraqi President Saddam Hussein and Libyan President Muammar Gaddafi and undermine the ability of their regimes to govern by attacking government buildings and private residences resulted in numerous civilian casualties and produced significant long-term reverberation effects on the stability of their societies after the war ended.

As mentioned earlier, many Israeli targets in Lebanon were the residences, economic enterprises, and political offices of Hezbollah supporters and members of their political party. Many of the attacks on public facilities and infrastructure was aimed at punishing the Lebanese population and government (which was officially neutral) for not reining in Hezbollah in the southern part of the country. These attacks resulted in significant collateral damage in both the short and long term.

The Consequences of Indifference

In each of the cases, the Western governments and their military organizations publicly treated the issue of civilian casualties and other forms of collateral damage with a mixture of indifference and denial. Although they often took steps to minimize civilian casualties during hostilities, they refused to publicly acknowledge noncombatant deaths when they occurred, except when they became a major political issue or were publicized in the mass media.

The official government positions on collateral damage followed a consistent pattern. First, political and military leaders issued statements bragging that they had taken greater precautions to protect civilians than any state had ever done during an armed conflict. The Gulf War of 1991 was "the most discriminate military campaign in history, to include extraordinary measures by US and Coalition aircrews to minimize collateral civilian casualties."[20] There had "never been an air campaign in history that has been discriminating against the military but in favour of civilians" as NATO's 1999 war against Serbia.[21] The US drone campaign was "the most precise and humane targeting program in the history of warfare."[22] And "the steps taken by Israel [in its 2006 war with Hezbollah] to address humanitarian considerations corresponded to, and often were more stringent than, those taken by many Western democracies confronting similar or lesser threats."[23]

Second, not only did all of the governments fail to acknowledge civilian losses during the conflicts, after the wars ended the officials failed to investigate the degree to which the boasts were accurate. In fact, none of them even attempted to document or verify any civilian casualties at all, except in the specific cases that became public political issues.[24] The Pentagon's final report to Congress on the Gulf War was 909 pages; approximately 10 pages were devoted to a discussion of collateral damage caused by coalition attacks. Most of the discussion in this area focused on the coalition's adherence to international law, the precautions taken by the military to avoid civilian casualties, and the culpability of the Iraqi government for coalition-induced civilian casualties.[25] Aside from justifying the attacks on dual-use facilities (which, the report acknowledges, had led to some collateral damage) and the al Firdos bunker, the report failed to account for the approximately 3,600 civilians killed by coalition action. Indeed, the report did not even offer an estimate of how many civilians were killed

or injured, nor did it discuss the extent of the damage to civilian infrastructure and other installations.

Similarly, NATO failed to investigate the civilian casualties or broader
collateral damage that they inflicted during its air war against Serbia. The
main report published by the US Air Force did little to verify or explain
noncombatant casualties. Indeed, it barely mentioned them aside from
ascribing them to the behavior of the Serbian government.[26]

Following its war with Lebanon, the government of Israel appointed
the Winograd Commission to investigate the circumstances that led to
the war, the performance of the Israeli Defense Force, and the decision-
making process within the government and military. However, the report
did not even mention the impact of the war on Lebanese civilians at all,
much less account for them, although it did discuss the effect of the war
on Israeli civilians.[27] The government had an opportunity to rectify this
in a written response to a report to Human Rights Watch, which had
charged Israel with demonstrating a callous disregard for the lives of the
Lebanese population. Rather than accounting for any civilian casualties
or even estimating a number, they blamed them all on Hezbollah.[28]

As discussed in chapter 6, for a long time the United States denied that
any civilians at all were killed in drone attacks against al Qaeda operatives
in Pakistan and Yemen. When they did finally acknowledge civilian casualties, the numbers were dramatically downplayed, estimated anywhere
from the single digits to insignificant.

Absolution Through Comparison

It is tempting to absolve the Western democracies of the collateral damage they inflict by comparing the numbers killed and injured in their military operations to the casualties that occur in bloodier conflicts where
combatants launch deliberate or indiscriminate attacks against civilians.
This is misguided in several ways.

First, it avoids the questions of whether the level of collateral damage produced in each case was preventable and excessive. In considering
this, the fact that more civilians may have been killed in other conflicts
or by one's adversary is irrelevant. The preceding chapters have demonstrated a direct link between the numbers of civilian casualties and the
strategies pursued by the attacking states. Few of the civilian casualties in

the four cases occurred in the heat of battle. The overwhelming majority
were produced during well-planned attacks that were executed by fighters who had the luxury of deliberation, consideration, and evaluation.
In this sense the casualties may have been inadvertent, but they were
neither unforeseeable nor usually necessary. Had the military organizations used different approaches—such as forgoing attacks on densely
populated towns or infrastructure, reducing strikes against political and
economic targets, or pursuing more limited political goals—they would
most likely have still prevailed but without producing the higher levels
of civilian casualties.

Second, comparing the conduct of one's own forces to those of war
criminals establishes a false standard. The military strategies promoted
by Liberian President Charles Taylor, the Rwandan Akazu, the Ugandan
Lord's Resistance Army, Serbian President Slobodan Milošević, the
Russian army in Chechnya, and Syrian President Bashar Hafez al-Assad
are not the benchmark by which compliance with the principle of civilian
immunity is measured. In adopting the tenets of international humanitarian law, the Western states have accepted civilian immunity as a fundamental principle to consider when planning and executing their military
strategies. It is this principle, not the behavior of brutal warriors, that
establishes the standard of behavior and comparison.

Third, it obscures the degree to which there were alternatives to the use
of military force in the first place. Political leaders consider a wide variety
of factors when weighing their options in the pursuit of a particular set
of goals. States with advanced military technology and dominant capabilities are more prone to use force as the preferred alternative because
their leadership believes it can achieve more through military action than
through other methods. This is made easier domestically by limiting the
cost to their own troops, and internationally by suggesting that they can
restrict most of the enemy casualties to combatants. By downplaying the
significance of civilian casualties and damage to civilian life, they can pro-
mote the military option as relatively cost-free. This is highly misleading,
however, bordering on disingenuous. If, as is clear from the preceding
pages, that even the most carefully orchestrated military operations will
kill and injure civilians, sometimes massively, the decision to forgo less
lethal options in favor of military force increases the culpability of those
who made the decision to pursue this alternative. The fact that a one's
military organization kills and injures fewer civilians that those waged by

tyrants does not in and of itself justify the use of force, particularly when such use produces significant collateral damage and when there were alternatives to military action.

Fourth, it trivializes the impact of collateral damage on the populations and societies that are forced to endure it. Attacks on Iraq's, Serbia's, and Lebanon's cities and infrastructure produced fewer devastating results than Syria's deliberate use of barrel bombs on civilian neighborhoods in Homs; however, not only did thousands of civilians die during these assaults, but in most cases those who survived lost the public facilities and institutions necessary for their future survival.

Fifth, because of the frequency that Western states have initiated armed conflicts since the end of the Cold War, their behavior has a greater impact on the welfare of civilians around the world than those of states who may kill more noncombatants during a particular conflict but who are involved in conflicts far less frequently. The Syrian government's military campaign against its rebel opponents has been both brutal and cruel, but once the civil war is resolved, it is unlikely to unleash similar violence against other populations. On the other hand, the United States, NATO, and Israel have been at war almost constantly over the past 25 years, in most cases conflicts that they have initiated. While they commit far fewer abuses of civilians in a particular conflict, they engage in far more conflicts than the average state and are therefore more often called upon to weigh the effects of their actions on noncombatants.

Re-evaluating Collateral Damage

Most people in and out of government and the military generally calculate collateral damage in terms of civilian deaths and injuries. Indeed this book has itself employed such statistical measures, and much of the case studies examined how and why civilians were killed or injured during military operations. But the cases also demonstrate that the side effects of the Western way of war go well beyond individual casualties. Massive assaults on political and economic institutions and infrastructure—a key component of effects-based targeting—have two other collateral effects: 1) medium- to long-term damage to, or destruction of, systems necessary for the survival and well-being of the civilian populace; and 2) the pervasive spread of terror and fear among the population.

Under IHL, it is prohibited to attack, destroy, or render useless objects indispensable to the survival of the civilian population "for the specific purpose of denying them for their sustenance value to the civilian population."[29] Since it was not the purpose of attacks by the military organizations studied in this book to specifically deny the population the means of survival, destroying these objects were not in and of themselves a violation of the laws of armed conflict. However, these actions often caused long-term damage to the social and economic fabric of civilian life, an impact that has endangered the populations' health, safety, and survival. These effects are more difficult to measure statistically—and are therefore often ignored—but they can be far more harmful to the civilian population overall than the individual deaths and injuries that are the immediate result of military attacks.

For example, according to a report issued by UN Under Secretary Marti Artisaari, who conducted a field investigation in Iraq immediately after the end of the Gulf War, allied bombardment,

> wrought near-apocalyptic results on the economic infrastructure of what had been, until January 1991, a rather highly urbanized and mechanized society. Now, most means of modern life support have been destroyed or rendered tenuous. Iraq has, for some time to come, been relegated to a pre-industrial age but with all the disabilities of post-industrial dependency on an intensive use of energy and technology.[30]

As a result,

> Iraqi rivers are heavily polluted by raw sewage, and water levels are unusually low. All sewage treatment and pumping plants have been brought to a virtual standstill by the lack of power supply and the lack of spare parts. Pools of sewage lie in the streets and villages.[31]

In addition, water purification ceased and hospitals and health center lacked adequate running water. This led to an alarming increase in water-borne diseases including cholera, typhoid, and severe gastroentitis, particularly in children. Coupled with the heavy damage to the transportation system, Iraq exhibited extremely high levels of malnutrition.[32]

Similar outcome resulted from Israeli attacks on the heavily populated Lebanese neighborhoods in and around Beirut and towns in southern Lebanon during the 2006 war with Hezbollah, as discussed in chapter 5. Israeli air and artillery strikes destroyed an estimated 130,000 homes and apartments, hundreds of public buildings, dozens of entire city blocks, bridges, and at least two dozen gas stations in the capital city of Beirut.[33] As a result tens of thousands of civilians were rendered homeless, food supplies were dramatically reduced, and many public services were eliminated. It took more than a year for many of these neighborhoods to recover, and some areas still have not.

Although the damage was less extensive in the Serbian cities of Belgrade, Nis, and Novi Sad, as a result of NATO bombing the population lost essential services, particularly economic and transportation infrastructure that was necessary for access to food and medical supplies. It also eliminated vital electrical power for months. As the *Washington Post* reported after the war:

> Yugoslavia is a shattered nation ... hundreds of its factories, buildings, bridges, houses, roads and railway lines are in ruins ... The Serbian landscape presents a vivid picture of the country's bleak future. Broken bridges in Novi Sad. The charred oil refinery, fertilizer plant and petrochemical complex in Pancevo. The smashed machinery factory in Kraljevo. The ruined auto plant in Kragujevac. The burned out and crushed office and government buildings in Belgrade. The main north-south highway is ruptured by downed overpasses. Broken trestles interrupt railroad lines. Fuel depots are blasted, electrical transformers damaged, central urban heating plants destroyed, water facilities out of commission.[34]

As discussed in chapter 4, the long-term damage to Libyan society far outweighed the hundreds of civilians killed and injured in NATO attacks. The destruction of Libya's political and security institutions not only eliminated most government services, it also made the postwar recovery virtually impossible. In the years following the attack, Libya had been without a functioning central government with any substantive authority within the country. No one has conducted a comprehensive survey of this long-term damage, but on-site visits by journalists reveal a lack of basic

services or security throughout the country. As a result, thousands of people have died, and a once stable and prosperous country has become a
failed state.[35]

In addition to the physical damage to vital civilian facilities wrought by
bombing campaigns in Iraq, Serbia, Lebanon, and Pakistan, the massive
numbers of sustained air attacks on populated areas also created widespread fear and terror among the civilian population in all four cases.
International humanitarian law prohibits "acts or threats of violence the
primary purpose of which is to spread terror among the civilian population."[36] To the extent that this was not the primary purpose of the aerial assaults by NATO, Israel, and the United States, they did not violate
the laws of armed conflict. However, as far as the populations were concerned, there was little difference. In Iraq, Serbia, Lebanon, Pakistan, and
Yemen, tens of thousands of civilians had to endure constant (sometimes
24-hour-a-day) bombardments in their communities, many close to their
homes and workplaces. As a resident of Ghundi Kala in Pakistan reported,
"the drone planes were flying over our village all day and night, flying in
pairs, sometimes three together."[37]

While precision bombing could spare a home and its residents from
destruction, it could not spare them from the panic and terror that accompanied these relentless assaults. The fact that the attacks were preplanned,
deliberate, and likely to be repeated only increased anxiety and fear within
the population. Moreover, the use of double-tap strikes (hitting a target
a second time soon after the initial attack) made it extremely risky for
neighbors and emergency workers to assist those injured or buried under
rubble. These effects were clearly present in all of the cases, and investigations by various research and human rights organizations documented
the state of terror that engulfed entire cities and communities. Indirect
terrorism is therefore a collateral effect of the Western strategies focused
on political and economic centers of gravity.

Finally, in virtually all cases, the catalog of deaths and injuries are that
are calculated by various organizations undercount the true numbers.
There are at five types of civilian casualties that can be attributed to military attacks and fighting: those killed or injured as a direct effect of the
war; those who die from indirect effects such as disease and malnutrition;
those uprooted as a result of armed attacks, for example, refugees and
internally displaced persons; those who are killed after the conflict has
ended as a result of the destruction of facilities vital to their survival; and

those killed or injured by ordnance left over from the conflict, for exam-ple, cluster munitions and land mines.

Most of the figures cited in this book address the first category and although they are very likely undercounted, they are the best we have and can be considered to be more or less accurate. The other four categories are difficult to count and even more difficult to trace to a particular bel-ligerent. Deaths from unexploded cluster munitions can occur years after the conflict has ended and long after the investigations into casualties have ceased, as has been the case in Serbia and Lebanon. Such weapons are reg-ularly used by advanced military organizations—for example in the Gulf War, Kosovo, and Lebanon—and deaths and injuries from these muni-tions are not considered to be part of their civilian casualty portfolios.

Similarly, death rates among refugees and internally displaced per-sons cannot easily be attributed to the actions of a particular belligerent. Although aerial bombings were certainly a major cause in the case studies, civilians relocate during wartime for a variety of reasons, and it is there-fore very difficult to make a direct connection. Moreover, we usually do not have any reliable figures to document deaths and injuries that result from the destruction of public facilities by Western attacks as described in the cases, and they are therefore excluded from most surveys. Sometimes the indirect effects can be estimated (such as the survey of deaths related to the destruction of public infrastructure taken in Iraq after the Gulf War), but because it is difficult in many cases to demonstrate a direct link to any specific act or attack, it is often excluded from evaluations of mili-tary behavior.

For this reason, with the exception of the few studies that are con-ducted well after the hostilities have ended, they remain hidden collateral damage.

Current and Future Wars

The preceding analysis is not only relevant for explaining past practices, but also provides a means for evaluating current and future actions. Between 2014 and 2017, a US-led coalition waged an aggressive air war against Daesh (also known as the Islamic State of Iraq and Levant, or ISIL) in Iraq and Syria. According to the US Air Force Central Command, this involved the release of 79,923 bombs over a two-and-a-half-year period.[38] It also resulted in a rough estimate of 3,100 civilian fatalities as a direct result of these attacks.[39] In what may have been the deadliest civilian death toll in a single incident, on March 17, 2017 a US warplane dropped a 500-pound bomb on a building in Mosul, in an attempt to kill two snipers reported to be on the rooftop. The blast killed between 105 and 278 civilians inside.[40] The numbers show a dramatic increase in civilian casualties between February and June 2017, following the adoption of newly elected President Donald Trump's order to significantly loosen the restrictions on US-led air operations.[41]

Although these numbers are still raw, the trend strongly supports the arguments made in the preceding pages regarding the causes and results of the Western way of warfare. The coalition used overwhelming force, relied on air attacks to reduce friendly casualties, and denied or downplayed the effect of their attacks on civilians.[42]

Similarly, various investigators have estimated that between 2015 and mid-2017, Saudi Arabia's air war against the Houthis in Yemen killed an estimated 9000 civilians.[43] These attacks were conducted in close consultation with, and direct support from, the United States and other Western governments, and have followed the standard Western approach to war.[44] For example, in October 2016, the coalition bombed a funeral reception in Sana, killing more than 100 civilians. The coalition later issued a statement saying that the attack had been based on false information.[45] These types of mishaps are likely to continue. President Trump reversed President Obama's suspension of precision munitions to Saudi Arabia that the former president had imposed because of concerns about civilian casualties that he attributed to poor targeting. Rather, President Trump has pledged his support for continued offensive operations by the Saudi kingdom, concluding an agreement to provide Saudi Arabia with billions of dollars in weapons, many of which are designed for use in its campaigns in the Middle East.

Implications

Since the end of the Cold War, the Western states have adopted an approach to armed conflict that has enabled them to wage war without facing the types of costs or constraints that have traditionally limited states' incentive to do so. The development of supersonic aircraft, precision-guided bombs and missiles, and high explosive ordnance has allowed their military organizations to launch attacks deep within the territory of their adversaries while facing minimal risk to their own soldiers and populations. Relying on superior air power and the advantage of not having to defend their own territory from significant retaliation, Western states have initiated 10 armed conflicts since 1989, most of them on the assumption that they could minimize the costs.

The costs, however, have not been minimal; they have been borne largely by the civilian populations of their adversaries. If one includes the long-term impact of the damage or destruction of public facilities and infrastructure in the target states, Western attacks have had a greater negative effect on civilians than on combatants in all of their operations. In fact, if we factor in the casualties produced by the secondary effects discussed in the last section, it is likely that Western attacks have killed more civilians than combatants in Iraq, Serbia, Libya, and Lebanon.

As the case studies suggest, although the Western armies avoid targeting civilian objects and often take steps to limit collateral damage, their approach to warfare makes significant noncombatant casualties inevitable. But in this case, inevitable does not mean unavoidable. The Western democracies can reduce the level of collateral damage they inflict on innocent civilians by changing their approach to armed conflict and re-evaluating the conditions under which they decide to employ military force in general. This will require the following changes.

First, political officials and military leaders must make the protection of civilians and their means of survival a high priority when planning military campaigns, particularly aerial attacks. This requires more than simply avoiding direct assaults on civilian objects and configuring attacks to minimize civilian harm. They must also change their military strategy to avoid practices that inevitably lead to high levels of collateral damage. This will mean forgoing aerial attacks on densely populated areas, abstaining from assaults on political targets that do not contribute directly to hostilities, and re-evaluating the degree to which dual-use targets such as transportation systems, infrastructure, and public utilities are militarily necessary.

The means and methods that define the Western way of war is not only problematic from a humanitarian perspective; it is unnecessary and in many cases counterproductive. The unrelenting attacks on Baghdad, the bridges over the Tigris and Euphrates, and the nation's electrical grid during Gulf War made the coalition victory easier, but they were not necessary for defeating the Iraqi army in Kuwait and southern Iraq. NATO's assaults on Serbia's cities and transportation systems enabled the alliance to achieve some of its political goals without risking its own soldiers; however, they did little to protect the Kosovar Albanians, ostensibly the goal of the war. Israeli's decision to rely on brutal air strikes on neighborhoods, businesses, and infrastructure throughout Lebanon punished the Lebanese population for their government's inability to restrain the growth of Hezbollah as a military force, but it did not help defeat Hezbollah; in fact it made them more popular domestically within Lebanon. The steady use of drones as the preferred means for the US targeted killing campaign eliminated a number of suspected al Qaeda operatives, but in the process alienated entire regions of Pakistan and Yemen and motivated hundreds if not thousands of their family members and neighbors to join or support al Qaeda and other anti-Western groups.[46]

Second, political leaders should re-evaluate the conditions under which they initiate or become involved in armed conflicts in the first place. Most of the conflicts studied in this book were wars of choice, inasmuch as there were alternatives to the use of military force. By avoiding discussion of collateral damage, or downplaying it when it is revealed, it is easier for Western states to stage attacks and wage war without acknowledging any danger to foreign civilians. Coupled with a policy of risk transfer, Western governments can publicly discuss initiating military action (for example, in Syria and North Korea in 2017) while assuring their own populations that the danger to their own soldiers and nonenemy combatants is minimal. As the previous chapters reveal, this is not an honest assessment, even if it makes the possibility of military action more palatable to the public. If the effect on foreign civilians is weighed as a serious factor, such an option should be viewed as less attractive.

It may be that given the Western way of war, the Western democracies cannot fight conflicts without causing a significant level of collateral damage. If this is in fact the case, it is incumbent on their governments to reconsider the utility of military force in circumstance where there are alternatives.

NOTES

Chapter 1

1. Department of Defense, *Dictionary of Military and Associated Terms,* Joint Publication 1-02, (Washington, DC: November 8, 2010, as amended through October 15, 2011), 55.
2. See Sarah Sewall, "Humanitarian Issues in Civilian Targeting Workshop," Carr Center for Human Rights Policy, Kennedy School of Government, Harvard University, March 7–8, 2002, 8 and Neta Crawford, *Moral Responsibility for Collateral Damage in America's Post-9/11 Wars* (New York: Oxford University Press, 2013). Jefferson Reynolds refers to the former as "voluntary" collateral damage, while the latter is "involuntary" collateral damage. See his "Collateral Damage on the 21st Century Battlefield: Enemy Exploitation of the Law of Armed Conflict, and the Struggle for a Moral High Ground," *Air Force Law Review* 56, no. 1 (2005): 89.
3. See, for example, United States Army, *The Targeting Process,* Field Manual no. 3-60 Washington, DC: November 26, 2010). For a good historical overview of the practice over the past few centuries, see Stephen J. Rockel and Rick Halpern, *Inventing Collateral Damage: Civilian Casualties, War, and Empire* (Toronto: Between the Lines, 2009). For a more recent historical treatment focusing on the Korean War and a potential nuclear conflict, see Sahr Conway-Lanz, *Collateral Damage: Americans, Noncombatant Immunity, and Atrocity After World War II* (London: Routledge, 2006).
4. See B. Graham, "Bugsplat Computer Program Aims to Limit Civilian Deaths at Targets," *Washington Post,* February 22, 2003, 1.
5. Reynolds, "Collateral Damage on the 21st Century Battlefield," 100–101.
6. Stockholm International Peace Research Institute, *SIPRI Yearbook 2011: Armaments, Disarmament and International Security* (Oxford: Oxford University Press, 2011).
7. The Malta Summit was a meeting between US President George H. W. Bush and Soviet Premier Mikhail Gorbachev on December 2 and 3, 1989, about three and a half weeks after the fall of the Berlin Wall. See "Transcripts from Malta Summit," at http://astro.temple.edu/~rimmerma/transcripts_from_malta_summit.htm.
8. First Protocol Additional to the Geneva Conventions of August 12, 1949, and Relating to the Protection of Victims of International Armed Conflicts, June 8, 1977, 1125 UN Treaty Series, 3.
9. For example, in 1987 President Regan's Legal Adviser to the State Department characterized the First Protocol as "no more than a restatement of the rules of conduct with which United States military forces would almost certainly comply as a matter of national policy, constitutional and legal protections, and common decency." Abraham D. Sofaer, "The Position of the United States on Current Law of War Agreements: Remarks of Judge Abraham D. Sofaer, Legal Adviser, United States Department of State," *American University Journal of International Law and Policy* 2 (Fall 1987): 461–462. See also Michael J. Matheson,

"The United States Position on the Relation of Customary International Law to the 1977 Protocols Additional to the 1949 6 Geneva Conventions," *American University Journal of International Law and Policy* 2, no. 2 (1987): 419–431.

10. Madelyn Hsiao-Rei Hicks, Hamit Dardagan, Gabriela Guerrero Serdán, Peter M. Bagnall, John A. Sloboda, and Michael Spagat, "Violent Deaths of Iraqi Civilians, 2003–2008: Analysis by Perpetrator, Weapon, Time, and Location," *PLoS Medicine*, February 15, 2011, Table 1 and Iraqi Body Count, "Database: Documented Civilian Deaths from Violence," at https://www.iraqbodycount.org/database. Similar numbers were cited by the highly respected website Iraqi Body Count, at https://www.iraqbodycount.org/database.

11. Amnesty International, "Lebanon: Deliberate Destruction or "Collateral Damage"? Israeli Attacks on Civilian Infrastructure" (London, August 2006), AI Index number: MDE 18/007/2006, 2. Similar numbers were reported by Human Rights Watch, *Why They Died: Civilian Casualties in Lebanon During the 2006 War* (New York, September 5, 2001).

12. Amnesty International, *Under the Rubble: Israeli Attacks on Inhabited Homes* (London, November 2014), Index number: MDE 12/03/2014.

13. Michael O'Hanlon, "A Flawed Masterpiece," *Foreign Affairs* 81, no. 3 (March/April 2002): 55; Carl Conetta, *Operation Enduring Freedom: Why a Higher Rate of Civilian Bombing Casualties,* Project on Defense Alternatives Briefing Report #13 (Cambridge, MA: Commonwealth Institute), January 18, 2002.

14. Marc W. Herold, "Counting the Dead," *The Guardian*, August 7, 2002, at https://www.the-guardian.com/world/2002/aug/08/afghanistan.comment.

15. Gen. Joseph W. Ralston, Vice Chairman, Joint Chiefs of Staff, estimates that 1,500 civilians died as a result of NATO attacks. See his AFA Policy Forum: "Aerospace Power and the Use of Force," September 14, 1999, at http://secure.afa.org/media/scripts/rlstn999.asp. Others, such as Human Rights Watch, put the civilian death toll at approximately 500 that they could verify, although they did not dispute the possibility that the actual toll is likely to be much higher. See William Arkin, *Civilian Deaths in the NATO Air Campaign*, Human Rights Watch Report 12, no. 1 (2000).

16. Beth Osborne Daponte, "A Case Study in Estimating Casualties from War and its Aftermath: the 1991 Persian Gulf War," *PSR Quarterly* 3, no. 2 (June 1993): 65.

17. The US Southern Command estimated 203 civilian dead, while the Panama government claimed more than a thousand. The most likely figure is close to the one offered by America's Watch, which is around three hundred. See Larry Rohter, "Panama and U.S. Strive to Settle on Death Toll," *New York Times*, April 1, 1990, A1.

18. The Bureau of Investigative Journalism, "Strikes in Pakistan," accessed March 1, 2017, https://www.thebureauinvestigates.com/projects/drone-war/charts?show_casualties=1&show_injuries=1&show_strikes=1&location=pakistan&from=2004-1-1&to=now.

19. Kareem Fahim, "Airstrikes Take Toll on Civilians In Yemen War," *New York Times*, September 12, 2015, 1.

20. Brian Bennett, W. J. Hennigan, and Alexandra Zavis, "Saudi-Led Yemen Air War's High Civilian Toll Unsettles U.S. Officials," *Los Angeles Times*, April 16, 2015, at http://www.latimes.com/world/middleeast/la-fg-us-saudis-20150417-story.html.

21. Christopher Coker, *Humane Warfare: The New Ethics of Postmodern War* (London: Routledge, 2001).

22. Carl Conetta, *Strange Victory: A Critical Appraisal of Operation Enduring Freedom and the Afghanistan War,* Project on Defense Alternatives Research Monograph #6 (Cambridge, MA: Commonwealth Institute, January 30, 2002), 7, 36.

23. See, for example, United States Air Force, Air Force Pamphlet 14-210, "USAF Intelligence Targeting Guide" (Washington, DC, February 1, 1998), section 4.5.2, 39; Israeli Defense Force, "Rules of Warfare on the Battlefield," Military Advocate General Corps Command, IDF School of Military Law, 2nd ed. (2006), 29; United Kingdom, "The Manual of the Law of Armed Conflict," Ministry of Defence (JSP 383) (London, July 1, 2004), para. 2.5-2.5.1. For a complete catalog of the official war-fighting policies of all states, see International Committee of the Red Cross, "Customary International Law Database," Part 2: Practice

(Geneva, December 2016), by country at http://www.icrc.org/customary-ihl/eng/docs/v2_cou.

24. See US Department of Defense, "Directive 2311.01E: DoD Law of War Program" (Washington, DC, May 9, 2006).

25. Department of the Army, "Civilian Casualty Mitigation," *Army Tactics, Techniques, and Procedures*, no. 3-37.31 (Washington, DC, July 18, 2012).

26. See Department of Defense, Chairman of the Joint Chiefs of Staff Instruction 3160.01, "No-Strike and the Collateral Damage Estimation Methodology," J-2 CJCSI 3160.01 (Washington, DC, February 13, 2009).

27. Jacquelyn S. Porth, Washington File Security Affairs Writer, "Coalition To Make Painstaking Effort To Avoid Iraqi Civilian Damage," US State Department Report, March 6, 2003, http://reliefweb.int/report/iraq/coalition-make-painstaking-effort-avoid-iraqi-civilian-damage.

28. See Andrew Bell, "Leashing the 'Dogs of War': Examining the Effects of LOAC Training at the U.S. Military Academy and in Army ROTC," *Proceedings of the Annual Meeting of the American Society of International Law* 108 (April 2014); and Colin H. Kahl, "In the Crossfire or the Crosshairs? Norms, Civilian Casualties, and U.S. Conduct in Iraq," *International Security* 32, no. 1 (Summer 2007), 7–46.

29. Colin H. Kahl, "How We Fight, *Foreign Affairs* 85, no. 6 (November–December 2006): 89; William Arkin, *Divining Victory: Airpower in the 2006 Israel-Hezbollah War* (Maxwell Air Force Base, AL: Air University Press, August 2007), 125.

30. Steven Komarow, "US Attorneys Dispatched to Advise Military," *USA Today*, March 11, 2003, 9A.

31. See Michael Schmitt, "The Principle of Discrimination in 21st Century Warfare," *Yale Human Rights and Development Law Journal* 2, no. 1 (1999): 174.

32. For a study that quantifies this in conflicts with insurgents, see Luke Condra and Jacob Shapiro, "Who Takes the Blame? The Strategic Effects of Collateral Damage," *American Journal of Political Science* 56, no. 1 (January 2012): 167–187.

33. Department of the Army, "Civilian Casualty Mitigation," 1–5 and 10–15.

34. Jessica A. Stanton, *Violence and Restraint in Civil War: Civilian Targeting in the Shadow of International Law* (Cambridge: Cambridge University Press, 2016).

35. O'Hanlon, "A Flawed Masterpiece," 55, emphasis mine. Herold's estimate is closer to 3,000–4,000. See his "Counting the Dead."

36. Gen. Joseph W. Ralston, Vice Chairman, Joint Chiefs of Staff, AFA Policy Forum, "Aerospace Power and the Use of Force," September 14, 1999, emphasis mine.

37. US Department of Defense, "Final Report to Congress: Conduct Of The Persian Gulf War, Pursuant to Title V of the Persian Gulf Conflict Supplemental Authorization and Personnel Benefits Act of 1991" (Public Law 102-25), April 1992, 177. Emphasis mine.

38. Carr Center for Human Rights Policy, Project on the Means of Intervention, John F. Kennedy School of Government, Harvard University, *Understanding Collateral Damage Workshop*, June 4–5, 2002, Washington, DC, 4.

39. Benjamin Lambeth, *NATO's Air War for Kosovo: A Strategic and Operational Assessment* (Santa Monica: RAND Corporation, 2001), xviii.

40. W. Hays Parks, "Air War and the Law of War," *Air Force Law Review* 32, no. 1 (1990): 5.

41. The name of the particular military officer who made this statement is not publicly known, since the Carr Center decided to publish only the ideas expressed during its collateral damage workshop, rather than attributing them to specific people. The identities of all participants, however, are listed at the end of the report. Carr Center for Human Rights Policy, *Understanding Collateral Damage Workshop*, 14.

42. Anthony Cordesman, *The Lessons and Non-Lessons of the Air and Missile Campaign in Kosovo* (Westport, CT: Praeger, 2001), 124.

43. For a good discussion of risk transfer, see David Luban, "Risk Taking and Force Projection," in *Reading Walzer*, ed. Yitzhak Benbaji and Naomi Sussman (New York: Routledge, 2014), 277–301.

44. Carl Conetta, *Strange Victory: A Critical Appraisal of Operation Enduring Freedom and the Afghanistan War*, Project on Defense Alternatives Research Monograph #6 (Cambridge: Commonwealth Institute, January 30, 2002).

45. The number of Serbian soldiers killed in the NATO bombings has never been conclusively determined. The Yugolav government officially uses the number 576 and no source has disputed it. See Steven Lee Myers, "Damage to Serb Military Less Than Expected," *New York Times*, June 28, 1999, 3.

46. Thomas A. Keaney and Eliot A. Cohen, *Gulf War Air Power Survey: Summary Report* Department of the Air Force, 1993, 249, at https://timemilitary.files.wordpress.com/2011/11/afd-100927-061.pdf.

47. Globalsecurity.org, "Operation Just Cause," accessed July 11, 2014, www.globalsecurity.org/military/ops/just_cause.htm.

48. Simon Rogers, "Wikileaks Iraq: Data Journalism Maps Every Death—Data Journalism Allows Us To Really Interrogate the Wikileaks Iraq War Logs Release," *The Guardian*, October 23, 2010, www.guardian.co.uk/news/datablog/2010/oct/23/wikileaks-iraq-data-journalism.

49. This is based on a death toll of approximately 500 Lebanese soldiers and Hezbollah militiamen. See Patrick Bishop, "Peacekeeping Force Won't Disarm Hezbollah," *The Telegraph*, August 22, 2006, 1.

50. Raphael Cohen-Almagor and Sharon Heleva, "The Israeli-Hezbollah War and the Winggrad Committee," *Journal of Parliamentary and Political Law* 2, no. 1 (December 2008): 28–29.

51. Amnesty International, *Under the Rubble*.

52. Bureau of Investigative Journalism, "Drone Strikes in Pakistan," at https://www.thebureauinvestigates.com/projects/drone-war/charts?show_casualties=1&show_injuries=1&show_strikes=1&location=pakistan&from=2004-1-1&to=now.

53. O'Hanlon, "A Flawed Masterpiece," 55.

54. Nese F. DeBruyne, "American War and Military Operations Casualties: Lists and Statistics," Congressional Research Service Report for Congress (Washington, DC, April 26, 2017), Table 18, 24.

55. Michael O'Hanlon, "Estimating Casualties in a War to Overthrow Saddam," *Orbis*, Winter 2003, 26.

56. Michael O'Hanlon and Ian Livingston, *Iraq Index: Tracking Variables of Reconstruction & Security in Post-Saddam Iraq*, (Washington, DC: Brookings Institution Press, January 31, 2011), 7, 10.

57. Israeli Ministry of Foreign Affairs, "Israel-Hizbullah Conflict: Victims of Rocket Attacks and IDF Casualties," July 12, 2005, http://www.mfa.gov.il/MFA/Terrorism-+Obstacle+to+Peace/Terrorism+from+Lebanon-+Hizbullah/Israel-Hizbullah+conflict-+Victims+of+rocket+attacks+and+IDF+casualties+July-Aug+2006.htm.

58. US Department of Defense, "Personnel & Procurement Statistics, Worldwide U.S. Active Duty Military Deaths, Selected Military Operations," http://siadapp.dmdc.osd.mil/personnel/Casualty/table13.htm.

59. The figures on NATO's air war against the government of Libya and incomplete and undercounted, because while there are partial statistics available concerning civilian casualties (thanks to Human Rights Watch and the United Nations Human Rights Council), there are no figures on the number of Libyan soldiers killed or wounded. It is unlikely that there ever will be.

60. Schmitt, "The Principle of Discrimination in 21st Century Warfare."

61. A. P. V. Rogers, *Law on the Battlefield*, 3rd ed. (Manchester, UK: Manchester University Press, 2013).

62. Israeli Ministry of Foreign Affairs, "The Operation in Gaza—Factual and Legal Aspects," July 29, 2009, 8 at http://www.mfa.gov.il/MFA_Graphics/MFA%20Gallery/Documents/GazaOperation%20w%20Links.pdf.

63. Kenneth Anderson, "Who Owns the Rules of War?," *New York Times Magazine*, April 13, 2003, 38.

64. Richard Rosen, "Targeting Enemy Forces in the War on Terror: Preserving Civilian Immunity," *Vanderbilt Journal of Transnational Law* 42, no. 3 (May 2009): 742.

65. Reynolds, "Collateral Damage on the 22st Century Battlefield," 75–77.

66. United States Department of the Air Force, "International Law: The Conduct of Armed Conflict and Air Operations," pamphlet 110-31 (Washington, DC, 1976). The US Army makes a similar claim in "Civilian Casualty Mitigation," 1–9.

67. Yoram Dinstein, *The Conduct of Hostilities under the Law of International Armed Conflict* (Cambridge: Cambridge University Press, 2010), 131; Margaret Artz, "A Chink in the Armor: How a Uniform Approach to Proportionality Analysis Can End the Use of Human Shields," *Vanderbilt Journal of Transnational Law* 45, no. 5 (November 2012): 1447–1487.

68. Steven Erlanger, "With Israeli Use of Force, Debate over Proportion," *New York Times*, July 19, 2006, www.nytimes.com/2006/07/19/world/middleeast/19israel.html?_r=1&oref=slogin.

69. IHL is part of a broader category of rules known as the Laws and Customs of Armed Conflict.

70. See Michael Schmitt, "Asymmetrical Warfare and International Humanitarian Law," in *International Humanitarian Law Facing New Challenges*, ed. Wolff Heintschel von Heinegg and Volker Epping (New York: Springer, 2007), 27.

71. This principle has become a basic tenet of international law. It has been articulated in most agreements that regulate armed conflict, dating back to the Hague Conventions of 1907, and has been cited repeatedly since. See the Convention Respecting the Laws and Customs of War on Land, annex art. 22, October 18, 1907.

72. United States Department of Air Force, "International Law—the Conduct of Armed Conflict and Air Operations (Washington, DC, 1976), 5–9.

73. Roger Chickering, "Total War: The Use and Abuse of a Concept," in *Anticipating Total War: The German and American Experiences, 1871–1914*, ed. Manfred Boemeke, Roger Chickering, and Stig Forster (Cambridge: Cambridge University Press, 1990), 13–28.

74. See Matthew Lippman, "Aerial Attacks on Civilians and the Humanitarian Law of War: Technology and Terror from World War I to Afghanistan," *California Western International Law Journal* 33, no. 1 (Fall 2002): 1–67.

75. Yoshiaki Yoshimi, *Comfort Women* (New York: Columbia University Press, 2002); Diana Lary, *The Chinese People at War: Human Suffering and Social Transformation, 1937–1945* (Cambridge: Cambridge University Press, 2010).

76. See David Held, *Global Transformations* (Cambridge: Polity, 1999), 124–126.

77. Michael Schmitt, "Military Necessity and Humanity in International Humanitarian Law: Preserving the Delicate Balance," *Virginia Journal of International Law* 50, no. 4 (2010): 806; Joseph Holland, "Military Objective and Collateral Damage: Their Relationship and Dynamics," *Yearbook of International Humanitarian Law* 7 (2004): 38.

78. Parks, "Air War and the Law of War," 76, 104.

79. Reynolds, "Collateral Damage on the 21st Century Battlefield," 79.

80. As Michael Reisman argues, including a treaty rule in a State's military manuals is evidence that the state regards the rule as legally binding. See Michael Reisman and William Lietzau, "Moving International Law From Theory to Practice: The Role of Military Manuals in Effectuating the Law of Armed Conflict," *International Law Studies: The Law of Naval Operations*, vol. 64 (Newport, RI: Naval War College Press, 1991).

81. This is the consensus of most legal scholars. See, for example, Jean-Marie Henckaerts, "Study on Customary International Humanitarian Law: A Contribution to the Understanding and Respect for the Rule of Law in Armed Conflict," *International Review of the Red Cross* 87, no. 857 (March 2006): 175–212.

82. *Prosecutor v. Norman*, Case No. SCSL-2004-14-AR72(E), "Decision on Preliminary Motion Based on Lack of Jurisdiction," (May 31, 2004), 22.

83. See, for example, Alexander Downes, *Targeting Civilians in War* (Ithaca, NY: Cornell University Press, 2008); Hugo Slim, *Killing Civilians: Methods, Madness and Morality in War* (New York: Columbia University Press, 2008); and Anthony Dworkin, Roy Gutman, and David Rieff, eds., *Crimes of War 2.0: What the Public Should Know* (New York: Norton, 2007).

84. John Tirman, *The Deaths of Others: The Fate of Civilians in America's Wars* (New York: Oxford University Press, 2012).

85. Neta C. Crawford, *Accountability for Killing* (Oxford: Oxford University Press, 2013).

86. Crawford, *Accountability for Killing*, 41.
87. These include the US invasion of Panama in 1989; the 1991 Gulf War; NATO's air war over Serbia, 1999; NATO's war in Afghanistan, 2001-present; US invasion and occupation of Iraq, 2003–2011; Israeli–Hezbollah war in Lebanon, 2006; Israeli–Hamas wars in Gaza, 2008–2009 and 2013; NATO's air war in Libya, 2011; the US war against al Qaeda and associated forces.
88. Although there are relatively reliable estimates of the total number of civilians killed and injured during this conflict, there are no concrete figures on how many of these casualties were specifically the result of military attacks by US or NATO forces. See Neta Crawford, "Civilian Death and Injury in Afghanistan, 2001–2011," Watson Institute for International and Public Affairs, Brown University, September 2011, http://watson.brown.edu/cost-sofwar/files/cow/imce/papers/2011/Civilian%20Death%20and%20Injury%20in%20 Afghanistan%2C%202001-2011.pdf.
89. Hick et al., "Violent Deaths of Iraqi Civilians, 2003–2008."
90. For a good discussion of the legal issues involved in "asymmetrical war," see Adreas Paulus and Mindia Vashakmadze, "Asymmetrical War and the Notion of Armed Conflict—a Tentative Conceptualization," *International Review of the Red Cross* 91, no. 873 (March 2009): 95–125.
91. Under international law, there are only two types of armed conflicts, international and non-international. Paulus and Vashakmadze proposed a third category, "transnational armed conflict," which he defines as a protracted armed confrontation occurring between a state and nonstate groups on the territory of more than one state. See Paulus and Vashakmadze, "Asymmetrical War and the Notion of Armed Conflict," 110. For a general discussion of the concept of armed conflict, see International Committee of the Red Cross, "How is the Term 'Armed Conflict' Defined in International Humanitarian Law?," Opinion Paper (Geneva, March 2008).
92. Parks, "Air War and the Law of War," 103.

Chapter 2

1. Alexander Downes refers to this type of strategy as "civilian victimization," while Robert Pape calls it "punishment." Ivan Arreguín-Toft uses the term "barbarism," which he defines as the deliberate and systemic harm of noncombatants in order to destroy their will to fight. Alexander Downes, *Targeting Civilians in War* (Ithaca, NY: Cornell University Press, 2008); Robert Pape, *Bombing to Win: Air Power and Coercion in War* (Ithaca, NY: Cornell University Press, 1996), 18; and Ivan Arreguín-Toft, *How the West Win Wars: A Theory of Asymmetric Conflict* (Cambridge: Cambridge University Press, 2008), 4.
2. See Hugo Slim, *Killing Civilians: Methods, Madness, and Morality in War* (New York: Columbia University Press, 2008), 121.
3. See Misha Glenny, *The Fall of Yugoslavia: The Third Balkan War* (New York: Penguin Books, 1996) and Mary Kaldor, *New and Old Wars: Organized Violence in a Global Era* (Redwood City, CA: Stanford University Press, 1999), 59.
4. Human Rights Watch, *Getting Away with Murder, Mutilation, Rape: New Testimony from Sierra Leone*, Human Rights Watch Report 3(A) (July 1999).
5. *People v. Suarez*, 6 N.Y.3d 202, 211 (2005).
6. I detail this approach in Bruce Cronin, "Reckless Endangerment Warfare: Civilian Casualties and the Collateral Damage Exemption in International Humanitarian Law," *Journal of Peace Research* 50 no. 2 (March 2013): 175–187.
7. See Council of Europe, Parliamentary Assembly, Committee on Legal Affairs and Human Rights, *Conflict in Chechnya—Implementation of Russia of Recommendation 1444*, Doc. 8700, April 5, 2000, http://assembly.coe.int/Documents/WorkingDocs/doc00/EDOC8697. HTM and Ib Faurby, "International Law, Human Rights and the Wars in Chechnya," *Baltic Defence Review* 7 (2002): 103–113.
8. In domestic criminal law, this is known as "reckless endangerment." See, for example, New York State Penal Law, Article 120.

9. Stockholm International Peace Research Institute (SIPRI), *Antipersonnel Weapons* (London: Taylor and Francis, 1978), 165 and 121.

10. See Preamble of the First Protocol Additional to the Geneva Conventions of August 12, 1949, and Relating to the Protection of Victims of International Armed Conflicts, June 8, 1977, 1125 UN Treaty Series, 3.

11. Article 52(2) of the First Protocol Additional to the Geneva Conventions.

12. See Yves Sandoz, Christophe Swinarski, Bruno Zimmermann, and International Committee of the Red Cross, *Commentary on the Additional First Protocols of June 8, 1977 to the Geneva Conventions of 12 August, 1949* (Geneva: Martinus Nijhoff Publishers, 1987), 53.

13. See Articles 48–59 of the First Protocol Additional to the Geneva Conventions.

14. United States Military Tribunal, Nuremberg, "The Hostages Trial: Trial Of Wilhelm List And Others," Case No. 47, Part IV, United Nations War Crimes Commission, Law Reports of Trials of War Criminals, Volume VIII (Nuremberg, 1949), 66.

15. This was one of the principles of the Lieber Code, which was established by Professor Francis Lieber as a guide to the Union forces at the request of President Lincoln during the US Civil War. This code became one of the main sources of the customary international law of war as it developed during the twentieth century. See Francis Lieber, "Instructions for the Government of Armies of the United States in the Field," article 14 (Washington, DC: Government Printing Office, 1863).

16. United States Military Tribunal, Nuremberg, "The Hostages Trial," 67.

17. Michael Schmitt, "Precision Attack and International Humanitarian Law," *International Review of the Red Cross* 87, no. 859 (2005): 457.

18. Program on Humanitarian Policy and Conflict Research at Harvard University, *HPCR Manual on International Law Applicable to Air and Missile Warfare* (Berne, 2009), 20–21.

19. Articles 51 (5b) and 57 (2iii) of the First Protocol Additional to the Geneva Conventions.

20. International Court of Justice, "Legality of the Threat or Use of Nuclear Weapons," Advisory Opinion of July 8, 1996, General List No. 95, Opinion of Judge Higgins, 587.

21. See A. P. V. Rogers, *Law on the Battlefield* (Manchester: Manchester University Press, 2004), 128 and William Boothly, *Weapons and the Law of Armed Conflict* (Oxford: Oxford University Press, 2009), 43.

22. Joseph Holland, "Military Objective and Collateral Damage: Their Relationship and Dynamics," *Yearbook of International Humanitarian Law* 7 (2004): 53.

23. Article 51 (8) of the First Protocol Additional to the Geneva Conventions of August 12, 1949.

24. Downes, *Targeting Civilians in War*, 53.

25. International Criminal Tribunal for the Former Yugoslavia, *The Prosecutor v. Zoran Kupreskic, Mirjan Kupreskic, Vlatko Kupreskic, Drago Josipovic, Dragan Papic and Vladimir Santic*, Judgment, Case No. IT-95-16 (The Hague, the Netherlands, January 14, 2003).

26. Luis Moreno-Ocampo, Chief Prosecutor, International Criminal Court, Letter, February 9, 2006, www.icc-cpi.int/library/organs/otp/OTP_letter_to_senders_re_Iraq_9_February_2006.pdf.

27. Martin Shaw, *The New Western Way of War: Risk Transfer and its Crisis in Iraq* (Cambridge: Polity, 2005).

28. Michael Ignatieff, *Virtual War: Kosovo and Beyond* (London: Chatto and Windus, 2000) and Colin McInnes, *Spectator Sport War: the New Ethics of Postmodern War* (London: Routledge, 2001).

29. See Major Charles K. Hyde, "Casualty Aversion: Implications for Policy Makers and Senior Military Officers," *Aerospace Power Journal*, Summer 2000. See also Yagil Levy, *Israel's Death Hierarchy: Casualty Aversion in a Militarized Democracy* (New York: NYU Press, 2012).

30. Janina Dill, *Legitimate Targets? Social Construction, International Law and US Bombing* (Cambridge: Cambridge University Press, 2015), particularly 350–351.

31. Reynolds, "Collateral Damage on the 21st Century Battlefield," 82.

32. See Brigadier General David A. Deptula, *Effects-Based Operations: Change in the Nature of Warfare* (Arlington, VA: Aerospace Education Foundation, 2001), 11 and Institute for

Defense Analyses, *New Perspectives on Effects-Based Operations* (Alexandria, VA: Institute for Defense Analyses June 30, 2001), 2–3.

33. David Deptula, "Parallel Warfare: What is It? Where Did it Come From? Why is it Important?," in *The Eagle in the Desert: Looking Back on U.S. Involvement in the Persian Gulf War*, ed. William Head and Earl Tilford (Westport: Praeger, 1996), 135.

34. David R. Mets, *Air Campaign: John Warden and the Classical Airpower Theorists* (Maxwell Air Force Base, AL: Air University Press, 1999).

35. Charles Dunlap, "Clever or Clueless? Observations About Bombing Norm Debates," in *The American Way of Bombing: Changing Ethnical and Legal Norms from Flying Fortresses to Drones*, ed. Matthew Evangelista and Henry Shue (Ithaca, NY: Cornell University Press, 2014), 116.

36. Deptula, "Parallel Warfare," 136.

37. Ward Thomas, "Victory by Duress: Civilian Infrastructure as a Target in Air Campaigns," *Security Studies* 15, no. 1 (January–March 2006): 1–33.

38. Office of General Counsel Department of Defense, *Department of Defense Law of War Manual* (Washington, DC, June 2015), particularly, 212–213.

39. Col. John Warden III, "Air Theory for the Twenty-First Century," in *Battlefield Of The Future: 21st Century Warfare Issues*, ed. Barry R. Schneider and Lawrence E. Grinter (University Press of the Pacific, 2002), 103–124.

40. Harlan Ullman and James Wade, *Shock and Awe: Achieving Rapid Dominance* (Washington, DC, National Defense University, 1996), 13.

41. Ibid., xxvii.

42. Ibid., 82.

43. Charles Dunlap, "The End of Innocence: Rethinking Noncombatancy in the Post-Kosovo Era," *Strategic Review* (Summer 2000): 9.

44. Robert Pape refers to this as "risk coercion." See *Bombing to Win*.

45. Henry Shue and David Wippman, "Limiting Attacks on Dual-Use Facilities Performing Indispensable Civilian Functions," *Cornell International Law Journal* 35, no. 3 (Winter 2002): 567.

46. See, for example, Department of the Air Force, *Air Force Basic Doctrine*, Document 1 (Washington, DC, September 1997).

47. See, for example, Office of General Counsel Department of Defense, *Department of Defense Law of War Manual* (Washington, DC, June 2015), particularly 210 and United States Navy, *Commander's Handbook on the Law of Naval Operations*, NWP 1-14M, MCWP 5-2.1, COMDTPUB P 5800.7, (Quantico, VA, July 2007), paragraph 8.1.1.

48. Quoted in Michael Schmitt, "Fault Lines in the Law of Attack," in *Testing the Boundaries of International Humanitarian Law*, ed. Susan Breaq and Agnieszka Jahec-Neale (London: British Institute of Comparative Law, 2006), 281.

49. US Department of Defense, Department of the Air Force, *International Law: The Conduct of Armed Conflict and Air Operations* (Washington, DC, 1976), 5–8.

50. Nils Melzer, *Interpretive Guidance on the Notion of Direct Participation in Hostilities Under International Humanitarian Law* (Geneva: International Committee of the Red Cross, 2009).

51. W. Hays Parks, "Asymmetries and the Identification of Legitimate Military Objectives," in *International Humanitarian Law Facing New Challenges*, ed. Wolff Heintschel von Heinegg and Volker Epping (New York: Springer, 2007), 100.

52. A. P. V. Rogers, "Conduct of Combat and Risks Run by the Civilian Population," *Military Law and the Law of War Review* 21, (1982).

53. Michael O'Hanlon, A Flawed Masterpiece," *Foreign Affairs* 81, no. 3 (March/April 2002): 52.

54. Thomas A. Keaney and Eliot A. Cohen, *Gulf War Air Power Survey: Summary Report*, Department of the Air Force, 1993, 13, www.afhso.af.mil/shared/media/document/AFD-100927-061.pdf.

55. Amnesty International received these figures from the Israeli Defense Force website.

56. Howard Zinn, "The Deadly Semantics of NATO Bombings," *Boston Globe*, May 28, 1999, A19.

57. Article 54(2) of the First Protocol to the Geneva Conventions specifically prohibit attacking, destroying, removing or rendering useless objects indispensable to the survival of the civilian population. This principle is also part of the military manuals of most of the states that have not signed the protocol and is viewed by the International Committee of the Red Cross to be part of the customary law of armed conflict. See Henckaerts and Doswald-Beck,

Customary International Law, Volume 1: Rules, rule 54, International Committee of the Red Cross (Cambridge: Cambridge University Press, 2005).

58. Jacquelyn Porth, "Coalition To Make Painstaking Effort to Avoid Iraqi Civilian Damage," *Washington File*,(US Department of State, March 6, 2003, http://reliefweb.int/report/iraq/coalition-make-painstaking-effort-avoid-iraqi-civilian-damage.

59. Michael Schmitt, "The Principle of Discrimination in 21st Century Warfare," 168.

60. "Bugsplat Computer Program Aims to Limit Civilian Deaths at Targets," *Washington Post*, February 26, 2003, 4.

61. Michael Ignatieff, *Virtual War: Kosovo and Beyond* (London: Chatto and Windus, 2000), 91–92.

62. Vernon Loeb, "An Unlikely Super-Warrior Emerges in Afghan War: U.S. Combat Controllers Guide Bombers to Precision Targets," *Washington Post*, May 19, 2002, A16, http://www.washingtonpost.com/wp-dyn/articles/A39171-2002May18_2.html. .

63. A. P. V. Rogers, "Zero-Casualty Warfare," *International Review of the Red Cross* 837 (March 31, 2000): 165–181.

64. Patricia Owens, "Accidents Don't Just Happen: The Liberal Politics of High-Technology 'Humanitarian' War," *Millennium: Journal of International Studies* 32, no. 3 (2003): 607.

65. Michael Schmitt, "Computer Network Attack: the Normative Software," *Yearbook of International Humanitarian Law* (Cambridge: Cambridge University Press, 2001), 82. The US Joint Chiefs of Staff refer to this as "collateral effects." See Chairman of the Joint Chiefs of Staff Manual, Joint Methodology for Estimating Collateral Damage and Casualties for Conventional Weapons: Precision, Unguided, and Cluster, September 20, 2002, A4.

66. Schmitt, "Fault Lines in the Law of Attack."

67. International Criminal Tribunal for the Former Yugoslavia, *The Prosecutor v. Zoran Kupreskic*.

68. Holland, "Military Objective and Collateral Damage," 62.

69. Reynolds, "Collateral Damage on the 21st Century Battlefield," 87.

70. Matthew C. Waxman, *International Law and the Politics of Air Operations* (Santa Monica, CA: RAND Corporation, 2000), 22.

71. See Michael Bothe, Karl Josef Partsch, and Waldemar Solf, *New Rules for Victims of Armed Conflicts: Commentary on the Two 1977 Protocols Additional to the Geneva Conventions of 1949* (The Hague: Martinus Nijhoff, 1982), 371–372.

72. See, for example, Ivan Arreguin-Toft, "How the Weak Win Wars," *International Security* 26, no. 1 (Summer 2001): 33.

73. W. Hays, Parks, "Air War and the Law of War," *Air Force Law Review* 32, no. 1 (1990): 163.

74. Article 51 (8) of the First Protocol Additional to the Geneva Conventions.

75. See Schmitt, "Fault Lines in the Law of Attack," 306.

76. Article 57 of the First Protocol Additional to the Geneva Conventions.

77. For an analysis of this concept as applied to the conflict between Israel and Hamas during Operation Cast Lead (2008–2009) and Protective Edge (2014), see Yagil Levy, "How Israel Shifted Risk from Soldiers to Gazan Civilians," *Washington Post*, August 18, 2015. For a similar focus on US behavior, see Martin Shaw, "Risk-Transfer Militarism, Small Massacres and the Historic Legitimacy of War," *International Relations* 16, no. 3 (2002): 343–359, https://www.washingtonpost.com/news/monkey-cage/wp/2015/08/18/how-israel-shifted-risk-from-soldiers-to-gazan-civilians/?utm_term=.fb4ad762d199.

78. See Thomas Smith, "Protecting Civilians . . . or Soldiers? Humanitarian Law and the Economy of Risk in Iraq," *International Studies Perspectives* 9, no. 2 (May 2008): 147.

79. United States Air Force, *Gulf War Air Power Survey*, Volume 5: A Statistical Compendium and Chronology (Washington, DC, 1993), Table 203, 641.

80. Michael Schmitt, "Military Necessity and Humanity in International Humanitarian Law: Preserving the Delicate Balance," *Virginia Journal of International Law* 50, no. 4 (2010): 823.

81. Charles Dunlap, "Kosovo, Casualty Aversion, and the American Military Ethos: A Perspective," *USAF Academy Journal of Legal Studies*, 10 (1999/2000): 95.

82. Rogers, "Conduct of Combat and Risks Run by the Civilian Population," 310.

83. Anshel Pfeffer, "IDF Officer: Gaza Civilians Risked to Protect Israeli Troops During War," *Haaretz*, March 2, 2010, at http://www.haaretz.com/news/idf-officer-gaza-civilians-risked-to-protect-israel-troops-during-war-1.262686.

84. Nils Melzer, *Interpretive Guidance*, 19.
85. Michael Gross, *Moral Dilemmas of Modern War: Torture, Assassination, and Blackmail in an Age of Asymmetric Conflict* (Cambridge: Cambridge University Press, 2010), 154.
86. Melzer, *Interpretive Guidance*, 19.
87. Richard Rosen, "Targeting Enemy Forces in the War on Terror: Preserving Civilian Immunity," *Vanderbilt Journal of Transnational Law* 42, no. 3 (May 2009): 736–737. I should note that the term "terrorist" has no legal meaning in this context and appears to be used more as an inflammatory characterization than a practical one.
88. Department of the Army, "Civilian Casualty Mitigation," section 1-46.
89. Department of the Army, "Civilian Casualty Mitigation." See in particular chapter 2.

Chapter 3

1. Williamson Murray, *Air War in the Persian Gulf* (Baltimore: Nautical and Aviation Publishing Company of America, 1995), i.
2. Thomas A. Keaney and Eliot A. Cohen, *Gulf War Air Power Survey: Summary Report*, (Washington, DC, Department of the Air Force, 1993), 13 at www.afhso.af.mil/shared/media/document/AFD-100927-061.pdf.
3. US Department of Defense, *Conduct of the Persian Gulf Conflict: An Interim Report to Congress* (Washington, DC, July 1991), section 2-7.
4. See Nicholas Fotion, "The Gulf War: Cleanly Fought," *Bulletin of Atomic Scientists* 47, no. 7 (September 1991): 24–29.
5. US Department of Defense, *Conduct of the Persian Gulf Conflict*, section 2-7.
6. Keaney and Cohen, *Gulf War Air Power Survey*, 46.
7. Kearney and Cohen, *Gulf War Air Power Survey*, vol. II, part II, chapter 6, 27.
8. The number of civilians killed during the Gulf war has long been the subject of controversy. In the immediate aftermath of the conflict, military analyst William Arkin estimated 2,278 civilian deaths, a figure that was generally accepted by military and media sources. See Kearney and Cohen, *Gulf War Air Power Survey*, vol. II, part II, chapter 6, 27. Human Rights Watch conducted a series of on-site interviews and investigations in Iraq and estimated civilian deaths to be between 2,500 and 3,000 (Human Rights Watch, *Needless Deaths in the Gulf War: Civilian Casualties During the Air Campaign and Violations of the Laws of War* [New York, 1991], 19). US Commerce Department demographer Beth Osborne Daponte subsequently conducted a more in-depth and comprehensive survey, raising the number to approximately 3,500. See "A Case Study in Estimating Casualties from War and its Aftermath: The 1991 Persian Gulf War," *The PSR Quarterly* 3, no. 2 (June 1993): 65. The study by Daponte appears to be the most comprehensive and reliable, in that it employs methods that are generally accepted among demographers; for this reason it is probably the best estimate available.
9. See Matthew Waxman, *International Law and the Politics of Air Operations* (Santa Monica, CA: RAND Corporation, 2000), 22, and Daponte, "A Case Study in Estimating Casualties from War and its Aftermath," 65. These figures were confirmed by other researchers.
10. Daponte, "A Case Study in Estimating Casualties from War and its Aftermath," 65.
11. US Department of Defense, *Conduct of the Persian Gulf Conflict*, section 27-1.
12. Rick Atkinson, *Crusade: The Untold Story of the Persian Gulf War* (New York: Houghton Mifflin, 1993).
13. John Andreas Olsen, *Strategic Air Power in Desert Storm* (London: Frank Cass, 2003), 37.
14. Lawrence Freedman and Efraim Karsh, *The Gulf Conflict 1990–1991: Diplomacy and War in the New World Order* (Princeton, NJ: Princeton University Press, 1993).
15. See UN Security Council Resolutions S/RES/662 (1990) and S/RES/678 (1990).
16. George H. W. Bush, "Address Before a Joint Session of the Congress on the Persian Gulf Crisis and the Federal Budget Deficit," September 11, 1990, from The American Presidency Project, at http://www.presidency.ucsb.edu/ws/?pid=18820.
17. See Barry Watts, Williamson Murray, Lt. Colonel Gary Cox, and Wayne Thompson, *Gulf War Air Power Survey: Operations Effects and Effectiveness* (Washington, DC: United States

Air Force, 1993), vol. II, 274–275; Rick Atkinson, "Allies to Intensify Bombing to Prepare for Ground War," *Washington Post*, February 8, 1991, 1.

18. Molly Moore, "War Exposed Rivalries, Weaknesses in Military," *Washington Post*, June 10, 1991, at https://www.washingtonpost.com/archive/politics/1991/06/10/war-exposed-rivalries-weaknesses-in-military/b9382685-ca58-4d30-9b0b-c8e3ee96b8a0/?utm_term=.21eb84a3a0ee.

19. Murray, *Air War in the Persian Gulf*, 153; Atkinson, *Crusade*, 233 and 273; Olsen, *Strategic Air Power in Desert Storm*, 233.

20. Martin Woollacott, "Iraq's Lost Generation," *The Guardian*, February 15, 1991, 25.

21. Quoted in Human Rights Watch, *Needless Deaths in the Gulf War*, 9–10.

22. Daniel Kuehl, "Thunder and Storm: Air Operations in the Persian Gulf War," in *The Eagle in the Desert: Looking Back on U.S. Involvement in the Persian Gulf War*, ed. William Head and Earl Tilford (Westport: Praeger, 1996), x.

23. See Watts et al., *Gulf War Air Power Survey*, vol. II, part II, chapter 6, 19.

24. Julie Bud, "Horner: Further Air Force Role in Gulf Not Needed," *Air Force Times*, March 18, 1991, 8.

25. Keaney and Cohen, *Gulf War Air Power Survey*, 36.

26. Murray, *Air War in the Persian Gulf*, 85.

27. Kearney and Cohen, *Gulf War Air Power Survey*, 44.

28. Ibid., *Gulf War Air Power Survey*, 45.

29. Olsen, *Strategic Air Power in Desert Storm*, 137.

30. Kuehl, "Thunder and Storm," 113; Atkinson, *Crusade*, 58–59.

31. John T. Correll, "The Strategy of Desert Storm," *Air Force Magazine* 89, no. 1 (January 2006): 27–33; Olsen, *Strategic Air Power in Desert Storm*, 102.

32. William Arkin, Damian Durrant, and Marianne Cherni, *On Impact: Modern Warfare and the Environment, A Case Study of the Gulf War*, report prepared by Greenpeace, for the Fifth Geneva Convention on the Protection of the Environment in Time of Armed Conflict, London, June 3, 1991.

33. Kuehl, "Thunder Storm," 114; Barton Gellman, "Allied Air War Struck Broadly in Iraq," *Washington Post*, June 23, 1991, A1.

34. Correll, "The Strategy of Desert Storm."

35. Kearney and Cohen, *Gulf War Air Power Survey*, 57.

36. Ibid., volume 5, 517.

37. Keaney and Cohen, *Gulf War Air Power Survey*, 73.

38. Harvard Study Team, "Harvard Study Team Report: Public Health in Iraq after the Gulf War," Harvard University, May 1991.

39. Arkin et al., *On Impact*, 92.

40. US Department of Defense, *Conduct of the Persian Gulf Conflict*, section 6-5.

41. Keaney and Cohen, *Gulf War Air Power Survey*, 92.

42. Human Rights Watch, *Needless Deaths in the Gulf War*, 159–168.

43. US Department of Defense, *Conduct of the Persian Gulf Conflict*, section 12-3.

44. Barton Gellman, "Allied Air War Struck Broadly in Iraq," *Washington Post*, June 23, 1991, at https://www.washingtonpost.com/archive/politics/1991/06/23/allied-air-war-struck-broadly-in-iraq/e469877b-b1c1-44a9-bfe7-084da4e38e41/?utm_term=.5233c2cfc288.

45. Human Rights Watch, *Needless Deaths in the Gulf War*, 102. For a more extensive list of bridge-related deaths, see 268–272. See also Arkin et al., *On Impact*, 88.

46. Human Rights Watch, *Needless Deaths in the Gulf War*, 5 and 219–223.

47. Ibid., 257.

48. Nora Boustany, "Bombs Killed Victims as They Slept," *Washington Post*, February 14, 1991, A1.

49. Human Rights Watch, *Needless Deaths in the Gulf War*, 128–129; Paul Lewis, "Effects of War Begin to Fade in Iraq, "*New York Times*, May 12, 1991, E2.

50. Human Rights Watch, *Needless Deaths in the Gulf War*, x.

51. Atkinson, *Crusade*, 276.

52. Human Rights Watch, *Needless Deaths in the Gulf War*, 104–105.

53. Ibid., 283.

54. Olsen, *Strategic Air Power in Desert Storm*, 252.

55. Harvard Study Team, "The Effects of the Gulf Crisis on the Children of Iraq," *New England Journal of Medicine* 325, no. 15 (September 1991): 977.

56. The Harvard Study Team was comprised of doctors and health professionals. They visited 11 major cities and towns in Iraq from April 27–May 6, 1991. This included inspections of 19 health facilities, 11 electrical generating plants, 10 substations, three water treatment plants, and four sewage treatment facilities.

57. US News and World Report, *Triumph without Victory: The Unreported History of the Persian Gulf War* (New York: Times Books, 1993), 274.

58. Arkin et al., *On Impact,* 56.

59. Lee Hockstader, "Baghdad Residents Face Health Crisis," *Washington Post*, March 4, 1991, A1.

60. Daponte, "A Case Study in Estimating Casualties from War and its Aftermath," 65. These figures were confirmed by other researchers.

61. Keaney and Cohen, *Gulf War Air Power Survey*, vol. II, part II, chapter 6, 26.

62. Atkinson, *Crusade*, 225.

63. US Department of Defense, *Conduct of the Persian Gulf Conflict*, section 2-6. "Hardships" is obviously an understatement.

64. Keaney and Cohen, *Gulf War Air Power Survey*, vol. II, part II, chapter 6, 27.

65. Atkinson, *Crusade*, 226.

66. See Human Rights Watch, *Needless Deaths in the Gulf War*, 90.

67. Rick Atkinson, *Crusade*, 226.

68. Barton Bellman, "U.S. Bombs Missed 70% of the Time," *Washington Post, 6,* March 16, 1991.

69. Bernard Debusmann, "No Havens Says Resident of Baghdad," *Washington Post*, February 4, 1991; and Human Rights Watch, *Needless Deaths in the Gulf War*, p. 246.

70. Quoted in John Morocco, "Looming Budget Cuts Threaten Future of Key HighTech Weapons," *Aviation Week and Space Technology*, April 22, 1991, 66.

71. Atkinson, *Crusade*, 224.

72. Ibid., 226–227.

73. Keaney and Cohen, *Gulf War Air Power Survey*, 16. Actually most of the bombers dropped their ordnance from 15,000–20,000 feet, and the B-52s from as high as 40,000.

74. Human Rights Watch, *Needless Deaths in the Gulf War*, 213.

75. Arkin et al., *On Impact*, 86; Human Rights Watch, *Needless Deaths in the Gulf War*, 274 and 211.

76. Human Rights Watch, *Needless Deaths in the Gulf War*, chapter 4.

77. US Department of Defense, *Conduct of the Persian Gulf Conflict*, section 12-17 and 12-18.

78. R. W. Apple, "UA Hits Hussein's Town, As War Hits Home in Iraq," *New York Times*, February 6, 1991, A28.

79. US Department of Defense, *Conduct of the Persian Gulf Conflict*, 96.

80. William Arkin, "The Difference Was in the Details," *Washington Post*, January 17, 1999, B1.

81. Atkinson, *Crusade*, 494.

82. Lawrence Feedman and Efraim Karsh, *The Gulf Conflict, 1990–1991* (Princeton, NJ: Princeton University Press, 1995), 437; and Arkin, "Tactical Bombing of Iraq Forces Outstripped Value of Strategic Targets," 62–63.

83. Olsen, *Strategic Air Power in Desert Storm*, 256.

84. Keaney and Cohen, *Gulf War Air Power Survey*.

85. "Bombing As a Policy Tool In Vietnam: Effectiveness," A Staff Study Based on the Pentagon Papers, Prepared for the Use of the Committee on Foreign Relations, United States Senate, Study no. 5 (Washington, DC, October 12, 1972).

86. Richard Davis, "Strategic Bombing in the Gulf War," in *Case Studies in Strategic Bombardment*, ed. R. Cargill Hall (Washington, DC: US Government Printing Office, 1998), 528.

87. Quoted in Human Rights Watch, *Needless Deaths in the Gulf War*, 82.

88. Keaney and Cohen, *Gulf War Air Power Survey*, 62.

89. Kuehl, "Thunder and Storm," x.

90. See, for example, US Department of Defense, *Conduct of the Persian Gulf Conflict* and Keaney and Cohen, *Gulf War Air Power Survey*.

91. "Saddam Has a Real Problem," *USA Today*, March 25, 1991, 7.

Chapter 4

1. During the period in question, Serbia was one of two political units (along with Montenegro) that comprised what was left of the Federal Republic of Yugoslavia. I use the name of Serbia in this chapter, however, because NATO's attacks were directed solely at Serbia, which was the dominant entity in the rump federation (Yugoslavia was formed as a federation of six republics. After it broke apart in the early 1990s, it remained as a federation of two: Serbia and Montenegro, thus a "rump" federation).

2. Lt. Colonel Michael Lamb, "Operation Allied Force: Golden Nuggets for Future Campaigns," Air War College, Maxwell, Paper No. 27, (Maxwell Air Force Base, Alabama, August 2002), 1.

3. Lt. Colonel Richard L. Sargen, "Deliberate Force Targeting," in *Deliberate Force: A Case Study in Effective Air Campaign*, ed. Robert Owen (Maxwell Air Force Base, AL: Air University Press, 2000), 284–285.

4. Independent International Commission on Kosovo, *The Kosovo Report: Conflict, International Response, Lessons Learned* (Oxford: Oxford University Press, 2000), 92; See also Statement of the Honorable John J. Hamre, US Deputy Secretary of Defense, before the US House Permanent Select Committee on Intelligence, Inadvertent Bombing of the Chinese Embassy in Belgrade, Yugoslavia, July 22, 1999.

5. These figures were first advanced by William Arkin, Human Rights Watch, *Civilian Deaths in the NATO Air Campaign* (New York, February 2000). Both the Federal Republic of Yugoslavia Ministry of Foreign Affairs and the US Department of Defense subsequently accepted these numbers as reasonably accurate.

6. Ivo Daalder and Michael O'Hanlon, *Winning Ugly: NATO's Air War to Save Kosovo* (Washington, DC: Brookings Institution Press, 2000), 103.

7. Andrew Bacevich and Eliot Cohen, eds., *War Over Kosovo* (New York: Columbia University Press, 2001), 1.

8. Ignatieff, *Virtual War*, 161.

9. Daalder and O'Hanlon, *Winning Ugly*, 108.

10. Anthony Cordesman, *The Lessons and Non-Lessons of the Air and Missile Campaign in Kosovo* (Washington, DC: Center for Strategic and International Studies, 2000), 27.

11. Lambeth, *NATO's Air War for Kosovo*, xvii.

12. US Air Force, *Initial Report: The Air War Over Serbia, Aerospace Power in Operation Allied Force* (Washington, DC, 2000), x.

13. Cordesman, *The Lessons and Non-Lessons*, 66.

14. Ibid., 101.

15. Department of Defense Report to Congress, *Kosovo/Operation Allied Force After Action Report* (Washington, DC, January 31, 2000), 24.

16. Rebecca Grant, "The Kosovo Campaign: Aerospace Power Made it Work," *Air Force Association Special Report* (Arlington, VA, 1999).

17. Daalder and O'Hanlon, *Winning Ugly*, 123.

18. The number of Serbian soldiers killed in the NATO bombings has never been conclusively determined. The Yugolav government officially uses the number 576 and no source has been able to dispute it. See Steven Lee Myers, "Damage to Serb Military Less Than Expected," *New York Times*, June 28, 1999, at http://www.nytimes.com/1999/06/28/world/crisis-in-the-balkans-the-toll-damage-to-serb-military-less-than-expected.html.

19. Hannah Fischer, "American War and Military Operations Casualties: Lists and Statistics," Congressional Research Service Report for Congress (Washington, DC: Library of Congress, 2005).

20. There is a large literature on the breakup of Yugoslavia. Josip Glaurdic's monograph draws on the most recent documentary materials that have been released: see *The Hour of Europe: Western Powers and the Breakup of Yugoslavia* (New Haven, CT: Yale University Press, 2011). See also Misha Glenny, *The Fall of Yugoslavia: The Third Balkan War* (New York: Penguin, 1996); Richard Holbrooke, *To End a War* (New York: Modern Library, 1999).

21. For details, see Steven L. Burg and Paul S. Shoup, *The War in Bosnia-Herzegovina: Ethnic Conflict and International Intervention* (Armonk, NY: M. E. Sharpe, 2000).

22. See Tim Judah, *Kosovo: What Everyone Needs to Know* (Oxford: Oxford University Press, 2008), chapter 8.

23. Department of Defense Report to Congress, *Kosovo/Operation Allied Force*, 7.
24. Message from Secretary of Defense William S. Cohen, to the Chair of Joint Chiefs of Staff Henry H. Shelton, in Department of Defense Report to Congress, *Kosovo/Operation Allied Force*.
25. Daalder and O'Hanlon, *Winning Ugly*, 116.
26. PEW Research Center for the People and Press, "Support for NATO Air Strikes with Plenty of Buts," March 29, 1999, www.people-press.org/1999/03/29/support-for-nato-air-strikes-with-plenty-of-buts.
27. A. V. Rogers, "Zero-Casualty Warfare," *International Review of the Red Cross* 837 (2000): 165–181.
28. Air Chief Marshal Sir Richard Johns, "Air Power in a New Era," *Royal Society of Arts Journal* 147, no. 5490 (1999): 99.
29. Adam Roberts, "NATO's 'Humanitarian War over Kosovo," *Survival* 41, no. 3 (August 1999): 112; UK House of Commons, Defense Select Committee, Fourteenth Report, "Lessons of Kosovo," October 24, 2000, 60.
30. William Arkin, "Smart Bombs, Dumb Targeting?," *Bulletin of Atomic Scientists* (May/June 2000): 50; William Arkin, "Operation Allied Force: 'The Most Precise Application of Air Power in History," in *War Over Kosovo*, ed. Andrew Bacevich and Eliot Cohen (New York: Columbia University Press, 2001), 7.
31. George Robertson, UK House of Commons, Select Committee on Defense, Hearings, March 24, 1999.
32. The Independent International Commission on Kosovo, *The Kosovo Report*, 93. Lambeth, *NATO's Air War for Kosovo*, xvi.
33. Ignatieff, *Virtual War*, 62; William Arkin, "Operation Allied Force," 9–10.
34. Wesley Clark, *Waging Modern War: Bosnia, Kosovo, and the Future of Combat* (New York: Public Affairs Publishing, 2002).
35. Daalder and O'Hanlon, *Winning Ugly*, 188; Cordesman, *The Lessons and Non-Lessons*, 25.
36. Dana Priest, "France Played Skeptic on Kosovo Attacks," *Washington Post*, September 20, 1999, A1.
37. NATO, "Statement on Kosovo Issued by the Heads of State and Government Participating in the Meeting of the North Atlantic Council in Washington, D.C. on 23rd and 24th April 1999," www.nato.int/docu/pr/1999/p99-062e.htm.
38. Cordesman, *The Lessons and Non-Lessons*, 130.
39. Grant, "The Kosovo Campaign," 17.
40. Eric Schmitt and Stephen Lee Myers, "Crisis in the Balkans: The Bombing. NATO Said to Focus on Serb Elite's Property," *New York Times*, May 25, 1999, A1; Cordesman, *The Lessons and Non-Lessons*, 169.
41. Schmitt and Lee Myers, "Crisis in the Balkans."
42. Arkin, *Civilian Deaths in the NATO Air Campaign*, 7.
43. House of Commons, Defense Select Committee, 14th Report (London, October 23, 2000), paragraph 99.
44. NATO Press Briefing, May 25, 1999, www.nato.int/kosovo/press.htm.
45. Craig Whitney, "The Commander: Air Wars Won't Stay Risk Free General Says," *New York Times*, June 18, 1999, A1.
46. Article 51(2) of the 1977 First Protocol Additional to the Geneva Conventions of 1948.
47. Amnesty International, "NATO/Federal Republic of Yugoslavia: 'Collateral Damage" or Unlawful Killings? Violations of the Laws of War by NATO During Operation Allied Force," Amnesty International Index, EUR 70/18/00 (London, June 2000), 2.
48. Arkin, *Civilian Deaths in the NATO Air Campaign*, 5. In his testimony before the House Select Committee on Intelligence, Deputy Secretary of Defense John Hamre claimed that there were only 30 incidents of collateral damage; however, he failed to produce any studies or data to back up this claim. See Statement of the Honorable John J. Hamre, US Deputy Secretary of Defense, before the US House Permanent Select Committee on Intelligence, July 22, 1999.
49. Arkin, *Civilian Deaths in the NATO Air Campaign*, 30.
50. Ibid., 25.
51. Grant, "The Kosovo Campaign," 21.
52. Lambeth, *NATO's Airwar for Kosovo*, 42.

53. The Independent International Commission on Kosovo, *The Kosovo Report*, 93.
54. James A. Burger, "International Humanitarian Law and the Kosovo Crisis: Lessons Learned or to be Learned," *International Review of the Red Cross* 82, no. 837 (2000): 129.
55. Steven Erlanger, "Reduced to a 'Caveman' Life, Serbs Don't Blame Milošević," *New York Times*, May 25, 1999, at http://www.nytimes.com/1999/05/25/world/crisis-balkans-belgrade-reduced-caveman-life-serbs-don-t-blame-milosevic.html; Philip Bennett and Steve Coll, "NATO Warplanes Jolt Power Grid," *Washington Post*, May 25, 1999, A1.
56. Arkin, *Civilian Deaths in the NATO Air Campaign*, 24.
57. Ibid., Appendix A.
58. BBC News Online, "NATO's Bombing Blunders," June 1, 1999, http://news.bbc.co.uk/2/hi/340966.stm.
59. Arkin, *Civilian Deaths in the NATO Air Campaign*, 63.
60. Ibid., 34.
61. Ibid., 25–26.
62. International Criminal Tribunal for the Former Yugoslavia (ICTY), "Final Report of the Prosecutor by the Committee Established to Review the NATO Bombing Campaign Against the Federal Republic of Yugoslavia," August 6, 2000, www.icty.org/sid/10052, 26.
63. ICTY, "Final Report"; Arkin, *Civilian Deaths in the NATO Air Campaign*, 26–27, 30, and 66.
64. Arkin, *Civilian Deaths in the NATO Air Campaign*, 3.
65. "Clinton Won't Back Down," CNN Online, April 15, 1999, http://articles.cnn.com/1999-04-15/us/9904_15_clinton.kosovo_1_clinton-nato-president-clinton-yugoslav-president?_s=PM:US.
66. Lambeth, *NATO's Air War for Kosovo*, 143.
67. Priest, "France Played Skeptic on Kosovo Attacks," A1.
68. See Arkin, "Smart Bombs, Dumb Targeting," 49.
69. Amnesty International, "NATO/Federal Republic of Yugoslavia," 3; Ignatieff, *Virtual War*, 62; Lambeth, *NATO's Air War for Kosovo*, 137.
70. ICTY, "Final Report," 17.
71. Arkin, *Civilian Deaths in the NATO Air Campaign*, Appendix A, number 49.
72. International Criminal Tribunal for the Former Yugoslavia (ICTY), "Final Report of the Prosecutor," paragraph 73.
73. Ibid.
74. Arkin, *Civilian Deaths in the NATO Air Campaign*, 30.
75. Helen Fawkes, "Scars of NATO Bombing Still Pain Serbs," *BBC News*, March 24, 2009, news.bbc.co.uk/2/hi/Europe/7960116.
76. Jonathan Steele, "Death Lurks in the Fields: Unexploded Bombs, Kosovo Tries to Clean Up After Air Strikes," *The Guardian*, May 13, 2000, at https://www.theguardian.com/world/2000/mar/14/balkans.
77. Cordesman, *The Lessons and Non-Lessons*, 89–90.
78. See United Nations Security Council Resolution S/RES/1973 (2011).
79. United Nations Human Rights Council, "Report of the International Commission of Inquiry on Libya" (March 2, 2012), A/HRC/19/88, 1–2.
80. United Nations Human Rights Council, "Report of the International Commission," paragraph 161.
81. C. J. Chivers and Eric Schmitt, "In Strikes on Libya by NATO, an Unspoken Civilian Toll," *New York Times*, December 17, 2011, A1.
82. Human Rights Watch, *Unacknowledged Deaths: Civilian Casualties in NATO's Air Campaign in Libya* (New York, May 2012), 102.
83. See, for example, Chivers and Schmitt, "In Strikes on Libya by NATO."
84. Ibid.
85. Ibid.
86. United Nations Human Rights Council, "Report of the International Commission," 16.
87. United Nations Security Council Resolution S/RES/1973 (2011), paragraph 4, authorized Member States "to take all necessary measures . . . to protect civilians and civilian populated areas under threat of attack in the Libyan Arab Jamahiriya, including Benghazi."

88. Chivers and Schmitt, "In Strikes on Libya by NATO."
89. United Nations Human Rights Council, "Report of the International Commission," 160–170.
90. BBC News, "Libya: Obama, Cameron and Sarkozy Vow Gaddafi Must Go," April 5, 2011, http://www.bbc.co.uk/news/world-africa-13089758.
91. UN Senior Military Adviser for the UN Human Rights Council's Independent Commission of Inquiry on Libya, Marc Garlasco, contacted NATO officials to discuss civilian casualties, but NATO refused to meet with him. See his account in "NATO's Lost Lessons from Libya," *Washington Post*, June 11, 2012 at https://www.washingtonpost.com/opinions/natos-lost-lessons-from-libya/2012/06/11/gJQAhkAoVV_story.html?utm_term=.11fb0d473e3b.
92. Chivers and Schmitt, "In Strikes on Libya by NATO." Emphasis mine.
93. Ignatieff, *Virtual War*, 108.
94. Arkin, *Civilian Deaths in the NATO Air Campaign*, 45.

Chapter 5

1. Quoted in Amos Harel and Avi Issacharoff, *34 Days: Israel, Hezbollah and the War in Lebanon* (New York: Palgrave, 2008), 76.
2. Ministry of Foreign Affairs, "Special Cabinet Communique-Hizbullah Attack," July 12, 2006, http://www.mfa.gov.il/mfa/pressroom/2006/pages/special%20cabinet%20communique%20-%20hizbullah%20attack%2012-jul-2006.aspx.
3. Nafez Qawas and Raed El Rafei, "Simiora's Cabinet Makes Clear it Had Nothing to Do with 'What Happened'," *Lebanon Daily Star*, July 13, 2006, https://web.archive.org/web/20060714183432/http://dailystar.com.lb/article.asp?edition_id=1&categ_id=2&article_id=73930.
4. Charge d'affaires a.i. of the Permanent Mission of Lebanon to the United Nations, Addressed to the Secretary General and the President of the Security Council, UN Doc. S12006/518, July 13, 2006.
5. Matt M. Matthews, *We Were Caught Unprepared: The 2006 Hezbollah–Israeli War*, The Long War Series Occasional Paper 26 (Leavenworth, KS: US Army Combined Arms Center Combat Studies Institute Press Fort, 2008), 50.
6. Benjamin Lamberth, *Air Operations in Israel's War Against Hezbollah: Learning from Lebanon and Getting It Right in Gaza* (Santa Monica, CA: RAND Corporation, 2011), 58.
7. William Arkin, *Divining Victory: Airpower in the 2006 Israel–Hezbollah War* (Maxwell Airforce Base, AL: Air University Press, 2007), 106.
8. See, for example, Israel, "Rules of Warfare on the Battlefield," Military Advocate Generals' Corps Command, Israeli Defense Force School of Military Law, 2nd ed., 2006; "Laws of War in the Battlefield," Manual, Military Advocate General Headquarters, Military School, 1998; Israeli Defense Force, "Conduct on the Battlefield in Accordance with the Law of War," 1986.
9. Arkin, *Divining Victory*, 42.
10. Amnesty International sets the civilian death toll at 1,183, one-third of who were children. See "Lebanon: Deliberate Destruction or Collateral Damage?: Israeli Attacks on Civilian Infrastructure" (London, August 2006), AI Index number: MDE 18/007/2006, 2. Israeli analysts Raphael Cohen-Almagor and Sharon Heleva cite 1,191 civilians killed. See their "The Israeli–Hezbollah War and the Winograd Committee," *Journal of Parliamentary and Political Law* 2, no. 1 (December 2008): 28–29. William Arkin uses the figure of 1,200 in *Divining Victory*, 150. Human Rights Watch estimates 860 civilian deaths, although they acknowledge that this is a significant undercount since their report only covers the period of July 12–27. See Human Rights Watch, *Why They Died: Civilian Casualties in Lebanon During the 2006 War* (New York City, September 2007), E, 2.
11. UNICEF, Sabine Dolan, "The Humanitarian Challenge in Lebanon," August 9, 2006, http://www.unicef.org/emerg/index_35274.html.
12. United Nations Human Rights Council, "Report of the Inquiry on Lebanon Pursuant to Human Rights Council Resolution S-2/1" (November 23, 2006), A/HRC/3/2, 49.
13. William Arkin obtained these figures from Megen David Adom, Israeli's national aid society. See his *Divining Victory*, x.

14. Cohen-Almagor and Heleva, "The Israeli–Hezbollah War," 28–29.
15. For a detailed account of Hezbollah's rocket attacks into Israel, including the toll on Israeli civilians, see Human Rights Watch, *Civilians Under Assault: Hezbollah's Rocket Attacks on Israel in the 2006 War* (New York, NY, August 2007).
16. Augustus Richard Norton, *Hezbollah: A Short History* (Princeton, NJ: Princeton University Press, 2014), 83–84.
17. Adam Shatz, "In Search of Hezbollah," *New York Review of Books* 51, no. 8, April 29, 2004.
18. Michael N. Schmitt, " 'Change Direction' 2006: Israeli Operations in Lebanon and the International Law of Self-Defense," *Michigan Journal of International Law* 29, no. 2 (2008): 134.
19. Shatz, "In Search of Hezbollah."
20. Harel and Issacharoff, *34 Days*, 91–92.
21. David Makovsky and Jeffrey White, "Lessons and Implications of the Israel–Hizballah War: A Preliminary Assessment," the Washington Institute for Near East Policy, Policy Focus #60 (Washington, DC, October 2006), 13.
22. Quoted in Harel and Issacharoff, *34 Days*, 177.
23. Makovsky and White, "Lessons and Implications of the Israel–Hizballah War," 11.
24. Jeffrey Collins, "A Problematic Duo? Airpower and Casualty-Averse Decision-Making: Israel and the Second Lebanon War," *RCMI (Journal of the Royal Canadian Military Institute)* 73, no. 1 (SITREP, January–February 2013): 11.
25. Israeli Ministry of Foreign Affairs communique, "Chief of Staff Halutz: 'We have no intention of hurting Syria or the citizens of Lebanon,' " July 27, 2006, at http://www.mfa.gov.il/mfa/foreignpolicy/terrorism/hizbullah/pages/chief%20of%20staff%20halutz-%20no%20intention%20of%20hurting%20syria%20or%20citizens%20of%20lebanon%2027-jul-2006.aspx.
26. Ibid.
27. Arkin, *Divining Victory*, 151–152.
28. Steven Erlanger, "Israel Vowing to Rout Hezbollah," *New York Times*, July 15, 2006, A1.
29. Quoted in Arkin, *Divining Victory*, 14.
30. Harel and Issacharoff, *34 Days*, 78.
31. Ibid., 114.
32. Makovsky and White, "Lessons and Implications of the Israel–Hizballah War," 39–41.
33. Arkin, *Divining Victory*, 246.
34. Human Rights Watch, *Why They Died*, 10.
35. Scott Wilson, "Israeli War Plan Had No Exit Strategy," *Washington Post*, October 21, 2006; Jeffrey Collins, "A Problematic Duo?," 121.
36. Amnesty International, "Lebanon," 9 and 16; UNHRC, "Report of the Commission of Inquiry," 38 and Arkin, *Divining Victory*, 75.
37. Amnesty International, "Lebanon," 2.
38. See Israel's response to the Human Rights report in Human Rights Watch, *Why They Died*, Appendix IV, 242.
39. Amnesty International, "Lebanon," 11.
40. See, for example, Cohen-Almagor and Heleva-Amin, "The Israeli–Hezbollah War and the Winograd Committee," 37; Benjamin Lambeth, *Air Operations in Israel's War Against Hezbollah* (Santa Monica, CA: RAND Corporation, 2011), 180.
41. Nils Melzer, *Interpretive Guidance on the Notion of Direct Participation in Hostilities Under International Humanitarian Law* (Geneva: International Committee of the Red Cross, May 1999), 19.
42. Melzer, *Interpretive Guidance*, 19.
43. See Ziv Bohrer and Mark Osiel, "Proportionality in Military Force at War's Multiple Levels: Averting Civilian Casualties vs. Safeguarding Soldiers," *Vanderbilt Journal of Transnational Law* 46, no. 3 (2013): 798. For a justification of this policy, see Asa Kasher and Amos Yadlin, "Military Ethics of Fighting Terror: An Israeli Perspective," *Journal of Military Ethics* 4, no. 1 (2005): 3–32.
44. For a detailed description of their research methodologies, see Human Rights Watch, *About Our Research*, at https://www.hrw.org/about-our-research.

45. See Human Rights Watch, *Why They Died*, Appendix I. Human Rights Watch compiled their statistics and analysis from on-the-ground field investigations, including interviews with witnesses, journalists, and medical personnel; on-site inspections; and information provided by hospitals, humanitarian organizations, and government agencies.

46. See Human Rights Watch, *Why They Died*, Appendix I.

47. Arkin, *Divining Victory*, Figure 5.3, 82.

48. UNHRC, "Report of the Commission," 32.

49. Mark Parker, "Tour of Terror in Beirut," *The Sun*, July 26, 2006.

50. Human Rights Watch, *Why They Died*, 139.

51. Harel and Issacharoff, *34 Days*, 162.

52. See UNSC, Resolution 8791, SC/8791, July 30, 2006.

53. UNHRC, "Report of the Commission of Inquiry," 33–34.

54. Norton, *Hezbollah*, 138.

55. Arkin, *Divining Victory*, Figure 5.3, 77.

56. Quoted in Human Rights Watch, *Why They Died*, 65.

57. Quoted in UN Human Rights Council, "Report of the Inquiry on Lebanon," 41.

58. Human Rights Watch, *Why They Died*, Appendix IV, 243.

59. Arkin, *Divining Victory*, 49.

60. Amnesty International, "Out of all Proportion: Civilians Bear the Brunt of the War" (November 2006), AI Index number: MDE 02/033/2006, 21.

61. Human Rights Watch, *Why They Died*, 66.

62. Arkin, *Divining Victory*, 120.

63. Amnesty International, "Out of All Proportion," 23; Human Rights Watch, *Why They Died*, 151.

64. Human Rights Watch, *Why They Died*, 69.

65. Ibid., 169.

66. Meron Rappaport, "IDF Commander: We Fired More Than a Million Cluster Bombs in Lebanon," *Haaretz*, September 12, 2006, http://www.haaretz.com/news/idf-commander-we-fired-more-than-a-million-cluster-bombs-in-lebanon-1.197099.

67. Human Rights Watch, *Flooding South Lebanon Israel's Use of Cluster Munitions in Lebanon in July and August 2006* (New York, NY, February 2008), 5.

68. Arkin, *Divining Victory*, 49.

69. Ibid., 109.

70. Human Rights Watch, *Why they Died*, 52.

71. Ibid., 45.

72. State of Israel, The Supreme Court Sitting as the High Court of Justice (Jerusalem, Israel, December 11, 2005), HCJ 769/02.

73. Harel and Issacharoff, *34 Days*, 80–82.

74. Protocol Additional to the Geneva Conventions of August 12, 1949, and relating to the Protection of Victims of International Armed Conflicts (Protocol I), June 8, 1977, article 51 5(b).

75. Government of Israel Response to the Human Rights Watch letter, in Human Rights Watch, *Why They Died*, Appendix IV, 241.

76. Final Report of the Commission to Investigate the Lebanon Campaign in 2006, Tel Aviv, January 30, 2008. English translation at, http://www.nytimes.com/2008/01/30/world/middleeast/31winograd-web.html.

Chapter 6

1. CFR Staff, "Al Qaeda in the Arabian Peninsula," Council on Foreign Relations, June 9, 2015, https://www.cfr.org/backgrounder/al-qaeda-arabian-peninsula-aqap.

2. See the National Commission on Terrorist Attacks against the United States, "9/11 Commission Final Report," Executive Summary, 4, http://www.globalsecurity.org/military/world/para/al-qaida.htm; and United States District Court for the Eastern District Of Virginia, Alexandria Division, *United States of America v. Zacarias Moussaoui*, December 2001, http://www.justice.gov/ag/indictment-zacarias-moussaoui.

3. See Martha Crenshaw, "There Is No Global Jihadist 'Movement': The World of Islamist Fighters Is Deeply Fragmented and Constantly Shifting," *The Atlantic*, March 11, 2015, at https://www.theatlantic.com/international/archive/2015/03/there-is-no-global-jihadist-movement/387502/.

4. David Kilcullen, "Countering Global Insurgency," *Small Wars Journal*, November 30, 2004, www.smallwarsjournal.com/documents/kilcullen.pdf.

5. Weekly radio address delivered by US President George W. Bush on September 29, 2001, http://en.wikisource.org/wiki/Presidential_Radio_Address_-_29_September_2001; and see President George W. Bush, address to a joint session of Congress, September 20, 2001, www.whitehouse.gov/news/releases/2001/09/20010920-8.html. Emphasis mine.

6. Ashley S. Deeks, "Pakistan's Sovereignty and the Killing of Osama Bin Laden," *Insights* 15, no. 11 (May 5, 2011).

7. Philip Alston, "Report of the Special Rapporteur on Extrajudicial, Summary, or Arbitrary Executions," *Human Rights Council* A/HRC/12/24/Add.6, 2010, 3. See also Nils Melzer, *Targeted Killings in International Law* (Oxford: Oxford University Press, 2008), 3–4.

8. There is an extensive literature debating the legal, moral, philosophical, and political aspects of targeted killing and drone warfare; however, these issues are beyond the scope of this chapter. For a good overview of the debate and issues involved, see Michael N. Schmitt, "Targeted Killings in International Law: Law Enforcement, Self-Defense and Armed Conflict," in *International Humanitarian Law and Human Rights Law: Towards a New Merger in International Law*, ed. Roberta Arnold and Noelle Quenivet (Leiden; Boston: Martinus Nijhoff Publishers, 2008), 525–554; International Committee of the Red Cross, "The Use of Force in Armed Conflicts: Interplay Between the Conduct of Hostilities and Law Enforcement Paradigms," report prepared and edited by Gloria Gaggioli (Geneva, November 2013); David Kretzmer, "Targeted Killing of Suspected Terrorists: Extra-Judicial Execution or Legitimate Means of Defence," *European Journal of International Law* 16, no. 2 (2005): 171–212; and Kenneth Anderson, "Targeted Killings in U.S. Counterterrorism Strategy and Law," in *Legislating the War on Terror: An Agenda for Reform*, ed. Benjamin Wittes (Washington, DC: Brookings Institution Press, 2009), 346–400; Claire Finkelstein, Jens David Ohlin, and Andrew Altman, eds., *Targeted Killings: Law and Morality in an Asymmetrical World* (Oxford: Oxford University Press. 2012); and Amos Guiora, *Legitimate Target: A Criteria-Based Approach to Targeted Killing* (Oxford: Oxford University Press, 2013).

9. W. Singer, *Wired for War: The Robotics Revolution and Conflict in the 21st Century* (New York: Penguin, 2009).

10. Mary Ellen O'Connell, "Unlawful Killing with Combat Drones: A Case Study of Pakistan, 2004–2009," Notre Dame Law School, Legal Studies Research Paper no. 09-43, July 2010, 4 and 5 and Marc Bowden, "The Killing Machines: How to Think About Drones," *The Atlantic*, September 2013, https://www.theatlantic.com/magazine/archive/2013/09/the-killing-machines-how-to-think-about-drones/309434/.

11. The Bureau of Investigative Journalism (TBIJ), https://www.thebureauinvestigates.com/category/projects/drones/drones-graphs. The raw data for US drone strikes in Pakistan can be found at https://docs.google.com/spreadsheets/d/1P1TSWNwr1j-0pX022Q2iLEZd2-IGoswD08unYSvCYaU/edit#gid=9. In addition to TBIJ, there are two other major sources of civilian casualty figures: the New American Foundation and the Foundation for Defense of Democracy/*Long War Journal*. Of the three, the Columbia Law School study concluded that the TBIJ was the most reliable, and after closely examining the three databases, I concur with their finding. See Human Rights Clinic at Columbia Law School and Center for Civilians in Conflict, "The Civilian Impact of Drones: Unexamined Costs, Unanswered Questions," 2012, 43–54. Neither the New American Foundation nor the Long War Journal update their statistics when new information is revealed, and therefore their figures are based on first reporting, much of which is often unreliable. Moreover, according to their website, the *Long War Journal* obtains most of its statistics from US intelligence sources and considers all casualties to be either Taliban or al Qaeda unless they are specifically identified as civilians by these sources. On the other hand, TBIJ not only updates the figures on its site on a regular basis, it lists each individual strike listed in its database. It compiles its estimates in Pakistan's Federally Administered Tribal Areas by analyzing data from thousands of reports including contemporaneous media reports, witness testimonies, and field research.

12. See, for example, Conor Friedesdorf, "CNN's Bogus Drone-Deaths Graphic," *The Atlantic*, July 6, 2012, http://www.theatlantic.com/politics/archive/2012/07/cnns-bogus-drone-deaths-graphic/259493 and Jo Becker and Scott Shane, "Secret 'Kill List' Proves a Test of Obama's Principles and Will," *New York Times*, May 29, 2012, A1.

13. See Scott Shane, "Drone Strikes Reveal Uncomfortable Truth: U.S. Is Often Unsure About Who Will Die," *New York Times*, April 23, 2015, A1.

14. These conditions for claiming self-defense were articulated in what is known in International Law circles as the *Caroline Case*. See Malcolm Shaw, *International Law*, 7th ed. (Cambridge: Cambridge University Press, 2014), 820.

15. See, for example, Saby Ghoshray, "Targeted Killing in International Law: Searching for Rights in the Shadow of 9/11," *Indiana International & Comparative Law Review* 24, no. 2 (2014): 355–419; and Philip Alston, "Report of the Special Rapporteur."

16. For a discussion of the competing paradigms of law enforcement versus hostilities, see Milzer, *Targeted Killings in International Law*.

17. International Criminal Tribunal for the Former Yugoslavia, *The Prosecutor v. Dusko Tadic*, Decision on the Defence Motion for Interlocutory Appeal on Jurisdiction, IT-94-1-A, October 2, 1995, para. 70.

18. Rohan Gunaratna, "The Post-Madrid Face of Al Qaeda," *Washington Quarterly* (Summer 2004): 95; James Risen, "Evolving Nature of Al Qaeda Is Misunderstood, Critic Says," *New York Times*, November 8, 2004, A18.

19. Human Rights Watch, *Between a Drone and Al Qaeda: The Civilian Cost of U.S. Targeted Killings in Yemen* (New York, October 22, 2013), 7.

20. Harold Hongju Koh, Legal Adviser, US Department of State, "The Obama Administration and International Law," speech given before Annual Meeting of the American Society of International Law, Washington, DC, March 25, 2010, http://www.state.gov/s/l/releases/remarks/139119.htm.

21. President Barack Obama, "Remarks by the President at the National Defense University," Fort McNair, Washington, DC, May 23, 2013, https://www.whitehouse.gov/the-press-office/2013/05/23/remarks-president-national-defense-university.

22. International Criminal Tribunal for the Former Yugoslavia, *The Prosecutor v. Boskoski*, Case no. IT-04-82-T, Judgement July 10, 2008, paragraphs 177, 199, and 200; and *The Prosecutor v. Dusko Tadic*, para. 70. See also International Committee of the Red Cross, "How is the Term 'Armed Conflict' Defined in International Humanitarian Law?," Opinion Paper (Geneva, March 2008), 3.

23. US Supreme Court, *Hamdan v. Rumsfeld*, 548 US 557, 2006. See also Supreme Court of Israel, *Public Committee against Torture in Israel v. Government of Israel*, Case No. HCJ 769/02, December 13, 2006.

24. See Resolution 1368, S/RES/1386 (September 12, 2001) and Resolution 1373, S/RES/1373 (September 28, 2001).

25. See "'Declaration of Jihad Against the Americans Occupying the Land of the Two Holy Mosques," *PBS News Hour*, http://www.pbs.org/newshour/updates/military-july-dec96-fatwa_1996; "Full Text: Bin Laden's 'Letter to America,'" *The Guardian*, November 24, 2002; and Norman Cigar and Stephanie E. Kramer, eds., *Al-Qaida After 10 Years of War: A Global Perspective of Successes, Failures, and Prospects* (Quantico, VA: Marine Corps University Press, 2015).

26. See Alberto Gonzales, "Decision Re Application of the Geneva Convention on Prisoners of War to the Conflict with Al Qaeda and the Taliban," Memorandum for the President, January 25, 2002.

27. President George W. Bush, "Military Order of November 13, 2001: Detention, Treatment, and Trial of Certain Non-Citizens in the War against Terrorism," *Federal Register* 66 FR 57833, November 16, 2001.

28. David Singer refers to this as a "light footprint" approach, while David Rohde calls it the "Obama Doctrine." See David Singer, *Confront and Conceal: Obama's Secret Wars and Surprising Use of American Power* (New York: Random House, 2013) and David Rohde, "The Obama Doctrine," *Foreign Policy* (March/April 2012): 64–69. See also Daniel Klaidman,

Kill or Capture: The War on Terror and the Soul of the Obama Presidency (Houghton Mifflin Harcourt, 2012).

29. Obama, "Remarks by the President at the National Defense University."
30. Obama, "Remarks by the President at the National Defense University."
31. Adam Entous, "Special Report: How the White House Learned to Love the Drone," *Reuters*, May 18, 2010, http://www.reuters.com/article/us-pakistan-drones-idUSTRE64H5SL20100518.
32. Obama, "Remarks by the President at the National Defense University."
33. Harold Hongju Koh, Legal Adviser, US Department of State, "The Obama Administration and International Law," speech given before Annual Meeting of the American Society of International Law, Washington, DC, March 25, 2010.
34. Jeh Johnson, "Speech on National Security Law, Lawyers and Lawyering in the Obama Administration," Council on Foreign Relations, February 22, 2012, http://www.cfr.org/defense-and-security/jeh-johnsons-speech-national-security-law-lawyers-lawyering-obama-administration/p27448.
35. Amnesty International, "Will I Be Next? U.S. Drone Strikes in Pakistan" (London, October 13, 2013), Index ASA 33/013/2013, 12.
36. See, for example, Amnesty International, "As if Hell Fell on Me: the Human Rights Crisis in Northwest Pakistan" (London, 2010), ASA 33/004/2010.
37. Christopher Faulkner and David Gray, "The Emergence of Al Qaeda in the Arabian Peninsula (AQAP) and the Effectiveness of U.S. Counterterrorism Efforts," *Global Security Studies* 5, no. 1 (Winter 2014): especially 11.
38. See Gregory S. McNeal, "Targeted Killing and Accountability," *Georgetown Law Journal* 102, no. 1 (March 5, 2014): 709.
39. Greg Miller, "Plan for Hunting Terrorists Signals U.S. Intends to Keep Adding Names to Kill Lists," *Washington Post*, October 23, 2012, at https://www.washingtonpost.com/world/national-security/plan-for-hunting-terrorists-signals-us-intends-to-keep-adding-names-to-kill-lists/2012/10/23/4789b2ae-18b3-11e2-a55c-39408fbe6a4b_story.html?utm_term=.b68fd382c50b.
40. Becker and Shane, "Secret 'Kill List,'" and Klaidman, *Kill or Capture*.
41. For an excellent discussion of this problem, see Marco Sassoli and Laura M. Olson, "The Relationship Between International Humanitarian and Human Rights Law Where It Matters: Admissible Killing and Internment of Fighters in Non-International Armed Conflicts," *International Review of the Red Cross* 90 no. 871 (September 2008): 599–627.
42. Milzer, *Targeted Killings in International Law*, 426–427.
43. International Committee of the Red Cross, *Interpretive Guidance on the Notion of Direct Participation in Hostilities Under International Humanitarian Law* (Geneva, 2009), 34.
44. This phrase is used by the International Committee of the Red Cross (ICRC) to determine who counts as a combatant in an armed conflict. See ICRC, *Interpretive Guidance on the Notion of Direct Participation in Hostilities Under International Humanitarian Law* (Geneva, May 1999), 19.
45. Rohde, "The Obama Doctrine"; Eric Schmitt and David Sanger, "Pakistan Shift Could Curtail Drone Strikes, *New York Times*, 5, February 22, 2008.
46. Klaidman, *Kill or Capture*, 41.
47. David Sanger, *The Inheritance: The World Obama Confronts and the Challenges to American Power* (New York: Three Rivers Press, 2010).
48. Paul D. Shinkman, "Obama, CIA Cornered Into Troubling 'Signature Strikes,'" *U.S. News and World Report*, June 18, 2015, https://www.usnews.com/news/articles/2015/06/18/obama-cia-returning-to-controversial-drone-signature-strikes.
49. Human Rights Clinic, "The Civilian Impact of Drones," 9.
50. Greg Miller, "CIA Didn't Know Strike Would Hit Al-Qaeda Leader," *Washington Post*, June 17, 2015, at https://www.washingtonpost.com/world/national-security/al-qaedas-leader-in-yemen-killed-us-signature-strike-us-officials-say/2015/06/17/9fe6673c-151b-11e5-89f3-61410da94eb1_story.html?utm_term=.0ac9daeb5614.
51. O'Connell, "Unlawful Killing," 6.
52. This is known as "latency."
53. Matt Martin, *Predator: The Remote-Control Air War over Iraq and Afghanistan: A Pilot's Story* (Minneapolis, MN: Zenith Press, 2010), 3 and 31.

54. The National Security Act of 1947 authorizes the CIA to conduct covert actions, which are not governed by the laws of armed conflict. The CIA is itself a civilian agency that tends to operate in places where the United States is not officially at war. The legal, political, and ethical questions concerning the CIA's involvement in areas that are designated as armed conflict zones is beyond the scope of this chapter; however, an interesting discussion of these issues can be found in Marshall Curtis Erwin, "Covert Action: Legislative Background and Possible Policy Questions," CRS Report for Congress, Congressional Research Service, April 10, 2013.

55. See Human Rights Clinic, "The Civilian Impact of Drones," 34–36.

56. Conor Friedesdorf, "CNN's Bogus Drone-Deaths Graphic," The Atlantic, July 6, 2012, http://www.theatlantic.com/politics/archive/2012/07/cnns-bogus-drone-deaths-graphic/259493; and Becker and Shane, "Secret 'Kill List,'" A1.

57. Jane Mayer, "The Predator War: What Are the Risks of the C.I.A.'s Covert Drone Program," New Yorker, October 26, 2009, 45.

58. Michael Hasting, "The Drone Wars" Rolling Stone, April 26, 2012, 40–82.

59. Human Rights Clinic, "The Civilian Impact of Drones," 30–31 and Adam Entous, "Drones Kill Low-Level Militants, Few Civilians: U.S," Reuters, May 3, 2010, http://www.reuters.com/article/us-pakistan-usa-drones-idUSTRE6424WI20100504.

60. John Keller, "Air Force Orders Eight MQ-9 Block 5 Reaper Attack Drones from Manufacturer General Atomics," Military and Aerospace Electronics, May 21, 2015, http://www.military-aerospace.com/articles/2015/05/reaper-attack-drones.html.

61. McNeal, "Targeted Killing and Accountability," 741–743.

62. Human Rights Clinic, "The Civilian Impact of Drones," 35.

63. Becker and Shane, "Secret 'Kill List.'"

64. Becker and Shane, "Secret 'Kill List.'"

65. Office of the Director of National Intelligence, "Summary of Information Regarding U.S. Counterterrorism Strikes Outside Areas of Active Hostilities," January 19, 2017, https://www.dni.gov/files/documents/Newsroom/Press%20Releases/DNI+Release+on+CT+Strikes+Outside+Areas+of+Active+Hostilities.PDF.

66. Scott Shane, "CIA Is Disputed on Civilian Toll in Drone Strikes," New York Times, August 11, 2011, A1.

67. Quoted in Chris Woods, Sudden Justice: America's Secret Drone Wars (New York: Oxford University Press, 2015), 7.

68. Adam Entous, "Special Report: How the White House Learned to Love the Drone," Reuters, May 18, 2010, http://www.reuters.com/article/us-pakistan-drones-idUSTRE64H5SL20100518.

69. Human Rights Clinic, "The Civilian Impact of Drones," 23.

70. Alice K. Ross and Jack Serle, "Most US Drone Strikes in Pakistan Attack Houses," Bureau of Investigative Journalism, May 23, 2014, https://www.thebureauinvestigates.com/2014/05/23/most-us-drone-strikes-in-pakistan-attack-houses/.

71. Ross and Serle, "Most US Drone Strikes in Pakistan Attack Houses."

72. Chris Woods, "CIA 'Revives Attacks on Rescuers' in Pakistan," Bureau of Investigative Journalism, June 4, 2012, https://www.thebureauinvestigates.com/2012/06/04/cia-revives-attacks-on-rescuers-in-pakistan.

73. International Human Rights and Conflict Resolution Clinic, Stanford Law School and Global Justice Clinic, New York University School of Law, Living Under Drones: Death, Injury and Trauma to Civilians From U.S. Drone Practices in Pakistan, September 2012, 25.

74. Human Rights Clinic, "The Civilian Impact of Drones," 68.

75. "Pakistan Drone Strikes, 2004–2013," Bureau of Investigative Journalism, 2013, https://www.thebureauinvestigates.com/drone-war/data/obama-2013-pakistan-drone-strikes.

76. Greg Miller, "CIA Didn't Know Strike Would Hit Al-Qaeda Leader," Washington Post, June 17, 2015, A1.

77. Amrit Singh, Open Society Initiative, Death by Drone: Civilian Harm Caused by U.S. Targeted Killings in Yemen (New York: Open Society Foundation, 2015), 81–85. As far as I can tell from my research, this appears to be the most comprehensive study of the drone campaign in Yemen, involving 96 interviews with survivors and witnesses covering nine specific drone attacks in 2013.

78. Human Rights Clinic, "The Civilian Impact of Drones," 62–63.
79. Singh, *Death by Drone*, 34.
80. Singh, *Death by Drone*, 34.
81. Human Rights Clinic, "The Civilian Impact of Drones," 57–59.
82. Human Rights Watch, *Between a Drone and al Qaeda*.
83. Chris Woods, "Get the Data: Obama's Terror Drones," Bureau of Investigative Journalism, February 4, 2012, https://www.thebureauinvestigates.com/2012/02/04/get-the-data-obamas-terror-drones.
84. Amnesty International, "Will I Be Next?," 28.
85. Woods, "Get the Data."
86. Amnesty International, "Will I Be Next?," 29.
87. See Aaron J. Klein, *Striking Back: The 1972 Munich Olympics Massacre and Israel's Deadly Response* (New York: Random House, 2007) and Simon Reeve, *One Day in September: The Full Story of the 1972 Munich Olympics Massacre and the Israeli Revenge Operation "Wrath of God"* (New York: Arcade Publishing, 2011).
88. Quoted in Gavin Cordon, "Former US Commander Stanley McChrystal Warns Afghanistan Could Descend Into Civil War When Foreign Troops Leave," *The Independent*, January 21, 2014, 1.
89. Quoted in "Don't Drone On," *The Economist*, September 1, 2012, 51.
90. Jack Serle, "CIA Drone Strikes in Pakistan Fall to Lowest Level in 8 Years, Bureau's Annual Report Reveals," Bureau of Investigative Journalism, January 7, 2014.
91. The White House, "Fact Sheet: U.S. Policy Standards and Procedures for the Use of Force in Counterterrorism Operations Outside the U.S. and Areas of Active Hostilities," May 23, 2013.
92. Obama, "Remarks by the President at the National Defense University."

Chapter 7

1. These principles are found in Articles 51 and 57 in the Protocol Additional to the Geneva Conventions of August 12, 1949, and relating to the Protection of Victims of International Armed Conflicts (Protocol I), June 8, 1977, and is also considered to be part of customary international law. See International Committee of the Red Cross, *Customary International Humanitarian Law*, Volume I: Rules (Cambridge: Cambridge University Press, 2009), Rules 1, 7, 9, and 14.
2. Benjamin Valentino, Paul Huth, and Sarah Croco, "Covenants without the Sword: International Law and the Protection of Civilians in Times of War," *World Politics* 58 (April 2006): particularly 371; Alexander Downes, "Desperate Times, Desperate Measures: The Causes of Civilian Victimization in War," *International Security* 30, no.4 (2006): 152–195; and James Fearon and David Laitin, "Ethnicity, Insurgency, and Civil War," *American Political Science Review* 97, no. 1 (February 2003): 75–90.
3. Downes, "Desperate Times, Desperate Measures."
4. See Gregory Fremont-Barnes, *A History of Counterinsurgency* (Santa Barbara, CA: Praeger, 2015).
5. US Department of Defense, *Final Report To Congress Conduct of The Persian Gulf War Pursuant To Title V of the Persian Gulf Conflict Supplemental Authorization and Personnel Benefits Act of 1991* (Public Law 102-25), April 1992, 698 and 701.
6. Human Rights Watch, *Why They Died*, 240–241.
7. Director of Central Intelligence, "Putting Noncombatants at Risk: Saddam's Use of 'Human Shields,'" January 2003, i.
8. Human Rights Watch, *Israel/Lebanon: Israeli Indiscriminate Attacks Killed Most Civilians: No Evidence of Widespread Hezbollah "Shielding"* (New York, September 5, 2007), https://www.hrw.org/news/2007/09/05/israel/lebanon-israeli-indiscriminate-attacks-killed-most-civilians.
9. Keaney and Cohen, *Gulf War Air Power Survey*, 62. Parenthetically, the US Senate vote on authorizing the war was 52–47—hardly a ringing endorsement, particularly since the vote was taken when there were already 400,000 American troops deployed in the Gulf and the war was scheduled to begin one week later.

10. See, for example, Guilio Douhet, *Command of the Air* (Berkshire: Express Publishing, 2013/ 1921) and Alfred F. Hurley, *Billy Mitchell: Crusader for Air Power* (Indianapolis: Indiana University Press, 2006).

11. This figure is drawn from an analysis of the reports issued by Human Rights Watch and other nongovernmental organizations, which detail each confirmed civilian death in Iraq, Serbia, and Lebanon.

12. See Marc Bowden, "The Killing Machines: How to Think About Drones," *The Atlantic*, September 20, 2013, at https://www.theatlantic.com/magazine/archive/2013/09/the-killing-machines-how-to-think-about-drones/309434/.

13. Ward Thomas, "Victory by Duress: Civilian Infrastructure as a Target in Air Campaigns," *Security Studies* 15, no. 1 (January–March 2006): 1–33.

14. John T. Correll, "The Strategy of Desert Storm," *Air Force Magazine* 89, no. 1 (January 2006): 1–33; Olsen, *Strategic Air Power in Desert Storm*, 102.

15. Iraq forces remained firmly entrenched in Kuwait even after six weeks of persistent attacks on its major cities and infrastructure. Rather, it was the relentless bombing of Iraqi troops in the desert, followed by a devastating ground assault in southern Iraq (neither of which produced any significant collateral damage), which forced Iraq to accept the coalition's demands.

16. Harel and Issacharoff, *34 Days*, 114 and BBC News, "Israel Hits Hezbollah Leader's HQ," July 14, 2006, http://news.bbc.co.uk/2/hi/middle_east/5179862.stm.

17. Jeremy Pressman, "The United States and the Israel-Hezbollah War," Middle East Brief, Crown Center for Middle East Studies, Brandeis University, November 2006.

18. Hamed Mousavi, "The Israel-Lebanon War of 2006 and the Failure of US Foreign Policy," *Journal of Politics and Law* 8, no. 1 (2015): 130–136.

19. See Steven Erlanger, "Crisis in the Balkans: The Targets; NATO Strikes Serb State TV; Casualties Seen," *New York Times*, April 23, 1999, http://www.nytimes.com/1999/05/25/world/crisis-balkans-belgrade-reduced-caveman-life-serbs-don-t-blame-milosevic.html.

20. US Department of Defense, *Conduct of the Persian Gulf Conflict: an Interim Report to Congress*, July 1991, section 12-3.

21. Statement by NATO spokesperson Jamie Shea. Quoted in Amnesty International, "NATO/ Federal Republic of Yugoslavia: 'Collateral Damage' or Unlawful Killings?, Violations of The Laws Of War by NATO During Operation Allied Force" (London, 2000), AI Index number: EUR 70/18/00, 15.

22. Human Rights Clinic, "The Civilian Impact of Drones," 35. Interestingly, in an op-ed piece in the *New York Times* published four years after this quote, Air Force General Michael Hayden uses almost the identical language. See his "The Case for Drones," *New York Times*, Sunday Review, February 21, 2016, 1.

23. Israeli Foreign Ministry, "Government of Israel Response to Human Rights Watch Letter," in Human Rights Watch, *Why They Died*, Appendix IV, 247.

24. Thus, for example, NATO acknowledged the loss of life caused by its misdirected attack on the Chinese Embassy in Belgrade after the Chinese government expressed outrage. During the Gulf war, the coalition expressed regrets at the casualties produced by their attack on the al Firdos bunker in Baghdad suburb of Amariyah once it appeared on CNN.

25. See "Conduct of the Persian Gulf War: Final Report to Congress, Pursuant to Title V of the Persian Gulf Conflict Supplemental Authorization and Personnel Benefits Act of 1991," Public Law 102-25, April 1992, especially 696–703.

26. US Air Force, "Initial Report: The Air War Over Serbia, Aerospace Power in Operation Allied Force," 2000.

27. Winograd Commission, Final Report of the Commission to Investigate the Lebanon Campaign in 2006.

28. Government of Israel Response to the Human Rights Watch letter, in Human Rights Watch, *Why They Died*, Appendix IV.

29. First Protocol Additional to the Geneva Conventions of August 12, 1949, and Relating to the Protection of Victims of International Armed Conflicts, June 8, 1977, Article 53(2).

30. United Nations, *Report On Humanitarian Needs in Iraq in The Immediate Post-Crisis Environment by a Mission to the Area Led by the Under-Secretary-General for Administration and Management*, March 10–17, S/22366, March 20, 1991, 5.

31. United Nations, *Report On Humanitarian Needs in Iraq*, 8.
32. Harvard Study Team, "The Effects of the Gulf Crisis on the Children of Iraq," *New England Journal of Medicine* 325, no. 13 (September 26, 1991): 978.
33. Arkin, *Divining Victory*, 125.
34. Daniel Williams, "Decades, Billions Needed to Restore Yugoslavia," *Washington Post*, June 5, 1999, A1.
35. See, for example, Seumas Milne, "Coups and Terror are the Fruit of NATO's war in Libya," *The Guardian*, May 22, 2014.
36. First Protocol Additional to the Geneva Conventions of August 12, 1949, Article 51(2).
37. Amnesty International, "Will I Be Next?," 19.
38. US Air Force Central Command, "Combined Forces Air Component Commander" 2012-2017 Airpower Statistics, Operation Inherent Resolve, Number of Weapons Released, at http://www.afcent.af.mil/Portals/82/Documents/Airpower%20summary/Airpower%20Summary%20-%20May%202017_Final.pdf?ver=2017-06-08-084015-140.
39. See Airwars at https://airwars.org/civilian-casualty-claims. Airwars is an investigative website operated by journalists, tasked with examining civilian casualties in current air operations in the Middle East. For a discussion of the group's methodology, see https://airwars.org/methodology-new-draft/.
40. Sarah Almukhtar, "U.S. Airstrikes on ISIS Have Killed Hundreds, Maybe Thousands of Civilians," *New York Times*, May 25, 2017. David Wood, "Trump's War to 'Annihilate' ISIS is Raising Civilian Casualties," *Huffington Post*, June 13, 2017, at http://www.huffingtonpost.com/entry/trump-isis-civilian-casualties_us_5939a2dfe4b0c5a35c9d76e5.
41. Leo Shane III, "Trump: I'm Giving the Military 'Total Authorization,'" *Military Times*, April 13, 2017, http://www.militarytimes.com/articles/trump-military-total-authorization-afghanistan-iraq.
42. The Pentagon claimed that no more than 352 civilians had been killed, and in response US Secretary of Defense James Mattis quipped, "civilians casualties are a fact of life in this situation." Wood, "Trump's War to 'Annihilate' ISIS is Raising Civilian Casualties."
43. Kareem Shaheen, "Yemen Death Toll Has Reached 10,000, UN Says," *The Guardian*, January 16, 2017, https://www.theguardian.com/world/2017/jan/16/yemen-war-death-toll-has-reached-10000-un-says; BBC News, "Yemen War: Saudi Coalition 'Causing Most Civilian Casualties,'" March 18, 2017, http://www.bbc.com/news/world-middle-east-35842708.
44. Brian Bennett, W. J. Hennigan, and Alexandra Zavis, "Saudi-Led Yemen Air War's High Civilian Toll Unsettles U.S. Officials," *Los Angeles Times*, April 16, 2015, at http://www.latimes.com/world/middleeast/la-fg-us-saudis-20150417-story.html.
45. Eric Schmitt, "Saudi Arabia Tries to Ease Concerns Over Civilian Deaths in Yemen," *New York Times*, June 14, 2017.
46. This observation has been made by a number of journalists and security analysts. See, for example, Gregory D. Johnsen, *The Last Refuge: Yemen, Al-Qaeda, and America's War in Arabia* (New York: Norton, 2012).

INDEX

absolving the Western democracies, 139–41
accidents as causes of civilian casualties, 25, 27, 41
aerial bombing
  as an act of terrorism, 144
  as the primary cause of collateral damage, 135
Afghanistan, casualties in, 5, 7, 9, 21, 38
air power
  effects of, 82
  theories of, 134
air wars
  in Iraq, 38, 42, 50
  in Kosovo, 77–89
  in Lebanon, 96, 100, 102, 104
  in Libya, 85–6
  as a tool for risk-transfer, 45
al Firdos bunker, 60, 62
al Qaeda, 5, 22
  criteria for membership in, 115–16
  as a global insurgency, 107
  goals and organization of, 107, 112
  U.S. armed conflict with, 110–13
al Qaeda in the Arabian Peninsula, 115–16
alternatives to war
  failure to consider, 135–7, 140–1
Ameriyya Shelter, 61
Amnesty International, 23, 83, 124
Anderson, Kenneth, 13
Andoni, Lamis, 67
Arkin, William, 62, 66, 90–1
armed conflict
  civilians as parties to, 89
  definition, 111–13
  Israeli-Hezbollah dispute as, 89
  U.S.-al Qaeda dispute as, 108
Artisaari, U.N. Under Secretary Marti, 142
Artz, Margaret, 4, 13
asymmetric conflicts
  definition of, 22, 42

Israeli-Hezbollah dispute as, 22, 89
  practices of weaker parties in, 42–3, 46
  responsibilities of stronger parties in, 43–4
asymmetry of position, 131
asymmetry of threat, 129
Atkinson, Rick, 64
Aziz- al Saud, King Fahd Abdul, 53

Ba'ath Party, 52, 54
Badinter Commission, 74
Baghdad
  attacks on, 57, 61–3, 66
  collateral damage in, 59
Basra
  attacks on, 57, 58, 62–3, 59, 61
Beirut, 92
  Israeli attacks on, 95, 100–1
Belgrade
  damage to, 27, 39, 89
belligerent. See combatant
bin Laden, Osama, 112
Bosnia, 26
  declaration of independence, 74
  and Operation Deliberate Force, 70
Bosnian Serb Army (Army of the Republika
  Srpska), 74
Brennan, National Security Advisor John, 121
Brookings Institution, 7, 24
bugsplat (computer software), 2
Bureau of Investigative Journalism, 5, 10, 24,
  110, 124
Burger, James, 80
Bush, U.S. President George H. W., 54, 63, 66
Bush, U.S. President George W., 22, 108, 113, 114

Carmon, Israeli Ambassador Daniel, 101
centers of gravity, 33, 35
  in Iraq, 55–7